Hesketh Prichard & Peter Carr

SPORT IN WILDEST BRITAIN
A Modern Perspective
Foreword by Lieutenant-General Sir Barney White-Spunner KCB CBE

"No one can get the highest enjoyment out of sport unless he can live over again in the library the keen pleasure he experienced in the wilderness."

THEODORE ROOSEVELT

AUTHORS
Peter Carr and Hesketh Prichard

EDITOR
Nicola Turner

DESIGN
Steve Dawson

COVER IMAGE
iStock

PHOTOGRAPHY
All transparencies either Shutterstock or iStock, except for: Chapter 1, page 27 –
Michelle Tribe; Chapter 3, page 86-87 – Andy Lee, page 88 – Peter Carr, page 91
– Peter Carr; Chapter 5, page 135 – Susan Nilsson; Chapter 10, page 222 – Andy
Morffew; Chapter 11, page 251 – Andy Lovel.

Copyright © 2014 Blaze Publishing Ltd / Peter Carr
First edition published in the UK in 2014 by Blaze Publishing Ltd
ISBN: 978-1-910247-15-0

A catalogue record for this book is available from the British Library

ISBN 978-1-910247-15-0

Printed in Europe by Cliffe Enterprise Print Partnership

Blaze Publishing Ltd
Lawrence House, Morrell Street, Leamington Spa, Warwickshire, CV32 5SZ
Tel: +44 (0) 1926 339 808 **Fax:** +44 (0) 1926 470 400
Email: info@blazepublishing.co.uk **Website:** www.blazepublishing.co.uk

Contents

Dedication

Dedicated to gamekeeper David Nesfield for showing me that humour and tenacity can overcome adversity and tragedy, and to all keepers who have provided sport in wildest Britain, then and now.

"The First World War is often cited as having been a watershed for the British countryside. Before the conflict, millions of men and women lived and worked on the land. More than 20,000 gamekeepers stalked the hedgerows and moors of the nation, and each one strived to destroy every predator on his given beat. After the treaty of Versailles, less than one third of that number returned to their former employment. Thousands had been killed in front line fighting, and landowners could no longer afford to employ surviving staff on a scale comparable to the pre-war years. The changes took some time to take effect, but when they did,
they were tremendous." Patrick Laurie – *The Black Grouse* by Merlin Unwin Books.

Britain's gamekeepers have been (and thankfully still are), the true custodians of our countryside since the time of the conqueror. I dedicate this book especially to those keepers who fell in the two world wars to save our isles from others who sought to invade, but also to the 'chosen men', the keepers of today who have followed in their footsteps, and taken up the baton of trust to safeguard our game and wildlife for the next generation. I've been very fortunate indeed to enjoy a variety of sport in the British Isles. None of it would have been possible without the dedicated skill applied by each and every one of those keepers that provided me with exceptional sporting opportunities and company. There are too many to mention individually by name, but this book is for you all. **PC**

Preface

Sport in Wildest Britain

This third edition of *Sport in Wildest Britain* has been a long time in coming; indeed nearly 90 years have passed since the second edition. But this current version is more than just a reprint; it contains additional chapters from Prichard not printed in the previous editions. Each chapter is also extended by the co-author Peter Carr, from a modern perspective. He adds his knowledge and experience to the ten quarry species selected by Prichard, and then augments the book with some of his own too.

In his chapter on widgeon and mallard, Prichard mentions a 'crawling carriage'. Growing up in Jersey, Prichard had hired a carpenter to make one – five shillings to be paid at Easter because all 'Christmas tips' had gone on the hire of an eight-bore and ammunition, plus the chippie gets half the bag of duck. A crawling carriage is like a covered go-cart. It lets you inch close to duck out on the sands. If you want to see a picture, says Prichard, read Colonel Hawker's *Instructions to Young Sportsmen*, page 394 of the sixth edition, he adds helpfully. I have a copy of that book at home, I pull it off the shelf,

turn back the marbled cover and it falls open easily on page 394, where a pencil line marks the section of text that interested Prichard, for this is his very own copy of the book.

It is a lovely feeling to touch a generation across a century with a discovery like that. I followed Prichard's footsteps across Labrador with a party funded by the Royal Canadian Geographical Society. We came across landmarks Prichard had photographed 100 years before and, because that landscape alters so little, we even found one of his camps, exactly as he had left it, stones still in a circle where he had cooked his last meal, precisely shown in his photograph.

He is my mother's grandfather. I met his wife, Lady Elizabeth Grimston, when I was a tot, whom I remember as grand and distant, as most of my family seemed at the time. Prichard admired her for the way she jumped a five-bar gate, but that was more than 60 years earlier. He remains a family legend and, like many families' legends, we have long forgotten any flaws. So I can only write about what a remarkable man he must have been. I met cousins who had met him, but his death in 1922 meant their memory must have blurred. With one voice they praised him, for his sportsmanship, his war record instigating and running the British Sniping School in France, his writing and his cricketing. I have heard how he he inspired EW Hornung's character AJ Raffles, how he was the basis for Arthur Conan Doyle's character Professor Challenger in *The Lost World*, how Captain Scott asked him to the Antarctic but he could not go because he was planning a hunting trip to Newfoundland, and it is history how his fictional character Don Q became the basis for the modern film superhero Zorro.

This was a time when the idea of the super-hero in fiction was just beginning. Characters like Don Q, Biggles, the Scarlet Pimpernel, Richard Hannay, Sherlock Holmes and Bulldog Drummond were dripping from the pens of 'clubland authors' such as Prichard. It was also a time when these men (Baroness Orczy apart) commanded the world. The Edwardian dream was at its height, the British Empire was as plump as a summer pigeon and their confidence supreme. There was nothing strange about Prichard's campaign for the rights of the Inuit, while being a prominent part of the empire-making machine. Today, the RSPCA is confident enough to gloss over how it was started by at least one foxhunting man. There was nothing unusual about Prichard shooting seals and birds, and campaigning for more legal protection for seals and birds.

Yes – seals. Seal-shooting is not to everyone's taste. Imagine my delight when

Image: Prichard Collection

Image: Prichard Collection

the co-author of this version of *Sport in Wildest Britain*, Peter Carr, told me he not only wholeheartedly approved of seal-shooting, but that he had a licence to do it. I felt he might be the right person to follow up and produce a modern version of what has always been my favourite of Prichard's books. But what does Peter know about capercaillie? Well, he took me to the place on the Airlie Estate where both he and Prichard had shot capercaillie – again, a century apart.

I am sure Prichard wrote articles in order to pay the bills. I do. However, Prichard assembled those articles into *Sport in Wildest Britain* in order to inspire a new generation of sportsmen.

Above: Prichard in later years on the lawn at Prae Wood

Right: Peter Carr ready for evening duck

Image: Blaze Publishing

Most or all of the book had already appeared in *Cornhill* and other magazines at that time. Peter has the same view about inspiring readers as Prichard did. The articles he puts into *Sporting Rifle* and *Shoot in Scotland* magazines, which he edits, are full of the derring-do that makes Prichard's writing so appealing. When Peter told me he was going to edit a trade magazine for gamekeepers, I suggested he fill it full of useful information about jobs and prices. He ignored me and filled it with inspirational hunting and shooting stories.

After reading Prichard's chapter about ducks and the grey seals, both Peter and I wanted to go to the islands of Causamull and Haskeir off North Uist and camp out on the rocks with rifles and shotguns. Should Peter have done this before attempting a book like this? I don't think so. *Sport in Wildest Britain* is an idea as well as a book. Peter has stuffed many new possibilities for future generations between these hard covers. Inspiration is a wonderful thing. We still will go to Causamull, Haskeir, the Big Bog and many other places besides.

When Prichard wrote this, he was a couple of years from death. The war had killed him – he was taking his time to die. The danger would have been, with a book like this, to allow the end of innocence that the First World War imposed to dampen his spirit of sportsmanship and adventure. It did not. Nor did it stop Prichard's charmingly childlike approach to what he does and who he meets along the way. He is a schoolboy at Fettes College where he has smuggled in a .410 disguised as an umbrella.

With it, one half holiday, he successfully shoots a lapwing, is caught by a policeman, bribes the man, gets his mother to hand over ten shillings to redeem the confiscated gun, and asks her to drop off the lapwing at the taxidermist. It was a good life, well started, sadly soon ended, but full of the stuff of stories.

Charlie Jacoby
Somerset
May 2014

Left: Charlie Jacoby, Hesketh Prichard's great-grandson

Foreword

By Lt. General Sir Barney White-Spunner

Shooting is worth £1.6 billion to the rural economy of these islands and supports the equivalent of 70,000 full-time jobs. Two million hectares are actively managed for conservation as a result of shooting, making us one of the great forces for the conservation of both our priceless native species and, as importantly, their habitat. Where would that extensive list of species originally listed by Hesketh Prichard be without us?

It is a pleasure to introduce a book whose authors write so fluently and with a knowledge and passion that only the most dedicated shot or stalker will be able to identify with. The original charming manuscript loses nothing from having been updated by Peter Carr in this third edition, and the places referred to will take many of us back to happy memories of past sport. I particularly like his dedicating a chapter to each of the wonderful species described. My particular favourite is Hesketh Prichard's chapter dedicated to the Causamull Ducks, but I won't spoil the read for everyone else by giving too much away!

Lt. General Sir Barney White-Spunner (ret'd) KCB, CBE
Executive Chairman of the Countryside Alliance
London
June 2014

Image: Prichard Collection

*Left: A newly-
commissioned Prichard
at the beginning of the
Great War*

Introduction

SIWB the **Modern Perspective**

I came across Hesketh Prichard as an author quite by chance, nearly two decades ago on a bookshelf in Well Bank shooting lodge. This lodge served the shooting and fishing guests that sought sport on the Earl of Airlie's vast Highland estates. I was alone in between shooting clients on a cold winter's evening, and in need of some literary entertainment. Old sporting books have always fascinated me, and on this particular occasion, when running a finger along the volumes that graced the lodge, my index digit hovered over a book entitled *Sport in Wildest Britain* by the said author.

What a revelation the book proved to be. Here was a like-minded sportsman, albeit living nearly a hundred years before me, who preferred the remoteness and solitude of Britain's wildest corners. Moreover, also like me, he favoured the more varied, unusual quarry; those species that are usually listed together in the various column of the game book, where all interesting incidentals shot on more formal shoot days are often recorded as one. But here was a book that actually dedicated whole chapters to them!

Right: Co-author Hesketh Prichard at his writing desk in the early years

Completely captivated by the book I read on through the night and the more I read, the more interested I became. I found Prichard and I had trod similar turf too. He had shot capercaillie not two miles from where I was reading his work, and I had shot caper but two glens over. We had both shot this prince of game birds in the same areas of Sweden and Norway, and shared a similar interest in the sporting pursuit of seals. Indeed, at the time I thought I was unique in my yearning to outwit this wary coastal quarry, the game which Prichard refers to as the 'herds of Proteus'. Two nights later I had finished reading the tome, and rated it as the very best of sporting books dedicated to the pursuit of wild game in our isles. I revisited it on many occasions, but a change in vocation took me from the glens and to a spell on a different continent, and the book was forgotten.

A decade after first reading SIWB a second chance encounter, this time with Hesketh Prichard's great-grandson – Charlie Jacoby – reawakened my interest in the book. Charlie was then the editor of *Sporting Rifle* magazine, and via another sporting editor, James Marching-

Image: Prichard Collection

ton, I had submitted an article on lion hunting to Charlie for consideration. This led to me securing a regular column in *Sporting Rifle*, and eventually taking over the reins from him as editor when he left to launch Fieldsports Channel.TV. Knowing my keen interest in Prichard and his sporting endeavours, Charlie gifted me an old out-of-print memoir penned by one of Prichard's contemporaries Eric Parker (a former

editor of the *Field*).

This memoir was titled *Hesketh Prichard DSO. MC. – Hunter: Explorer: Naturalist: Cricketer: Author: Soldier*. It tells the story of a remarkable man, who was, in his short lifetime, a prominent explorer, and leading naturalist, one of the best bowlers England has produced, an exceptional author of various genres, crowned by a unique military career during his temporary commission in the Great War. Indeed by the end of that war he had gained his majority, been twice mentioned in dispatches, and won both the Military Cross and the Distinguished Service Order. He had become one of the war's most effective snipers, killing more Germans to his own rifle than any other British serviceman during that conflict. Appalled at British losses to German snipers at the war's start, by its end he had founded an effective sniping school against great opposition, and totally turned the sniper war against the Germans. By 1918 Major Prichard's sniper corps had virtually paralysed the opposition, to such an extent that hardly a German sniper dared lift his rifle. But it is that first accolade to which Eric Parker relates to Prichard in the sub-heading of his memoir that concerns readers of this book, and that is, of course, Prichard as a hunter.

I see in Prichard's great-grandson much of the old Edwardian adventurer: the great gangly height, comparable facial features, and a most admirable moral ethic on sport. He also shares a similar skill with the pen as his ancestor, and is nearly as fair a mark with the rifle, but then again definitely not with the shotgun – I'm sure he will forgive me for that, although I'm not sure Prichard would. To make up for his inconsistent skill with the shotgun, Charlie is, to his credit, an absolute master with the trout rod. He is an adventurer too, and has undertaken three noteworthy expeditions in his own right. Two of those in the footsteps of his great-grandfather though Canada's trackless Labrador, and in search of the giant sloth in Patagonia. His other expedition entailed traveling in an old, clapped-out Land Rover from the ex-clave of Ceuta, North Africa, through various countries to Cape Town, South Africa. This interesting adventure may be read in CJ's book *In Search of Will Carling*. I have enjoyed many a sporting foray in the company of Charlie Jacoby, and he is featured quite often in these pages within my own anecdotes, and occasionally by his own pen.

Hesketh Prichard fathered two sons, and a daughter: Alfgar, Michael and Diana. Both boys would follow in their father's footsteps and serve their country when war returned to Europe. They would also emulate their father by gaining their own majorities during World War Two. Alfgar was sadly lost in action under mysterious circumstances while serving with the SOE. He was head of the Czech Section, and had trained the agents to conduct the assassination of Reinhard Heydrich. Alfgar was posthumously awarded the MC for his work with Tito's partisans. Michael fortunately survived the war, and thanks to him and his daughter Venetia, much of the Prichard papers, diaries, game books, articles, photographs and other memorabilia have been saved. The family library also contains many of the books that formed Prichard's own source of inspiration to take up the gun and rifle in pursuit of sport. The first time I visited the library and leafed through the books therein, and read Prichard's personal papers, I was astounded. Many of the books had been gifted to him by leading authors of his time, most of them true adventurers. The likes of Selous, Roosevelt, Cumming, Conan Doyle, Millias, Nansen, etc. had contributed copies to his collection, many with personal inscriptions inside their covers. It really was a treasure trove of sporting discovery.

During my research for this book I was allowed unlimited access to the Prichard papers, and I shall be forever grateful to both Charlie and his aunt Venetia for that privilege. Furthermore, I discovered in Prichard's own hand the original synopsis of *Sport in Wildest Britain*, and two previously unpublished chapters on golden plover and black grouse. These have been included in full in this third edition. Golden plover were, of course, covered in the original edition but only touched on in an abridged form within the chapter: 'Where the Snipe Drums'. This wonderful wader now shares a complete chapter dedicated to both it and the smallest of our ducks, the teal, in equal measure.

There are three sporting tomes in Prichard's library that stand out above all others for two very good reasons. Firstly, the three of them seemed to have had more use then the rest of the books in the library put together, and they contain many small pencil notes or underscores, presumably by Prichard himself. Secondly, he quotes these authors occasionally in SIWB. Not surprisingly, they were principal works of their time during the Victorian and Edwardian regencies, and were then every shooting man's must-have.

These works are: *Instructions to Young Sportsmen in all that Relates to Guns and Shooting* by Colonel Peter Hawker (born November 1786 – died 1853), first published in 1814. This book was an all-encompassing book on sport, particularly wildfowling, to which Prichard paid much attention as a boy. Hawker kept a diary from the age of sixteen and this forms much of his writings. He was a remarkable man, first following a military career, he purchased a cornet's commission in the 1st Royal Dragoon Guards, and quickly gained his captaincy. He is famously quoted as saying: "I was a Captain of Dragoons soon after I was seventeen years old, but paid dearer for it than anyone in the service". He served under Wellington in Spain and Portugal and led his squadron valiantly, but was badly wounded at the battle of Talavera. Hawker was then compelled to resign his commission and spend the rest of his life as a sporting squire, mostly shooting and maintaining a dairy of his gunnery exploits.

The Moor and the Loch by John Colquhoun (born March 1805 – died 27 May 1885) first published in 1840. Colquhoun was an exceptionally keen sportsman and also a superb observer of nature. Indeed at that time it was frowned upon if the sportsman was not also a naturalist; to be one without the other made the shooter a mere killer of game and not very gentleman-like at all. Prichard and all of his close acquaintances certainly subscribed to that school of thought. Colquhoun acquired vast experience in matters of Scottish sport and natural history, which was really quite exceptional, as he had hunted over most of mainland Scotland during his sporting lifetime. This book, along with the following work by St John, set the benchmark for future sport-

Right: Co-author Pete Carr at his desk writing Sport In Wildest Britain

ing writers. Prichard was one of the few that surpassed them.

Short Sketches of the Wild Sports and Natural History of the Highlands by Charles William George St John (born 1809 – died 1856) first published 1893. Written by an English naturalist and sportsman, son of General the Hon. Frederick St John, this work was recognised as that of an accurate observer and a writer of talent. As a sportsman, St John thought no obstacle too great, and loved to work for his sport. He often took more delight in seeing his dogs work well, pursuing more varied wilder game, than in securing large bags of partridges and pheasants. He would certainly have appealed to Prichard, who shared similar outlooks on sport. His style is clear and direct, sober details based on factual experience are wrapped in a genuine appreciation of scenery. His writings incentivised many a Victorian and Edwardian lover of wild sport to visit the hills and moors of the north.

There, then, are three classic books of sport that were found well-used in the Prichard library. However, two other interesting titles penned by Prichard's contemporaries are also worthy of note. The first of these is *The Wildfowler in Scotland*, by J.G. Millais (born March 1865 – died March 1931) published by Longmans, in 1901. Prichard had a great respect for Millais as naturalist, artist and sportsman, and he appears in SIWB. And it was J.G. Millais who introduced Prichard to Balranald estate in North Uist, where much of Prichard's wildfowling and seal hunting was done. The second title

is *Autumns in Argyleshire with Rod and Gun*, by Hon. Alfred Erskine Gathorne-Hardy (born 27 February 1845 – 11 November 1918), also published by Longmans but a year earlier in 1900. This book I personally believe set the style for SIWB. It is a collection of 30 years' worth of sporting reminiscences, at Poltalloch estate in Argyll. Many of the honourable gentleman's musings had been previously published in the *Field* and *Cornhill* magazines. Similarly, SIWB is mostly a collection of Prichard's published articles, but added to greatly during the war and after, to be eventually completed just before his death in 1922.

The author of *Autumns in Argyleshire with Rod and Gun*, is also the father of Prichard's great friends – Alfred (Jnr), and Geoffrey Gathorne-Hardy – who feature significantly in SIWB as either A. or G. Both brothers were firm friends with Prichard and had accompanied him on many a shooting foray and on some of his expeditions, and the two of them also served with him during the Great War. Alfred had crawled across no man's land with Prichard one dark night to successfully secure a sample of German breast plates to test the British rifle bullet's effectiveness. Unfortunately, Captain Alfred Gathorne-Hardy was killed during the fighting at Loos, valiantly leading his troop of Cameronian Scottish Rifles, between 25th and 26th September 1915. His death badly affected Prichard, and he wrote the following to his wife Lady Elizabeth: "I only heard in your letter (of the death of Alfred Gathorne-Hardy). Of course it is hard to realise – anyone here but him, yes. If it is any satisfaction,

I shot a German between the eyes at 5 o'clock today. I waited an hour and a quarter for him; he never knew I existed. I cannot write of A. I wish I could get a shot at one of those who made the war. I was applying for Alfred to help me."

Two days later, Prichard writes again to tell in detail the death of the German sniper and closes with the confirmation that he: "is to have Geoffrey Gathorne-Hardy as his assistant". The hand of war had clearly touched Prichard when he was writing parts of SIWB at the front. Occasionally, this could be seen in his jottings and letters as both negative and positive. The following is a good example found at the end of his chapter on the common seal: "Finally here is a story of the war which would not be well regarded by the Prussians. Who have, we are led to understand, undertaken this war in part with the hope of delivering the world from the ideals of the British sportsman, in order to re-place them by that "Kultur'" [sic German] which is the birth right and monopoly of the "children of Odin." A young British officer, wounded in the thighs, announced the fact thus: "Dear —, — Both legs down. Coming home with the Pickers up." That injured officer was Captain Geoffrey Gathorne-Hardy. His wounds would eventually heal, but he would lose a foot during the process, (he'd already lost a finger in the Boer war). Geoffrey finished the Great War with both the MC and the Croix de Guerre (Belgium).

Other notables who feature in SIWB are Eric Parker as E. He was a highly respected naturalist, sporting columnist and author who would later write Prichard's biography and become editor of the *Field*. Prichard's brother-in-law, Lord James Walter Grimston, who would become the 4th Earl of Verulam, often shot with Prichard, and it is he who accompanies him on occasion in SIWB. Confusingly, his other brother-in-law Major Geoffrey Barnett also features as another G. He was the willing participant in a last-ditch blood transfusion attempt at saving Prichard's life when the doctors had run out of answers.

I have always felt that SIWB wasn't a complete work, and the discovery of the original synopsis and the two previously unpublished chapters confirmed that my initial feelings were indeed correct. However, even if we include these two newly-discovered chapters, a number of sporting species that live wild in Britain are still omitted. The most obvious one is red deer. Prichard certainly pursued them, and mentioned stag stalking almost as a side-line in his chapter on ptarmigan. Was it perhaps that he considered stags inferior to the greater game of caribou and moose? The latter two of which he has written of in depth in various journals and other books on sport. It is the same with the roe deer, and here I am most certain it is because he subscribed to the Edwardian mindset that roe deer were definitely lesser game to be shot with the shotgun. I have included separate chapters of my own to cover both of these two very sporting species.

Woodcock and red grouse are also noted by their absence in the original work. They too deserve their place, and I have added my own anecdotes on woodcock to Prichard's chapter:

'Where the Snipe Drums', to form a new chapter alliance called: 'Where the Snipe Drums and the Woodcock Falls'. Indeed, this particular chapter contained as much on teal and lapwing as it did on snipe. I have therefore also stripped out all mentions concerning these two species and formed another separate chapter: 'With Teal and Plover'. Included in this is the first of Prichard's newly found work on golden plover added to the original text on teal and lapwing. Similarly, I have added my thoughts and experiences on red grouse to Prichard's second newly discovered chapter detailing the black grouse and its sporting attributes in the new chapter: 'Heath and Moor Game'. Finally, there is a chapter on ground game. Prichard's game books show he shot thousands of rabbits and hares. In recognition of this, I thought it fitting that they too should have a chapter of their own as they are both often found in the most desolate and wildest corners of Britain. Prichard's original two chapters on the grey and common seals I have amalgamated into one. It has been necessary for reasons of space to offer these in shortened form. The rest of Prichard's original work is reproduced here in full, including two new chapters, with the exception of one paragraph on whimbrel omitted from the curlew chapter.

I have extended all of Prichard's original chapters with anecdotes of my own concerning the relative species and their pursuit from a modern perspective – that is, during my lifetime to the present day. This work is therefore two books within one; it is a double memoir of two very different sportsmen, from two very different worlds, a century apart with a common interest and love for the chase of our varied game pursued in the wildest corners of Britain.

Like Prichard, I have been fortunate enough to engage big game around the world on four different continents, and earn a living writing about those experiences. However, as exciting these far-flung places have been during my extensive travel with gun, rod and rifle, I have always had a strong urge to return to Blighty. Be it the mountains, lochs, and firths of Scotland, Ireland's bogs and mosses, the rugged defiant Welsh coast, or England's dramatic moorlands and foreshores, all have touched the heart in the most moving of ways when out in the pursuit of sport, and long may it continue.

But you too can sample most if not all of this sport (apart from the curlew, and black geese). Class boundaries are now mostly gone. The rise of the middle class has enabled most of us who want to work to earn a reasonable living that will allow some shooting indulgence. Since Prichard's day all field sports have become more available. Now no longer the sole preserve of the aristocracy, and officer class, any safe, polite shoulder-gunner can follow the path of Nimrod if he so chooses. Wild sport is out there, you just have to find it. But please remember there is no becoming a sportsman by book alone; you may find inspiration and direction to that end within these pages, but it is by adherence to the rules, respecting one's quarry, and the experience thus attained that hopefully should qualify the tyro to become a respected sportsman before he ascends Valhalla. **PC**

Ptarmigan

on the **High Tops**

The ptarmigan owes much of the security it enjoys to the red deer. All through the stalking season he cannot be hunted, because the firing would disturb the high ground sacred to the big stags. Hard and barren as are his surroundings, it is surprising that he does not increase in numbers, or rather that he did not before the war, when vermin were killed down more completely than is now the case.

During the war [WW1] the ptarmigan had a bad time, and no doubt great numbers were killed by foxes; but this does not appear to have made much difference, and if one could only shoot the ground, it would be possible to-day to make as big a bag of ptarmigan as ever it was.

Like many other men, I have seen an immense number of ptarmigan and shot very few. Abroad I once made a journey across the great table-land of Labrador, where often a single ptarmigan alone stood between our little party and hunger. The curious thing about the ptarmigan which we met on that journey was their extreme wildness, especially on windy days. We used a .22 rifle to shoot them with, and when the wind was blowing high it was extremely difficult to get a shot at all; in fact, except in the lee of some great basaltic fragment, the birds rose and flew at eighty yards.

On a still evening all this was quite changed, and I remember once, when we were fishing, my comrade, Gathorne-Hardy, spotted a ptarmigan and left me to look after it and keep my eye on it while he went back to camp and brought the rifle. So I was left alone to contemplate the shades of evening with the ptarmigan. It was a very peaceful evening only spoiled by several million mosquitoes. I remember that when my friend returned my first intimation of his approaching presence was gained from a great pillar of these mosquitoes which towered high in the air above him, so that before his head appeared over the skyline, I knew that something living, either man or caribou, was on the move.

When my friend arrived, I pointed out the ptarmigan which I was "minding,"

whereupon he stalked and killed it.

At one other time or another we saw a good many coveys on the table-land, but we only killed eight. Still, in a hunger-march of this kind, eight ptarmigan are not to be despised.

However, to change the scene from Labrador to Scotland – and if you were to put down suddenly without knowing where you were, you might easily mistake one country for the other – I was once stalking on the hills of Inverness-shire, from which it is said on a clear day you can see the sea both east and west. We had spotted our stag long before, not a particularly exciting animal, but a distinctly shootable beast: black in colour, and with a heavy head of six or eight points. I was at the time utterly unfit, being only just out of hospital, so that I was quite grateful when a volume of mist appeared over the hill. We went forward in the direction of the stag for some time, and then lay down behind a rock to wait for the weather to clear. The old stalker evidently was not sure that this would happen, for he kept looking to windward and shaking his head mournfully. At first all

around was silent, and then quite close we heard the croaking cry of ptarmigan, which was repeated from lower down the hill. There could be little doubt that there were two or three coveys close to us, and though we could see nothing of them, a bird here and there kept calling ... At length, after we had waited half an hour – to be exact thirty-five minutes – the wind rolled away the mist, leaving the sun to shine down with all his northern power upon the huddle of mountains and the great green corrie at our feet.

My first glance was for the stag, and there he was right beneath us, about five hundred yards away. I was in full view, so I did not move but sat still as the stones that strewed the hillside. Then ten yards from me on my left front was a covey of nine ptarmigan, and not much farther off, straight ahead, another of eleven. I could not count them at once, because they were among the grey stones with which they harmonise so well, but as the time passed the birds became distinct. To get away without disturbing them was almost impossible. Anyhow we sat for a few minutes looking down on the scene. In the course of my travels I have looked upon many a wild and beautiful scene: the Andes rising thousands of feet above the lakes which lie at their base, with the immense forests of black Antarctic beech which clothe their slopes mirrored in the lakes; the great icebergs which float upon these lakes. That is a beautiful scene, but like the fiords

of Norway, or the huge cliffs of Labrador, its sense of vastness is too great.

But Scotland is quite different, and there is a friendliness about her hills and glens which in these other vaster lands is quite absent.

As we crawled away we put up one of the coveys, which disappeared round the knoll with its curious diving flight. The other covey meantime had run out of sight. Whenever I think of ptarmigan that scene comes back to me. I do not know how what is the record bag

of ptarmigan, but he is essentially the bird for an off day. No one wants to kill many ptarmigan, indeed, few people invade his solitudes, where he lives a more or less haunted life, crouching under the eye of birds of prey, and often hunted in that particular glen of which I write by the golden eagle.

The actual shooting of ptarmigan is usually easy, but a high wind makes them rise, as I have said, wild. They have also a habit of flying across from one high top to another, a matter of a few moments to them, but entailing perhaps a two hours' climb to whoever is pursuing them. They have exactly the same habit on the grey rolling table-land of Labrador, where they will fly from ridge to ridge in a manner that will soon tire one out. In fact, in Scotland, ptarmigan shooting generally consists of few shots and far between. The coveys are sometimes, however, very considerate, and fly around the same top instead off launching themselves into space. I do not think there is any bird which can be more considerate or more exasperating.

On some days everything is easy, on others, each flight of the birds is made as though they had an uncanny knowledge of the disabilities of man. Sometimes it is possible to drive ptarmigan, but as far as my experience goes, this is merely a matter of getting one or two shots. The line of flight of a covey is by no means certain, and the deer-stalkers do not pay much attention to its direction. Why should they? It is only once in every three years or so some crack-brained sportsman desires a day's ptarmigan shooting after the stalking season. Still, these impromptu drives are, are to my mind, more interesting than the set drives of the lower lands. I yield to no one in my joy in a day's ptarmigan driving, for – especially as I grow older – my mind goes back with just as much, perhaps more, pleasure to the little days, when one lurked behind a rock and a single attendant drove the top. **HP**

Above: The author enjoying success on the high flats of Coignafearn

Right: Head keeper Sandy Dey's remarkable Labrador retrieving a brace of ptarmigan

I have pursued the ptarmigan in Scotland, Scandinavia and Greenland. It is no secret that the snow grouse is my favourite of game birds, and I have been fortunate to have shot a good number. That said, I have been very careful not to over-shoot them in their sanctuaries, preferring only to shoot a brace or two from any given area. And as I like to be about the high-tops, my path has crossed that of the ptarmigan more often than most sportsmen.

In Prichard's time during the Great War, he clearly feared for this bird's survival in Scotland. In his own words he was convinced "the foxes had done them great harm," when the keepers were away at the front fighting for king and country.

On this point I would have to say his fears were unfounded. Only once have I have found evidence of sustained targeting of ptarmigan by hill foxes. This was at one particular den entrance. Outside the offending cairn, I found precious little else but ptarmigan wings, which the cubs had evidently been dining on. The vulpine parents of the said cubs had, on this occasion, tuned into searching the high ground for snow grouse. In my experience, the fox has a tendency to hunt downhill rather than uphill, and when you look at it from a fox fodder point of view, there is precious little prey on the high-tops other than ptarmigan. Interestingly, that particular year was a good one for ptarmigan, and no doubt the vixen and her beau recognised that fact, and changed hunting tactics to suit nature's bounty. I have seen this with hares on the low ground, when in good years there is a glut of leverets, and the foxes switch almost exclusively to hunting the young hares during the few weeks of *Lepus* abundance.

That said, the above was an isolated case, and I have only heard of one other similar occurrence. In light of this, I don't think that foxes take too many ptarmigan, and Prichard's concern was perhaps a little misplaced. Foxes will kill them by chance of course, but eagles and maybe the occasional falcon are the only predators that actively hunt ptarmigan. They will certainly kill more than Reynard in any one season I'm sure. Ravens and hoodies taken to high altitude foraging may destroy an odd clutch of eggs or chicks, but the bird's real enemy must be the increasing threat of climate change.

If not over-shot, most estates that host this delightful game bird will continue to have a shootable harvest for those who like their sport wild, and expect to work for it. But if weather patterns continue to get milder, ptarmigan populations may suffer irreversibly, and then it will be a different story. An example of this may be seen if we look at Arran, which once hosted the lowest and southernmost population of ptarmigan in Britain. Worryingly, the bird now seems to

Image: Peter Carr Collection

have disappeared from this isolated ptarmigan outpost off Scotland's south west coastline. It would be a tragedy to lose the pluckiest of game birds from Britain's fauna to milder weather patterns. As a species it has adapted over millennia to tackle the harshest of weather, and developed near as perfect a camouflage that nature could create in the unique environment that it lives in. If the snow doesn't come in the winter months, this bird's winter plumage would actually work against it, advertising rather than disguising its presence to every predator with hooked bill, tooth or claw.

The title of Britain's hardiest game bird has to got to go to the ptarmigan. Pronounced with a silent "P", it is a corruption of its Gaelic name *Tàrmachan*. In the Germanic tongues it is simply known as the *Schneehuhn* – which translates to snow hen or snow grouse. It is an apt description of this hardy bird that thrives above the snow-line, and one that I think I prefer to the Gaelic corruptive. A close but slightly smaller cousin of the red grouse, ptarmigan only thrive on the highest of Scottish mountain tops in Britain. It is a resilient little game bird that almost defies its very existence in such a harsh and unforgiving environment, but it seems this is just what ptarmigan prefer as an abode.

I was inspired in my youth by reading the exploits of that old ptarmigan shooting sage, Robin Rolfe, to eventually try out a day on the high tops in pursuit of the snow grouse. And when that inaugural ptarmigan shooting foray finally came round, it was the start of many adventures on great estates such as Coignafearn, Invercauld,

Glenshee, Glenshero, Tulchan, Black Mount, and Glen Etive. Furthermore, that initial encounter with ptarmigan proved to be the best day out I have ever experienced to the present day in pursuit of those wonderfully elusive snow grouse.

The sportsman cannot reasonably expect big bags of these birds and a brace per gun nowadays should be more than enough for the ethical sportsman. However, like the grouse, ptarmigan populations do fluctuate and in bumper years more birds may then be shot. My first foray after ptarmigan was just such a bumper year, and many moons ago, I and five friends were heading out onto the hills of Coignafearn estate, full of youthful enthusiasm.

We had squeezed into two Argocats and were about half way up the barely visible mountain track before eventually stopping and all gladly piling out of the cramped Argos. Leaving the semi-amphibious all-terrain vehicles behind, we fell in behind the keeper, Sandy Dey, and struck out for the scree line. Soaring higher than the great granite cathedrals that towered above us, a solitary golden eagle surveyed his dominions.

Heather and peat soon gave way to stone and scree, when we began to line out toward the ridge-line, dropping off intermittently as our group pushed on up the slope. My position was about mid-way and, while waiting for the line to be completed, I heard my first ptarmigan. Often described as sounding like a rusty door hinge being worked, I could think of no better description of this hardy bird's creaking call. As I watched on and listened intently, our quarry's melancholic call was the only sound to be heard in this desolate, almost lunar-like landscape, other than the occasional noise of my companions hop-scotching across the loose scree. Then from nowhere a wind whipped up around us, breaking the scene's solitary spell, and dispersing the soaring eagle to his eyrie in a sheltered cornice somewhere across the glen.

Just as we started forward, the now foreboding looking heavens opened in deluge and almost immediately we flushed a large pack of ptarmigan. In flushing they certainly took us all by surprise, struggling as we were through the heavy rain squall that stung our faces. In the midst of this flush one gun brought down an impressive

left and right which were quickly retrieved by the keeper's Labrador. The going underfoot on these mountain tops is hazardous to say the least in fine weather, but in rain and wind it is absolutely treacherous and one must take every precaution. Working the ridge side forward very slowly due to the difficult terrain, we soon flushed another pack. Erupting between me and the next gun the air was suddenly full of white wings. I cleanly folded one bird, as did my neighbour, and I soon had my first ptarmigan safely ensconced in the game bag. It was self-evident that the inclement weather was the reason for the birds being packed up as they were. Surprisingly, they were

Below: John Stevenson proudly displays his hard-won prizes on the high tops

Image: Peter Carr Collection

Image: Peter Carr Collection

Above: A good day in the early 1990s on Glenshero. 12 ½ brace ptarmigan, 9 ½ brace grouse and 4 mtn. hares. Author front row, first left

also far wilder than we ever expected that they would be. Due to them packing up there was only a slim chance of doing much by walking them up.

The keeper decided that he would attempt to drive the windswept ridge that we were on in an attempt to share out the shooting. This seemed a fine idea and he and his under keeper, along with the two Labradors, disappeared over the ridge while we remained stood in line in anticipation of the impromptu drive to come. Sometime after, the ptarmigan's white wings once more filled the foreboding sky. Flying as fast as the best driven grouse the first pack was gone, followed by another, and then the drive was finished as quickly

as it had started. The result for an undisclosed number of shots was one bird, but what fun we had had.

A change of tactics was once more agreed upon, and we all walked across the ground just driven to the opposite side of the hill to walk up what birds we could find into the wind. Hopefully the ptarmigan would then flip back over our heads, and again this should share out the shooting. While some of these white grouse would be swept forward around the buttresses of their rocky citadel, we would be sure to encounter them again before too long. This ruse worked a treat, and while this beat lasted the shooting was as wild and sporting as a roving gun could desire. Being as we were now on the lea side of the mountain, and out of the worst of the windy conditions, it couldn't have been more favourable. The rain had also abated, and was followed by a welcome display of rare Scottish sunshine to dry out one's sodden tweeds.

Moving forward once more the shooting was intermittent, but on occasion fast and furious, with birds swinging past one or over one's head. Sometimes the ptarmigan would alight within view, only to be flushed again and if unscathed alight once more. The large packs were not as evident at this side of the ridge, and birds were mostly broken into smaller coveys, some pairs and the occasional singleton. Obviously disorientated, a few single birds took to crouching tamely and we passed them by as being too easy victims and therefore unsporting.

This final beat passed by all too quickly as we picked our way cautiously among the big boulders and the loose scree. The walking gun on a ptarmigan beat has to be extra careful about both ricochets and the relative position of himself to his neighbouring guns. He also has to tread carefully on the treacherous lichen-clad rocks. Few dogs are needed for this type of shooting; indeed two are enough to help flush and retrieve dropped birds in this steep, slippery and unforgiving environment.

Our total tally when our united game bags were turned out produced 14 brace of ptarmigan, one brace of grouse and three and a half couple of blue hares, the latter taken on our final walk back to the Argos. The collective count under the circumstances represented an excellent bit of walked-up wild bird shooting that I have never bettered. Indeed, there can be no better earthly enjoyment for any roving shoulder gunner than the pursuit of ptarmigan in the wildest corners of Great Britain.

During the hunting of ptarmigan in Britain, Scotland's most jaw-dropping Highland vistas will become apparent on a clear day, and this I assure you will inspire the most adventurous of hunters. To me, the ptarmigan is the premier of Scottish game birds, pursued among some of the wildest and most dramatic landscapes in Britain. A denizen of the high tops, it never ceases to amaze me how the bird actually manages to scratch a living from the lichen covered scree slopes. And what tenacity it must have to survive on such bland diet, supplemented only by seasonal berries, insects or what few sparse heather shoots can be found in this challenging habitat on top of the world. When choosing a home, the species clearly had in mind that great mantra of real estate – location, location, location.

One has to be reasonably fit to hunt in this mountainous environment, where the fickle moods of the weather make all the difference, not just to success, but also to one's well-being and, occasionally, survival. Be ready for the worst, and wear sensible clothing and comfortable, well worn-in footwear. A compass and a map are an absolute must if you like your birds unguided, and even in experienced company, having them with you is good insurance against all eventualities. Two very different ptarmigan shooting forays stand out in the memory that underline a couple of the points mentioned above.

The first was on the Glenshee beat of Invercauld estate on a shoot marshalled by keeper Grahame Kerr. This estate is one of the few where it is possible to drive up to the scree line in the Land Rovers. Our party included a few characters straight out of Punch magazine. Two are seared into the memory like no others. Desperate was the MD of a scaffolding firm who had made a fortune out of scaffolding from the top down on many of our city's tallest buildings. He was a man known for his forthright opinions, and even better known for his propensity to share them vocally at every opportunity.

Dennis, on the other hand, was a quiet, dry-humoured Hull fishmonger, a wheeler-dealer type, with a quick eye for making a quid. Indeed he once thought the price of pub beer was so extortionate, that he allegedly opened a private drinking club – in a similar vein to the drinking dens of prohibition Chicago. But I remember Dennis better from my days keepering the Paull Shoot on the banks of the Humber. As a regular guest, Dennis was always a source of personal amusement. No more so than when he used to follow me round post-shoot when I paid the beating staff. I would hand over the beaters' hard won wonga, and Dennis would do his best to relieve them of it by attempting to sell them fingerless mittens, leather belts, caps, gaiters, et al. You name it; Dennis usually had it in his van for sale and, on the rare occasion he didn't, he would take orders – but only if secured with a deposit.

Dennis and Desperate had two other things in common; both were excellent shots, and were, shall we say, a tad portly due to good living. As we debunked from the Rovers and I explained the forthcoming operation, Dennis's demeanour changed from jovial to doubtful. "You mean this is a walk-up, not a driven shoot?" he questioned in disbelief, and visibly gulped as he looked up at the formidable ridge above us. "Of course," I replied, getting more nervous by the minute as realisation set in that someone had sold Dennis a pup. To this day I am not sure which one of the group had told Dennis the ptarmigan hunt was as an easy driven day with next to no walking involved, but I suspect it might have been someone he'd sold some item to without a guarantee.

Desperate, who can shoot from the lip as quick as he can execute a springing teal, didn't relive any of Dennis's concern with his next gem. "Dennis, I'm gonna struggle mate but you'll be f_____d for good if you attempt that ridge. Make no mistake you will flat-line before you get halfway up, and I ain't carrying ya." Dennis, clothed in best bib and shod in the finest of brogues, considered his options. "I tell you what" he finally said, "I'll tak the bottom of the line on the scree edge – in case of owt going back," thankfully averting a possible public relations disaster.

Fitness and correct clobber is the moral of that story, but I'm happy to say that Dennis, and Desperate, actually got the best of the shooting on what turned out to be an excellent day. For whatever reason, the rising birds went forward, dipped a wing and curved downhill to turn back over the bottom of the line. Desperate had sensibly opted for the next position up from Dennis and their formidable marksmanship accounted for some of the most sporting ptarmigan I have

ever seen shot. It was a fine display indeed, with the birds breaking back on the wind and keeping their height too. They came over the two guns like the best of driven grouse, and Dennis had the last laugh because as events went, he got his driven ptarmigan day after all.

The second anecdote I am about to relate is a good example of how the weather can quickly change in the Highlands. Gary Sharp and I were to attempt an old drover's route up the Highlander which, if we found it, would shave off a couple of hours hiking to the ptarmigan. Previous attempts by the then-keeper Ian Dingwall had failed to locate the old overgrown path.

Gary was a retired businessman who had done well in the chemical industry, and sold his company to enjoy the rest of his time doing what he wanted to. This mostly meant shooting and fishing, and as one of the boys he was always a good companion and keen for an adventure. Therefore when I suggested an attempt on the old drover's route up the Highlander, he was as keen as I to shave off a couple of hours that potentially would allow us more shooting.

The day dawned well with a good forecast, and as a front was due on the morrow, we decided to take advantage of the current weather window. Heading out along the march between Glen

Above: Another day in the early 90s, this time on Glenshee, 11 ½ brace ptarmigan, 2 brace grouse. Author kneeling

Image: Paul McGreevey

A ptarmigan melted into form atop of a rock not ten yards from us. Unseen thanks to its perfect camouflage, it had no doubt been eyeing us suspiciously, as we took our victuals. The increased movement made by us as we prepared to begin the hunt had unnerved the bird, and its own movement had given it away. It stretched and walked to the edge of the rock, ready to take to the wing as I marvelled at the close encounter. Then enough was enough, it was gone before Gary had even seen it, whisked away on the wind that had again come from nowhere.

No longer transfixed, I was aware that the scene of September tranquillity had gone with the ptarmigan. Replaced, it seemed, in just a few seconds by great billowing overcast clouds that had raced in from the west when I had been preoccupied with my close encounter. With the wind came a sudden drop in temperature, and I noticed the first hint of concern from Gary. He was checking his GPS was working, and the battery strength on his international rescue beacon. I ribbed him about his lack of confidence in his guide (me), and we spaced out to walk the ground into the strengthening wind.

A golden plover got up almost at my feet, and sped back like a bullet. Swinging the gun through with a good lead, I managed to bring the wader down first barrel. Made up with my performance I gave Gary the thumbs-up and headed back to pick the bird, and then the snow came. In no time at all we stood in two inches of snow, and I failed to find the bird.

Disgruntled at having to leave the bird despite an intense search we moved off again, but

Etive and the neighbouring estate of Dalness, we began our ascent. More by luck than design we soon found the remnants of the path. It petered out every now and then, but close scrutiny of the contours revealed where it was hidden in the heather. Despite a few checks and false starts, we made good time, and before long topped the ridge we would walk for ptarmigan.

Breaking out the flasks for a tea and a sandwich we stretched out on the granite slabs and surveyed the scene. The mid-September duck-egg-blue sky couldn't be faulted, and an occasional call of a golden plover added to the serene majesty of our location. Normally the plover had gone to the coast by now, but their wistful calls told us a few of their kin had stayed behind. Plover always excite me and I was keen to be on.

the biting wind on my windward side had cut the circulation to my hand. Unable to safely shoot, Gary (who can be relied upon to have every bit of kit about him), gave me an air activated hand warmer. This soon brought the feeling back and we carried on, it what was now a white-out. Gary now repeatedly questioned me about our whereabouts, and was clearly worried we wouldn't get off the mountain.

A covey of ptarmigan flushed and my two barrels brought down a bird that dropped over the ridge. In a normal situation it would have been easily picked, but safety considerations deemed it was better left. I made the decision that the sport should be curtailed and we should make haste our descent. It would have been foolish to return the way we had come, I knew if we kept the ridge to our right we would eventually come to a buttress that would mark the path down from Glas Bheinn Mor – if the limited visibility allowed. If we missed it, we would end up on Blackmount and run out of ridge. One thing for sure, I wasn't about to use Gary's rescue beacon and call in Thunderbirds just yet. Thankfully, despite Gary's doubt, I knew exactly our whereabouts and the buttress soon came into view, marking our way down onto the pony path that would take us back to the lodge. It wasn't a close run thing because I was in charge of the situation – not the situation in charge of us – but it certainly could have got serious, and if nothing else proves the fickleness of the Highlands and weather.

I have made an annual pilgrimage to the Highlands in pursuit of ptarmigan since that first fateful day on Coignafearn 20 years ago. The flame of excitement has never dimmed, indeed it is brighter than ever, and I look forward to the growing anticipation I always feel the closer I get to the Highlands. As I've said earlier, a brace of birds per gun is a more than adequate return for the sweat, tears and blisters often involved in the pursuit of ptarmigan. But believe me when I say, successful or not, a hunting hike up to the high tops will always be an unforgettably exhilarating experience.

The past few years I have spent most autumns in Argyllshire with gun, rod or rifle in hand, but increasingly I have favoured the gun, as the call of the ptarmigan, plover or grouse has won over the stag's roar, or the temptation to try a fly across and down the salmon pools. Of course this is all relative, and when the river is falling, with promise of new fish in the system after a storm-fed torrent subsides – it may be quite a different thing.

But enough of wistful thinking. Last season I was staying at Glen Etive Lodge and looking out through my bedroom window in the small hours at the mountain opposite. It was a perfect moonlit night with a clear star-studded sky, almost as clear as daylight. The particular peak I was staring up at in awe, known locally as the 'Highlander', was like an old friend to me. It is a Munro (a mountain over 3,000ft), and one of those hills with a hidden summit that seems to move farther away as you top consecutive ridges. We would be ascending it at dawn for a go at the ptarmigan, and the excitement was the reason for my insomnia. It is the same every year, until after a few days of exertion, followed by a late evening dram or two, I eventually settle into a more regular sleep pattern.

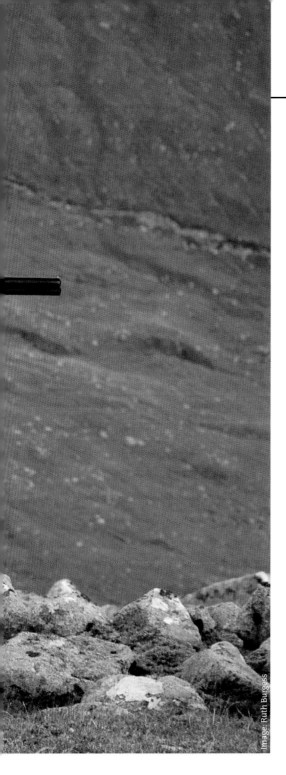

Four of us set out from the lodge at first light the following morning, with high expectations – touched with a little trepidation at the arduous climb ahead. We started at sea level and each foot of the 3,000ft ascent would be hard won. There would be no Land Rover or Argocat to shorten the distance, as the ground was just too rough for such vehicles. The entire journey would be on foot.

Splashing across the river ford, I took a longing look up the steep corrie, and struck out along the pony path that was the first leg of our journey. We would pass by the Robbers Waterfalls and eventually up to the first cairn built in the dip that forms the high pass between the peaks of Glas Bheinn Mor and our destination the Highlander. It would be here where, at last, the guns could be un-slipped at the scree-line.

Three hours later we were approaching the gods. At ptarmigan height and with guns in hand at last, we began the final pull up the mountainside. Lining out and keeping in some sort of a line is not easy on such inclines; the scree is slippery underfoot, and you quickly learn not to take balance for granted. Dropping my companions off one by one on the ascent, I struggled uphill and finally reached the ridgeline. Forming an evenly-spaced, downhill line, some 30 yards apart, four eager faces waited for the wave that would start proceedings.

After a few moments to recover my breath, I gave the eagerly-awaited signal and we collectively moved forward, eyes searching for the perfectly camouflaged mountain bird that is

Left: Andy Lovel dressed light for the high tops and in action

just too easy to pass by unoticed. Ptarmigan do not see too many two-legged predators, but are more used to the much more benign hiker. They are therefore relatively tame when shot lightly. Often, they will simply clamp down tight among the rocks and wait for possible danger to pass, which is their usual defence when threatened by their nemesis – the golden eagle. Therefore it is very important not to walk around the difficult scree sections of the terrain, as this is where the birds are most likely to be. One or two biddable dogs are all that is needed – mainly for retrieving work – if one is to hunt to a dog at all. If so, then Fido must be biddable and worked tight if chances are not to be spoiled. A headstrong or unruly dog will lift birds too far out in front, and this is a heart-sinking sight after such a difficult hike. Better to keep the dog at heel and work the ground carefully to maximise your chances of success. The only exception to this would be a good pointer or setter. Unfortunately, ptarmigan ground is rarely suited to these specialists. That said, there are a few rare places, with high flat-topped, wide ridges, in which shooting ptarmigan over pointers or setters would be pure perfection.

Approaching the second cairn, I noticed a single bird at the same moment as Andy Lovel, my adjacent gun. The ptarmigan had clamped down true to form as we cautiously moved ahead. If it broke left it would be mine, but if it went forward or to the right, it would be Andy's shot. The excitement of my neighbour was strange to watch. It was his first bash at

Image: Ruth Burgess

Left: First ptarmigan for Mr Lovel and congratulations are in order

Opposite: The author admires another snow grouse after a successful shot

hunting ptarmigan and he could barely control his anticipation. He edged ever nearer to the flush with his legs shaking in a strange manner, which would henceforth be forever known as 'the Lovel shuffle'. Finally the grey, speckled mountain grouse had had enough, and lifted into the air in flurry of snow-white wings. Andy instantly shouldered the gun and folded the first ptarmigan of the day with a well-practised snap shot. The bird was more or less safely retrieved by Billy, our attendant black Labrador, and token gun dog for the day. After admiring Lovel's prize, it was slipped into the game bag, before we all moved forward once more.

Dropping into some dead ground, I caught the unmistakable sound of nervous ptarmigan. There was an unseen covey nearby, and I cautiously alerted Andy to pass the message along. The ptarmigan's creaking call is similar to the sound of the aforementioned rusty hinge, and is used by the birds to communicate in mist or when about to flush. Seconds later, a whirr of wings a few yards out in front saw the covey erupt and bank hard left downhill. Wrong-footed, I missed with both barrels, and had my eye wiped again by Andy, who confidently took a neat right and a left to take his tally to an impressive hat-trick. Behaving impeccably, the covey flew the gauntlet right down the line past the third gun Ruth Burgess who, like me, also fluffed it, and finally to the last gun, James Folkard, who took out the trailing bird before they disappeared across the glen to quieter pastures.

With two brace safely ensconced in the game bag, the line moved on again and two more coveys lifted well out of range as we climbed the last rise and out onto the flats that led to the summit. We were rewarded for our earlier climb as the going was much easier now, and we picked our way cautiously among the big boulders and over the loose scree. At last a singleton rose before me, and I executed a fine first barrel shot to add another bird to our haul. Half an hour later we reached the abrupt end of the massif, and a rapidly sinking sun reminded us it was time to begin our descent from the heavens. Turning about we headed back along the broken ridge and flushed a few smaller coveys, two pairs and another singleton, without touching a feather. With a final tally of two and a half brace, we slipped our guns, and four very contented shooters began the arduous descent from the high tops as the sun slipped below the western horizon.

One of the most enjoyable ptarmigan jaunts I ever experienced at Glen Etive was with Prichard's great-grandson, Charlie Jacoby. As editor of *Shoot in Scotland* magazine, I commissioned him to write a feature about it, which arrived, as always from Charlie, an hour before deadline. Furthermore, he had let his literary bent run away with him, and the feature actually arrived as a short chapter rather than the requested two-page article. An abridged version made it to press, after some frantic subbing and cutting. The following anecdote is the original work in its entirety, written with a good dash of Charlie's trademark wit:

Left: Success with the snow grouse on the Highlander at Glen Etive

If you don't know Glen Etive, picture rough Scottish coastline in your mind, see hills rising to 3,000ft straight out of the sea and fancy, of all the places along the Argyllshire shore, the one most likely to win an award for drama and beauty, and there you have it. The estate has its own river, the Etive, running into its own little firth and behind it a good stag forest with the chance of not just grouse but ptarmigan, and the odd black cock.

Glen Etive is sufficiently brooding to have been the star location of the last of the Harry Potter films – just when the storyline goes a bit dark and everybody starts to die. And you would need magic to keeper ptarmigan. You would need to be Hagrid. In Scotland, they are only happy over 3,000ft where they appear to live off the rock and stones they look like. Where you can do a reasonable job on grouse by medicating grit and

shooting foxes, the only sure-fire way to encourage ptarmigan is to reverse climate change and shoot ramblers, only one of which is Scottish Government policy.

It is always wise for a writer to blow a little smoke the editor's way, and in this case I am doubly grateful to the esteemed Mr Carr, not just for asking me to write this piece but for asking me to come on what turned out to be my most entertaining sporting day of that year. It was his 'week' at Glen Etive.

Think editor and you doubtless see a man of stern outlook and serious demeanour, so imagine my surprise that Peter Carr's keenest interest in the lodge was which room Emma Watson slept in when they were filming. Once he had got over that, he set to work making our time there as interesting as he could. There was fishing when there was ever a chance of fish. Another guest and sporting writer, young Byron Pace, was there too. This is before he grew a beard, so we were stunned when the child started pulling out salmon like rabbits from a hat. That was one misspent toddlerhood, which would rapidly get worse under the guiding wing of Peter Carr esq.

Pete's background includes a large dose of gamekeeping and not a little work on commercial trawlers. I could see him turning round in his mind more effective methods of fishing as he watched the other guests thrash the water. Happily, the sportsman in him prevailed and his greatest joy was to take a trout rod up the hill to find the little lochans that teemed with wild but moody brown trout.

So it was the evening before our last full day,

Right: Charlie Jacoby prospecting for wild hill trout at Glen Etive

Below: Snow often caps the peaks at Glen Etive, even early in the season

Image: Paul McGreevey

Chapter One
Ptarmigan on the High Tops

after most had left – indeed it was only Pete and I – and we were discussing what to do.

"Another stag?"

Pete felt he had done stags.

"Chance of a grouse?"

It would mean a long walk with little reward.

"How about take everything on a long walk with little reward?"

So that's what we decided to do, and saluted said decision with a number of fine flavoured drams.

There is a lochan half way up one hill, Bloody Loch, where the Campbells allegedly washed off the Macdonald blood after the massacre at nearby Glencoe. It holds small Scottish brown trout, what lazy fishing writers call 'hungry trout', what the great Scottish poet Robbie Burns calls 'wanton trout'. On the right day, they can be easy fishing.

We went up there with the keeper in the estate Argo. I know it is cheating to do the first 1,000 feet like this, but we would have another 2,000 feet to go on foot before we summited, and we were laden with rifle, shotgun, rods, sticks, lunch, wine and my two spaniels. I'm not sure why Pete brought glass Paris goblets from the lodge. They did not survive the journey.

This was the wrong day for the trout. They were not easy at all. My standard-issue fly choice for these lochs is grey wulff to represent the white moth that floats off the heather, Dick Walker's mayfly nymph to imitate the stonefly larvae they feed on underwater, and black gnat or zulu to be almost everything else that survives long enough here to make up its mind to try drowning. It was

Image: Peter Carr Collection

Above: The author and the co-author's great-grandson enjoying elevenses alongside the Bloody Lochan

a warm day but not the kind of bright and blowy one when the grey wulff does best. The nymph was the taker. As a north-countryman, Pete often fishes a team of wet flies behind a bubble without shame. He catches fish.

After landing a brace he left to try another lochan. I spotted two duck on the other side of Bloody Loch – a hen teal, strangely paired with a mallard drake. I swapped rod for 20 bore and started one of my longest stalks of the year. From behind a glacial relic boulder, I had to wait until the birds were sufficiently hidden by the overhanging heather and peat on the edge of the loch before I could move. The last 20 yards were across open bog, so it was a question of striding that

part purposefully and manfully, as if to reach the duck and ask them directions or somesuch, but certainly to wrongfoot them into thinking I cannot be here for the duckshooting. The ducks looked at the tweed-monster marching towards them and paused just too long before they took off. The first shot was a clean miss over the top of the mallard, the fastest rising bird, but the second shot hit the teal and the dogs raced forward in unruly style to win the honour of retrieving it.

By lunchtime Pete had returned, and we had half a dozen fish each, a teal, and we were swigging wine out of the bottle. We made our decision then. In the immortal words of Yazz, 'The only way is up'. Leaving rods, rifle and the bag-so-far to go down the hill in the vehicle – taking sticks, dog and the shotgun – we decided on ptarmigan.

I like walking but I am not a good walker. I am an especially bad walker when carrying anything up a hill heavier than the suit I am wearing. The same slopes that would win prizes for their landscaping are sods to ascend. I am reduced to counting 100 steps, pausing every tenth for three breaths, and again pausing on the century for a full half a minute – it works for me.

The last time I shot ptarmigan was in the barren grounds of Canada. Called 'The Labrador' by previous generations of fearless sportsmen, this is a big flat country, riddled with lakes, that starts at 1,500ft above sea level. There are only a few places in the area where we landed our canoes that it is possible to climb out of the river gorge, and on to the barren grounds. It was a 10-week trip and, at the start of it, carrying 60lb packs, four of us would average an hour per 1,000ft ascent.

By the end of it, we were down to 30 minutes per 1,000ft.

Here in Scotland, even with just 20lb of extra weight about me, I was more than an hour per 1,000ft. But we made it.

Half way up, we met a Soay ram, with a full curl on his horns and ticks the size of large marbles. He was standing firm on the narrow path and didn't like the look of us at all. As we advanced he charged, Pete, who shooting from the hip, sent him on his way downwards with a flourish. Olé. The ram was not supposed to be on this hill, but he must have lived here for years. His head was soon in Pete's game bag.

The summit attempt was achieved, and we found the unpromising pile of grey stones that ptarmigan like to call home. It is the same in Labrador. Generally, the first you know of a covey is the burst of birds near your feet as up to half a dozen stones grow wings and throw themselves into the air. If you are sharp-eyed, before they launch, you will see one or two of them poking up necks out of the rocks like little Loch Ness monster silhouettes.

It is a few seconds after the covey takes off that you see ptarmigan at their best. All the grouse species are dramatic in flight, the red grouse for the way it skims the heather towards you, and the black grouse and capercaillie for the way they race over the tops of trees, looking like lumbering Lancaster bombers with deceptive speed. Where the ptarmigan scores is its backdrop. You generally see Scottish ptarmigan flying below you, which means there is usually a mile of empty space both below and behind them

to the next hillside. That perspective is one of the reasons I love ptarmigan.

Back in Labrador, they were not hard to shoot. To keep the weight of the packs down, I carried a single-barrelled .410 and, because we were hungry most of the time, tended to shoot the birds on the ground if I could. Even if a covey took off, and even with my poor marksmanship, it was usual to hit one. Maybe I wasn't hungry enough after comfortable lodge-living but, once the birds started flying up here, I could not hit one, however hard I tried.

Pete and I shared the gun. We would walk 20 yards apart and we put up a lot of birds. After more than a dozen had flown down the hill complaining about my ineffective shooting as much as Pete was, Pete spotted one of those grey necks looking out from the rocks. He took the gun and disappeared behind a rise. I did not see the action but there was a bang and a puff of feathers drifted towards me as if he had shot a small but expensive scatter cushion at close range. Whatever his story, he had his ptarmigan and I did not.

We had two cartridges left and Pete generously gave them to me, but without much hope I would do anything useful with them. As the next bird got up, the gun came to shoulder, and down went my first Scottish ptarmigan. The dogs were delighted – but not as happy as me, and even that paled into insignificance compared to Pete's bliss at the bird's ill-luck.

We kept the last cartridge in case of any grouse, or more duck on the way down, and we started our descent. We saw none, but a walk with a gun is so much better than just a walk. It's like turning up the volume on the landscape.

Ptarmigan shooting is for the fit, and it is when you start to go down the hill, that your fitness, or lack of it, comes home to roost. My heart was happy, I had my three T's: teal, trout and ptarmigan (silent 'P' so it counts), and so did Pete: Tenacity, Temperament and Tolerance. And yet, going through my mind were the words of friends, relations and doctors from long ago that this or that about me, usually brought about by some self-inflicted abuse ranging from too much butter on toast in my teens to too much of everything else enjoyable 'will give you trouble in later life'. They were right.

I had my ptarmigan just in time. This is later life.

As far as wild sport goes, ptarmigan shooting cannot be beaten, but as Charlie outlines above, you have to be reasonably fit. They are a hardy, resilient game bird living in an unforgiving environment, but that is only part of their allure. The sportsman has to work hard for his chances, and when presented make the most of the few he is given. Furthermore, this is the most exquisitely flavoured game bird on Britain's quarry list, all the more enjoyable for the pain, sweat and sometimes tears involved in getting it to the plate. In short, ptarmigan shooting is always an adventure and one that all dedicated but fit bird shooters should sample at least once in a lifetime.

The record bag of Ptarmigan was achieved on 25th August 1866 by the Hon. Geoffery Hill, who shot 112 ptarmigan to his own gun at Achnashellac, Rosshire. This total does not seem to have been beaten even by a party of guns who shot 112 on a day's driving in 1901 at Gaick, Invernesshire. **PC**

Right: Charlie Jacoby finally claims his ptarmigan on Ben Maol Chalum with Minor and Muffin in attendance

Image: Peter Carr Collection

Capercaillie

Prince of the Pine Forest

Concerning the derivation of the word capercaillie, there are differences of opinion so well marked as to claim the distinction of a controversy. With regard to the second part of it we are all agreed. It comes from the Gaelic word *coille*, a wood, but the first offers to scholar's opportunity for one of those differences of opinion which make up in bulk the fascination of philology.

Cabhar means an old bird, *Gabhar* means a goat; and in this connection it is interesting to note that *Gabhar-athar* = the snipe = the goat of the air, so called doubtless from its bleating cry; or *Cabhar-athar* = bird of the air, in which case we get *Cabhar-coille = Capercaillie =* bird of the woods. On the other hand the word cabhar is by no means idiomatic, and the noun has long since passed out of use. The Encyclopaedia Britannica has it "*Cabhar*, an old man, by metaphor an old bird, which is the old bird of the wood, the capercaillie."

That is one view. The other starts at *Capull*, a horse; *capull-coille* = the horse of the woods. In *Desc. Reg. Scotiae* (1578) we read: "*In Rossia*

quoque Louquhabria (Lochaber?) *atque allis montanis locis non desunt abietes, in quibus avis quaedam rarissima capercalze; id est Sylvester equus vulgo dictum frequens sedit, corvo illa quidem minor, quae palatum edentium sapore longe gratissimo delinit.*"

To this derivation I personally incline, since, having weighed the evidence, as far as one ignorant of the Gaelic tongue may, I agree with him who wrote: "It is called horse of the woods because of its size, strength and beauty, as compared with other wood birds." These seem good reasons enough; so let the mighty bird enjoy his high sounding title.

The standard work upon the capercaillie is Harvie Brown's *Capercaillie in Scotland*, a book which it is safe to say will have its readers as long as there are sportsmen in this country.

Mr. Harvie Brown writes: "Of the occurrence of the capercaillie in earlier historic times and prior to the extinction of the species in Scotland, there is not so much to relate which has not been quoted"; but after stating that the bird was known to the ancient Britons as *Ceiliog Coed*, he goes on to assign to Hector Boetius (1526) first mention of the species.

In *Old. Stat. Acct. of Scot. XX.* 473, may be found the following illuminating and delightful letter written by James VI to the Earl of Tullibardine: *"James, Right trustie and right well-beloved cosen and counsellor, we greet thee well. Albe-it our knowledge of your dutiful af-fection to the good of our service and your countries credite doeth sufficentlie persuade us that you will earnistlie endeavour yourself to express the same be all means in your power; yet there being some things I that behalf requisite, which seem not-withstanding of so meane moment as in that regaird, both you and others might neglect the same, if our love and care of that native Kingdom made Us not the more to trie their na-ture and necessity, and accordingly to give order for preparation of every thing that may in any sort import the honour and credite thereof. Which consideration, and the known com-moditie yee have to provide, Capercaillies and termiganties, have moved us very earnestlie to request you to employ both your oune paines and the travelles of your friendis for provision of each kind of the saidis foules, to be now and then sent to us by way of present, be means of our deputy-treasurer; and so as the first sent thereof may meet us on the 19th of April at Durham, and the rest as we shall happen to meet and rancounter them in other places on our way from thence to Berwick. The raritie of these foules will both make their estimation the more pretious, and confirm the good opinion conceaved of the good cheare to be had there. For which respectis, not doubting but that yee will so much the more earnestlie endeavour your-self to give us good satisfaction anent the premises, as yee will do us acceptable service. We bid you farewell. — At Whitehall, the 14th of Marche, 1617."*

Surely it calls for no great stretch of the imagination to picture the Earl's "oune paines" and the "travelles" of his friends. The caper was doubtless even then a wary bird and a lover of the high woods, nor were the weapons of the day such as to command success. Doubtless the wild hunters who were Tullibardine's clansmen trusted more to snare than missile. This brings us to an interesting question. Were wildfowl such as snipe and woodcock much less sophisticated in the days of yore of which we read when thousands were taken? Could such success attend a saner setter of to-day?

Another point of interest is raised by the letter of King James. Evidently the royal palate recked [sic] not of the "turpentiny" flavour which would probably cause the modern "gun" to decline with thanks, in the unlikely event of his

host offering him to have a brace of caper "put into the motor."

Of course our ancestors had excellent digestions, and also were catholic in their tastes.
"Pages with ready blade, were there
The mighty meal to carve and share.
O'er capon, heron-shew and crane,
And princely peacock's gilded train,
And o'er the boarhead, garnished brave,
And cygnet from St. Mary's wave,
O'er ptarmigan and venison
The priest had spoke his benison."

This bill of fare gives good evidence of their capabilities, and it is highly improbable that capercaillies were absent from that groaning board. Except under the title "giant grouse" no one has (as far as I know) succeeded in putting them into poetry.

"And from the pine's high top brought down
The Giant Grous, while boastful he displayed
His breast of varying green, and crow'd and clapp'd
His glossy wings."

The date – March the fourteenth – of King James's letter enables us to fill in the subsequent slaying of the capercaillies destined for the royal table. The messenger left Whitehall on the Ides and rode north. The birds which (we may suppose) arrived in Berwick on April 19th may or may not have begun to pair, but all shot or taken after almost certainly had, a fact which must have rendered the task of the Earl and his friends the easier.

The caper appears to have been welcomed as an addition to the Royal menu on another recorded occasion. From the *Black Book of Taymouth: "To the Right Worshipfull, his much honoured friend the Laird of Glenorquhy, this – much honouredSir, Immediatelie after the receat of your letter on Saturday, I went and shew your capercailizie to the King in his bed-chamber, who accepted it weel as a raretie, for he had never seen any of them before. — (signed) Jo. Dickson. Perth. The 3 of Februar. 1651."*

The question of the distribution of capercaillie in the British Isles prior to their temporary extinction is naturally of interest, but it is also a matter upon which details are meagre. As early as 1528 they are mentioned by inference as existing upon the lands of the Earl of Atholl, and again in Taylor's *Visit to the Brae of Marr*, as existing there as well as in Sutherlandshire and other counties. It is also quite clear that the birds were to be found in some numbers in Ireland, but to attempt to define their range in the one country or other would be absurd. Their presence is referred to by many writers of the sixteenth, seventeenth, and eighteenth centuries; but midway through the last the caper had become a very rare bird indeed.

The fact remains that in 1745 the last capers disappeared from Strathespey, and about the same time but a few were left near Thomastown in Tipperary. Roughly speaking, we may assume that in the year 1780 at latest (and probably considerably earlier) no caper "display'd his breast of varying green" in woods Irish or Scottish. In which country he lingered the longer, who can be sure? The evidence on this point is mostly of authors who were born after the disappearance of the last of the capers. Let us leave the old breed with a quotation from the Rev. L. Shaw, who goes more into detail concerning the caper than does any other early author:

"Caperkylie (called also Cock of the Wood); in Latin *Capricalea*, as if he infested the goats; but properly in Erse, *Capal-coil-ie* – the Wood horse, being the chief fowl in the woods. He resembles and is the size of a turkey-cock, of a dark grey, and red about the eyes; he lodges in bushy fir trees, and is very shy; but the hen, which is much less in size, lays her eggs in the heather, where they are destroyed by foxes and wild cats, and thereby the Caperkylie is become rare. His flesh is tender and delicious, though somewhat of a resinous fir taste."

So from the 1760 until the year 1836 the caper ceased to be counted among the gamebirds of Britain. During these years the shooting of two or three specimens is chronicled; but, as the best authenticated of these took place about 1810, it is more than probable that the victims were strayed imported birds. It is dimly possible that, somewhere in the rugged pine woods, a few brace may have survived, but we have no real evidence of the fact.

The reason of their extinction in Scotland and Ireland is purely a matter of conjecture. On this subject Harvie Brown writes:

"What appears to be the most likely factors were as follows: The proable destruction of great forest tracts by fire (evidence of the destruction of great tracts of forest country are frequently to be met with in early history. Thus to get rid of wolves, a large pine forest extending from the western braes of Lochaber to the Black Water and Mosses of Rannoch was burned to expel the wolves) ...the cutting down of the same by man as late as the days of Cromwell, and the wasting away of forests from natural causes... It was not until the beginning of the eighteenth that any arboriculture became general in Scotland."

At which we may leave it, and passing by the years when the Giant Grouse was absent from Scottish woods, let us trace the story of his restoration. During the first thirty years of the nineteenth century certain efforts were made to reintroduce the capercaillie. They failed. The birds, which were brought over from Sweden in very small numbers, did not thrive. In 1827 Lord Fyfe [sic] imported a cock and hen. The hen died after reaching Montrose Bay. The year 1829 saw another importation of a cock and hen at Mar Lodge. This time the hen laid twenty-four eggs – all addled.

And now we must let L. Loyd, the author of delightful works on Scandinavia, tell the epic of a success in attaining which he himself was largely instrumental:

"It is fortunate that for the sporting world that the Capercali, after the lapse of more than a century, is once more included in the British fauna, and I feel proud in having been a contributor in a small degree to so desirable an event...

"For a long while no one would move in the matter, but at length in the autumn of 1836 the late Sir Thomas Fowell Buxton, then recently returned from Taymouth Castle, where he had been much struck with the great capabilities of the woods for the naturalisation of the Capercali, took up the affair in good earnest.

"'Influenced by the desire, in which I am sure you will concur,' so he wrote to me, 'to introduce these noble birds into Scotland, coupled with that of making Lord Breadalbane some return for his kindness to me, I request you to procure for his Lordship, at whatever cost, the requisite number.' He at the same time placed his head keeper at my disposal – no slight sacrifice for a Norfolk game-preserver. It was indeed, indeed, an onerous commission, as prior to this time it had been a matter of difficulty to procure even a brace of living Capercali in Sweden; but by

distributing placards throughout the country offering ample rewards, and by instructing the peasants how to knot their snares so as not to kill the birds, my object was at length gained, and within a few months receipt of the Baronet's letter, twenty-nine Capercali, followed up shortly after by twenty more, were on the their way from Sweden to Taymouth Castle, and with the exception of a single one killed by accident, all reached their destination in safety.

"The arrival of this magnificent collection in Scotland caused quite a sensation; every one was delighted that matters thus far had gone well… In September 1837, not very long after the arrival of the twenty-nine, he (Sir Thomas Fowell Buxton) wrote me as follows: 'I have just returned from Taymouth, where I have been reminded of you very frequently by the Capercali. I saw eighteen of them in excellent health and plumage a few days ago; the other ten, six hens and four cocks, were turned out and there is reason to hope that they are doing well – so that, thanks to your energy in collecting them, Larry's care in bringing them over, and Lord Breadalbane's anxiety for their welfare, our experiment is likely, I trust, to succeed; and Scotland to be re-stocked with this noble bird. They are greatly admired by every one, and very deep interest is felt about them… Nothing can surpass the woods into which they are to be turned out, and the protection they will receive,' the writer then goes on to say; 'and as Lord Breadalbane's territory is so large, I hope they will not be disposed to leave such excellent quarters.'"

A letter from Lord Breadlabane to Mr. Loyd dated five years later reads as follows:

"I have great pleasure in informing you that the Capercali have thriven most excellently. The experiment of putting the eggs under the Grey Hen was attended with perfect success, and there are now a goodly number of these birds hereabouts."

Mr. Loyd continunes: "It is very satisfying to add that the Capercali have subsequently flourished in the Highlands in an extraordinary manner. Less than four years ago, indeed (1862), Lord Breadalbane himself told me he imagined there was fully one thousand of these birds on the Taymouth property. His head keeper, moreover, in a letter to a friend estimated them at double that number."

Taymouth, although it was first, was not the only point at which the caper were reintroduced. They were imported at Tulliallan and at Lathirsk, but not into Arran, where a few birds have nevertheless been shot. In 1860 they were "put down" on the hills at Cortachy, where they have thriven exceedingly and seem to be still increasing. In October 1911, during the course of a short walk with the beaters of some ten minutes' duration through an outlying portion of the woods of Tullo Hill, we saw no less than eleven of the grand birds; and in January of this year in driving the same hill about thirty were seen (or heard) by the writer, and probably double that number broke back. In 1856, or four years before the Cortachy importation, caper were observed at Lindertis, near Kirriemuir, thirty five miles from Taymouth. Indeed it is from Taymouth that all the neighbouring country has been re-stocked, the birds have spread mostly east and south to a distance of fifty and sixty miles and even farther. It is said by observers that the wandering or colonising propensity is strongest in the hens, which sometimes suddenly appear and settle down in districts where caper are unknown. The cocks do not follow until a year or two later, with the result that in the springs before their advent the caper hens nest with the blackcock. The hybrid is a beautiful and very pugnacious bird.

It is probable that every year sees an advance in the distribution of capercaillie, and though in their choice of abode they are very arbitrary, yet the rough rule may be laid down that they prefer and thrive best upon hillsides having a southern exposure. Their lines of demarcation are very clearly marked, and caper will live their lives within easy flight and sight of woods which they can never be induced to visit, and yet when the spirit seizes them they are great wanderers, as is proved by the fact that one was identified in Mansion House Road on the outskirts of Edinburgh in May 1876.

Having now traced the history of the caper from early times, and having seen him flourish, become extinct, be reintroduced and flourish once more, lets us consider him as a game-bird, an aspect under which I humbly submit that he is neither properly appreciated nor at all fairly treated.

For some reason the caper has been left as nearly outside the law as any bird not included under the head of vermin can be. He comes in, so to speak, with the crowd under the Wild Bird Protection Act, which allows him to be shot from August 1st to the end of February, thus giving him but five months' protection. This lack of protection is a sad mistake; for to permit the murder of caper fledglings in August is both senseless and short-sighted. The caper hen does not lay her eggs much before the end of May, and – as her period of incubation is twenty six to twenty-eight days – the young are not hatched until the latter end of June. What then of the law that permits these immature birds to be shot on August 1st, when barely two months old? And what kind of sport do they give? Young unwieldy bodies rising slowly from thick undergrowth present marks which must either be let alone or riddled with shot. Of course I am quite aware that the fortunate owners or lessees who have caper on their ground do not permit this sort of thing as a general rule. They know too well what a difference a couple of months will make to that lumbering mass of feathers. Then he will be in beautiful plumage, and, dashing out above the pine trees before the beaters, he will probably give the gun who essays him as sporting a shot as he can desire, and the chances are – more especially if the movements of the said gun are owing to his position, at all cramped or confined – will leave him wondering how he missed so big a bird so clean and fairly.

But many people who have leases of shootings which last only a couple of months; more still find it necessary to go south in September, and in such cases the caper sometimes fare badly. "I've paid for them," argues the lessee, "so, hang it all! I may as well have them," and so he does. But it is all a sad pity, and unquestionably a law should be passed protecting caper until the 1st of October. Against such a proposal would probably be arrayed the quota of keepers and game-preservers who believe in destroying caper at every opportunity. These people say that caper drive away pheasants and black game, and do great harm to the woods. In those allegations there is just enough truth to make them dangerous, and we will return to a consideration of them later.

By far the greater number of caper killed each year in Scotland are brought to bag when the woods are driven late in the year. It is usual to shoot both cocks and hens, and although on some estates this is a reasonable policy, upon others it is a mistake. In this connection everything depends upon the lie of the land of the estate. In most of the famous caper counties of Scotland there is a proportion of wild wooded land, clothing gullies and hillsides, which would not repay an organised drive. These places are practical sanctuaries to the caper, and where such exist both cocks and hens may be shot in woods of the lower ground without damaging the stock too much. But where woods are of small, or comparatively small, extent, and fairly easy of access, the caper must be shot in a very discriminating manner, or one fine October morning the owner will find that the birds have been exterminated on his ground. The young caper – for all the strength he may later attain – is a weakly thing during

his first month of life, and it is probable that the hen which rears three chicks to maturity is doing more than average good work.

In the vast forests of Norway and Sweden the caper seem to hold their own fairly well, notwithstanding the toll taken from their numbers by a large variety of creatures of prey. The caper hen nesting on the ground has little chance in saving her brood from the keen nose of the wandering lynx. Also in Norway a good many caper are shot when the snow is deep. At this time of year a hunter on a ski can cover a large extent of ground, and as he invariably fires from long ranges (Kristian Fiskum, the most skilful elk-hunter of the Namsos Valley, who annually kills a good many caper, told me that he rarely fired under one hundred and fifty yards) he can, by shooting the birds on the lower branches first, sometimes kill three or four without moving. But to do this a man needs to be a good shot. On the other hand, the woods of Norway are so vast and so continuous that they provide a splendid refuge. No doubt there are large quantities of caper in them, though I personally have never seen more than nine birds in a day. But the case of Norway is by no means on all fours with that of Scotland, and it is I fear, a fact that the spread and increase of our most lordly bird of chase has been both hampered and damaged by the actions of the ignorant and the narrow-minded.

It is deeply to be regretted, for what an addition the chance of shooting a caper makes to one's enjoyment of a good day's driving of some dark wood of the north! Not long ago I found myself on a high hill facing such a wood.

The snow was on the ground, and all day we had been occupied in driving the pheasants, the roe, the caper and the ground-game which inhabited it into the last beat. Below me I could see the next gun perched on the sheer of the hillside attempting to kick himself a footing, nor was he, so far as I could judge, succeeding very well. Above him towered the wall of the wood, and I was trying to calculate the distance a bird would have to travel between coming over the wood into his sight and its attainment of the angle behind him at which it would be impossible to shoot. It was not a long space, giving hardly time for a snap shot – no more – and I must say that, looked at from my standpoint, the dash of the caper cocks over this space seemed to constitute as difficult shooting as I have seen. A woodcock and the pheasants flashed out fast enough, but the caper cocks were quicker far. Once upon that same hill at the same drive, taken, however, at a different angle I saw three pheasants coming wide of the guns, when a caper cock rose behind them. On that occasion I could not make out as they approached that the caper was faster, but over the valley between the twin hills the flight of the larger bird was certainly more direct and swift and purposeful. The caper is a magnificent bird, well worthy of all the law in both senses of the word that we can give him.

I remember one day, to be marked for ever with a red underline in the game-book of memory. There was snow on the Norsk hills, not deep, but it was freezing, and a cold wind was blowing in the isolated edges of the forest. One outlying gulley – so my hunter told me – generally held an elk. As the travelling was very noisy owing to the frost, I instructed him to go round and drive the place, as it was probable that any animal which might be disturbed would seek the lower levels rather than face the gale on the heights. Meantime I found a fallen tree, a fir, behind which I ensconced myself. The time was late afternoon and the sun was giving its last lights to the desolate upland world before sinking behind the forest.

It was very, very, cold. Looking ahead I saw a raven rise from the woods that were being driven by the single beater, and go swinging down the wind. A long wait followed, and then one by one three cock caper rose, at first as small as bats against the white backgrounds, but developing as they came into enormous black fowl, which whizzed by me so close that I could see the red in their eyes, and even the startled optics themselves. Later, another hustled out of a pine and followed them. I had nothing but my rifle, and no wish to shoot at any game save elk, but I rarely think of capercaillie without seeing again that chill Norwegian sunset and the great sudden birds looking so large that they might be such fowls as Thor hunted on his journey through Jotunheim.

I have sometimes heard sportsmen (not themselves averse from fledgling-shooting in August) speak with scorn of the methods of caper-shooting so popular in Austria and other continental countries. As is well known, the caper cock, which is polygamous, flies in the early dawn to the pairing ground and there utters his *spel*, or love song, and at the same time puffs out his plumage and makes a brave challenge. It is then that the hunter attempts to approach him.

The finest description of what occurs is undoubtedly that given in by the author of *The Game Birds of Sweden*, and since for clarity and picturesqueness, as well as correct detail, the modern may not hope to compete with it, I shall quote:

"He (the hunter) should be there," we are told, *"by the first dawn of day, when the Woodcock begins to* rode, *and the shrill notes of the Woodlark* (Alauda arborea, Linn.) *– hence called the* Tjäder klockan, *or the caper-cali-watch – are heard in the forest. Here the man listens in profound silence until he hears the spel of the cock, then, for the most part, perched on or near the top of a pine. Sheltering himself as much as possible, behind trees and other cover, he stealthily approaches the bird; but, owing to the imperfect daylight and the thickness of the wood, he is often unable to see it until close upon it. So long, however, as the first and second notes,* knappningen *and* klunden, *last, he must remain stationary, and, if in an exposed position, immovable as a statue. But when the bird's third note,* sisningen, *commences, which, as said, continues only a very short time – and in the while the bird is all but blind and deaf – he takes three or four steps, or rather strides, in advance, when he again halts. Should all remain perfectly quiet, however, the bird almost immediately recommences its spel, and, when it once more comes to* sisningen, *the man, as before, moved forward several steps; and, by thus alternately halting and advancing, he, at length, arrives within gunshot of the Capercali, whose fate is then soon sealed.*

"The Capercali during its spel is very watchful; and the fowler must, therefore, be exceed-

ingly guarded in his movements whilst thus stealing up on it; and, at such times as the bird is heard, although not seen, he should of all things avoid looking about him. Want of caution on the part of the fowler in this matter has saved the lives of many Capercali. Its eye, indeed, is said to be so piercing as more readily to discover the face and hands of the man, if they be uncovered, than his person; and some, therefore, deem it advisable, not only to wear gloves, but to hold down the head.

"The fowler should also be careful never to advance until the sisningen has actually commenced, for an old Capercali cock that has previously been persecuted will, perhaps, when one imagines it is on the very point of beginning the last-named note, suddenly stop in its spel; and, if one then advances, will most assuredly take wing. When again the man halts after the sisningen, it should be in an easy position; so that, however long he may have to wait before the bird recommences its spel, it will not be needful for him to change it for another.

"During the early part of the spring, when the cock carries on his spel quite alone, he runs the greatest risk of his life; but when, at an after-period, he is joined by the hens, they act the part of his guardian angels. On the least appearance of peril, they, to put him on his guard, utter a peculiar kind of cackle; and should this not suffice to attract his attention, one or other of them will straightaway fly past the tree on which he is perched, and at times so near him as apparently to strike him with the tip of

her wing, which unmistakable hint he cannot but comprehend, and, as a consequence, moves off at once 'in the wake' of his kind monitress.

"Happily but few hens, comparatively, are shot at the Lek-ställe, partly because they are more wary than the cock, but chiefly, I take it, owing to the fowler having other and better game in view. Indeed, were a proportionate slaughter to take place amongst them, the breed, in parts of Scandinavia, must soon become extinct. As it is, the cocks are so ruthlessly shot down during the pairing season that a large proportion of the hens are unable to find mates; and hence the number of barren birds (Gall-Hönor) one meets in the forest. Were people to refrain from killing the cocks until the spring is well advanced, and pairing for the most part over, no great harm would be done, and they might still have ample amusement; for the cocks, especially the young ones, continue, they say, to spel until the middle of May, or it may be even longer.

"The number of Capercali – of the cocks I speak – that a man may thus kill at the Lek-ställe within a given time depends very much on the circumstances. If, for instance, the weather be boisterous, or there be a crust on the snow, which in the more northern parts of Scandinavia often remains on the ground until late in the spring, it may happen that even the most experienced chasseur will hardly kill a bird in a week; but under favourable circumstances, on the contrary, a good deal may be done. I myself have known more than one man to shoot from five to six of these birds in the course of the morning and evening of the same day – but one or two is a more usual number. A peasant in the interior, however, who knows what he is about and devotes much of his time to the purpose, as many do, will probably kill from fifteen to twenty cocks in the course of the spring. I was, indeed, assured by an acquaintance of mine, who resided in the heart of the Wermeland Finn Forest, that one particular spring he shot no less than twenty-nine. This is in a country where nearly every one carries a gun, will give some idea of the havoc that is thus annually made amongst these noble birds.

"In the northern parts of Scandinavia the Capercali is generally shot at the Lek-ställe with a small pea-rifle; but in the south the shot-gun is almost universally used for the purpose.

"Though the capercali is large a bird as to be thought impossible to miss, it nevertheless not seldom escapes the fowler, even though provided with a shot-gun. Several causes contribute to this. In the first place, it is usually very dark when one fires; secondly, it is not always that an unobstructed view of the bird can be obtained; and last, 'a good dose' is required to bring it to the ground.

"Accidents, and those of a serious nature, sometimes occur at the Lek-ställe; for when, at early dawn, the fowler is stealing on the Capercali in a bent position, a brother sportsman similarly engaged may take him for a bear or other wild beast, and send a ball into his body, many instances of which are on record."

As a matter of fact, even in the days when Lloyd wrote the above account, caper shooting at the Lek-ställe was contrary to law in Scandinavia; but at the present time the sport (for sport it undoubtedly is) has been brought to a high pitch of excellence on the estates of other continental countries. There the cocks, having been persecuted upon their pairing grounds for generations, have developed an extraordinary acuteness of sight and hearing, so much so that British, as well as most native sportsmen, rank the caper very high as a quarry, not so far indeed behind the stalked deer and chamois, and above either of these animals when obtained by watching of some mountain pass to which they are driven.

Certainly no great harm is done to the stock of capercaillie provided that shooting is not carried to extremes (as it never is on well-managed estates) until late in the pairing season. Provided this rule be rigorously observed it is difficult to imagine any more adequate way of killing off the old cocks; and if a light rook rifle be the weapon used, the hunter will find that he deserves any bird he is fortunate enough to kill. There is, of course, a natural feeling in the Briton against shooting any bird during the spring, but is should always be remembered that the old cock-caper is a polygamist and the very reverse of mindful of any parental feelings. He probably does not even remember where the nests of all his wives are placed. In any case it must be acknowledged that he who shoots with a .250 rook rifle shoots a caper in the pine-dusk of the early dawn as the noble bird breaks into his ecstasy, is responsible for a far better and more praiseworthy action than he who puts an ounce and sixteenth of No.6 shot into a skinny fledgling flapping from a bed of bracken only to fall into it again, unfit for food and slain long, long ere his prime. **HP**

The current plight of the capercaillie in Scotland could not be a better example of how anti-shooting conservation bodies can get it so wrong. Gamekeepers are the true experts on bird conservation, the real custodians of the countryside. They do not need a PhD beside their name to tell those who will listen what has to be done. Neither do keepers need to pander to the purple rinse brigade – people who the RSPB are at pains not to upset; fearing the endless dripping tap of pound coins would cease to swell their coffers. Deer fences, coupled with predation by buzzards, goshawks, foxes and pine martens, are the real reason this iconic game bird has so rapidly declined since being taken off the quarry list. Indeed since the protection of the caper has been mostly taken out of the keeper's hands after the ban, its fortunes are a disgrace to those who profess to be bird protectionists.

Let us not forget, as Prichard wrote in great detail, that the caper has been extinct once already in Britain. I continue to read with dismay report after report, rehashing hearsay and half-truths, blaming hunting for the last extinction of this great game bird. The overriding evidence actually points to forest clearance by large-scale burning as the real reason for the loss of the caper back then, but I guess that doesn't sell newspapers.

Thankfully, a dedicated number of Victorian sportsmen set about its reintroduction in 1836 and it was successfully returned to our fauna. Gamekeepers and devoted sportsmen, through their tenacity, practical knowledge and due diligence, were solely responsible for the only ever successful re-introduction of an extinct native bird

to our Isles. The next generation of Edwardian sportsmen nurtured and preserved the capercaillie to expand its range. I shudder to think what those great guns of yesteryear would think of the species' plight today. Prichard must be turning in his grave! It now seems our shooting forefathers' lasting legacy in wild game conservation will be consigned to the history books, antiquities of literature to be treasured only by the fortunate few who realise the value of their knowledge, and what adversity was overcome to reinstate this avian prince to his Caledonian pinewood principality. This 170-year-old sporting success story is all but doomed, any hope now it seems, dashed by bias and bigotry from the likes of the RSPB hierarchy – prejudice really is the enemy of the rational argument in this instance.

The giant grouse's fortunes started to slide in the 1970s, persecuted by foresters and not by sportsmen as many reports would have the ignorant believe. A propensity to nip off the buds and shoots of young conifers encouraged little favour towards the caper from those trying to restock native pines. In truth, the bird didn't deserve the persecution it received for a crime at best unproven, or at worst exaggerated beyond all proportion.

However in areas where the caper was preserved, i.e. sporting estates, it fared fairly well until predator protection – indeed encouragement – was adopted by many conservation bodies. The population quickly became more and more fragmented, and when former sporting estates – some still strongholds of the species – came under the ownership of protectionists, this bird's fate was irreversibly sealed.

Left: Jost Arnold pays his respects to a superb trophy cock caper

Image: Peter Carr Collection

Above: Chris Beadle's first bird is an old hen, treed and marked by a spitz

Right: The Finnish spitz hound marking a cock caper high in the tree above

Some aspects of decline have been identified and addressed, fence strikes for instance, and much deer fencing has been removed in sensitive areas – but this is too little too late. Also, some protectionist bodies have now sanctioned crow control at last! But they have to get hard on all predators in caper populated areas, if they really want to revive any realistic optimism of saving this species. Unfortunately, most of these self-declared experts cannot agree on the colour of shite. I recently read one who suggested that pine martens are not a significant threat to caper – using Sweden's thriving population of this bird as an example of how they can happily co-exist. For Christ's sake, Sweden has almost endless acres of perfect pine forest and blueberry understorey ideal for capercaillie. In no way can this be used as a fair comparison of Scotland's few fragmented populations – where predators definitely make much more of a negative impact, and local extinction is a grim reality. Furthermore, the few remaining suitable habitats left in Scotland are as equally disjointed as the precarious populations themselves. Nest predation by pine martens has also been proven beyond all doubt to be the most significant cause of nest loss in Scotland.

It will be a sad day indeed when the "tok… tok… tok," sound of a caper's new season spel, declaring his sovereignty of the pines, and mating potential, will no longer be heard in the remnant woodland of old Caledonia. I really fear the haunting sound of spring silence that will mark a second Scottish extinction, but in all probability it will happen in my lifetime.

Imagine my surprise and incredulity, when I recently read a news story in *Keeping the Balance* magazine that detailed the Vincent Wildlife Trust's plans to supplement Wales' currently small pine marten population, with animals imported from Scotland. One of the trust's officers, David Bevan, responded to some sensible questions from the National Gamekeepers' Organisations' (NGO) two regional chairmen in Wales, David Pooler and Brian Hardcastle. I won't dwell long on the subject, but some of Bevan's answers really do beg belief. When asked if the VWT envisages any negative conserva-

tion impacts arising from the re-introduction of pine martens, he initially answers with a well-rehearsed political parry. "In Wales pine martens would be released to reinforce an existing population, compared with a reintroduction where the species had gone extinct." He then recites the age-old, fundamentally flawed rhetoric about martens co-existing with other woodland dwellers on the continent without any significant adverse impact, before he delivers a real pearler: "an increase in pine marten numbers is likely to be beneficial for our other native species; for example, pine marten predation of grey squirrels could be beneficial to red squirrels". Does he really think the pine marten will differentiate between the two species when it comes to filling its belly? No, I think not.

The real concern of course is for the caper's cousin, the black grouse, that is already struggling to hold on in Wales. Bevan is asked whether he thinks the release of pine martens will have any

Image: Peter Carr Collection

impact on black grouse in Wales *vis-à-vis* their impact on capercaillie in Scotland. He replies with an equally audacious answer as the one above. Firstly, he reiterates the continental co-existence claptrap, and then claims that black grouse populations have increased within the pine marten's Scottish range, before saying there is no evidence to support pine marten predation as an influential factor in the caper's decline, despite absolute evidence readily available to the contrary. This smacks of blinkered opinion based on selective evidence and an absolute disaster waiting to happen to another of our iconic game birds if the project is allowed to go ahead.

But enough of despondency; let me pull Prichard up on a few points of note. I have researched in great detail the reintroduction of capercaillie that Prichard also goes into in some depth. He was wrong to record that no birds were introduced "into Arran, where a few birds have nevertheless been shot". My research shows that seven caper were actually sent to Brodick Castle, Arran in 1843, and further reinforced with 10 more Swedish birds in 1846. These founded a small, self-sustaining colony that rose to 70 birds or so in 1865, but had died out owing to disease by 1910.

Prichard also attributes colonisation of central Scotland to the Marquis of Breadalbane's Taymouth Castle birds. They most certainly did spread fast along the wooded valleys of the southern Highlands, reaching as far as Blair Drummond in 1860, but their range was increased by other releases too. Though Prichard does mention an introduction at Cortachy that same year by the then Earl of Airlie, the idea was rapidly taken up by a number of lairds and landowners across Scotland. All and one keen to add this turkey-sized bird to the available game on their estates. No less than 25 attempts at reintroduction to the Highlands alone occurred after 1860. Prior to this, earlier releases all failed at The Earl of Fife's estate near Braemar in 1827, Glenapp, Ayrshire with birds and eggs from Taymouth, Lochnabo, Morayshire in 1852 with Norwegian imports, and at Castle Grant Morayshire in 1860.

Interestingly, there was a lot more to the well-celebrated introduction of caper at Taymouth Castle – on the whim of the Norfolk Baronet Sir Thomas Fowell Buxton. Apparently he had wanted to repay Lord Breadalbane's kindness by gifting him some of the giant grouse. However, Sir Thomas had long wanted to reintroduce the bird, indeed, he had already attempted to establish capercaillie on his own Norfolk Estate in 1822 into what proved to be unsuitable woodland. This was one of six failed attempts to establish the bird in England. Buxton, however, was committed to bringing the bird back to Britain, and after seeing that the Marquis had ideal caper habitat at Taymouth, he put all his energies and efforts into making it happen. Therefore a kindness returned was also an ambition fulfilled. The name of that stalwart of a Norfolk gamekeeper tasked with transporting and preserving the original Taymouth imports from Sweden was one Lawrence Banville, an Irish-born keeper employed by Buxton.

Post-1860 the release of adult birds, and the placing of eggs in greyhens' nests by diligent keepers, had caught on as the best methods of release. Prichard briefly mentions two other points

Left: Peter Kenworth, rightly proud of a perfectly feathered old cock caper

of introduction at "Tulliallan and Lathirsk, Fife" in 1862 and 1874 respectively and successful. I have found a record of further successes at Drumtochty, Kincardineshire 1870, Clunas, Morayshire 1884, Balmoral, Aberdeenshire 1885, Brahan, Ross-shire 1889, Gordon Castle, Morayshire 1897, and Strath-nairn between 1894 and 1900. Birds were also released on the Stirlingshire shore of Loch Lomond in the early 1870s. The same result occurred at Sanquhar, Dumfriesshire with eggs from Arran, some were put in a pheasant's nest and recorded as "destroyed by crows", and Douglas Lanarkshire in the 1860s.

After 1900 the novelty had worn off and far fewer capers were released. Eggs set under greyhens and bantams at Broughton, Peebleshire, failed between 1902 and1904. However, three birds seen at Tynron, Dumfriesshire, in November 1905 and the one shot in December 1905 at Tarbolton Moss, Ayshire, may owe their origins to these birds hatched at Broughton. Birds introduced to Bute in 1922 and to the Isle of Islay a little later in the 1920s, and Coulin, Ross-shire about 1929, all failed.

It seems that F.R.S. Balfour, after failing to raise birds from eggs in in 1929 and day-old chicks in 1930, made the last serious attempt at release in 1930, until I tried a similar experiment 70 years later at the start of a new millennium. Balfour re-leased a pair of old birds brought south from Dee-side in August 1930, seven Finish imports – four in November the same year, and three the following October. These established a small population that increased up to 1938 but declined to only a handful in 1948 before dying out altogether soon

after. This latter loss was blamed on the wartime felling of trees and subsequent loss of anything like suitable habitat. My experiment with 21 eggs placed in two pheasant nests, and one greyhen nest at Glen Trusta, Angus, all failed. A wildcat killed the greyhen on the nest – the one I had pinned all hopes on – and hooded crows predated the remaining two clutches under the questionable pheasant surrogates. The idea had been born after I took up the stalking lease, and found one forlorn caper in residence. A well-meaning hiker gave my captive laying stock their liberty, and they quickly dispersed. Soon after this, I was also forced to shoot the solitary cock caper, and that was the end of the experiment.

Three glens over, I once flushed a hen caper and her brood when walking the hills of Glen Prosen. Interestingly, Cortachy – one of Prichard's old haunts and a successful site of an 1860s release – was situated between the two estates. When shooting with the present Earl of Airlie on a partridge day I questioned him about the loss of caper stocks on Cortachy, and he told me that they had mostly died out by 1980. He did say that the Tullo Hill was their favoured area and last stand. This was the same hill mentioned by Prichard. Almost a century after Prichard had last shot this place, I took his great-grandson Charlie Jacoby through the old pine trees to the top of Tullo hill, where the Airlie monument now stands. It was a moving moment to tread in the footsteps of the old adventurer.

I also, in all probability, have the questionable distinction of shooting the last capercallie cock bird in Britain. It happened by chance on the last Satur-

day of the season before it was prematurely closed by a Scottish Statutory Instrument, which came into effect on 4 November 2001. The lone caper I mentioned earlier was one of only three I have shot in Scotland. Unfortunately, it had some discarded bail twine wrapped around its legs, and was clearly in some distress. As I approached it flapped lazily away for a short distance before alighting again in the heather. I was walking the forest edge at the time, checking the deer fence, and had the shotgun with me on the off chance of bagging a black cock. As it happened the game bag was filled with his bigger cousin, because the next time the caper rose on approach; I raised the gun and put him down for welfare reasons alone, and a little bit of unfortunate history was made. Staying with the bad luck theme, I also remember the last caper being killed on Blackmount, Argyll and Bute. It was the first year I had stalked on the neighbouring estate of Glen Etive, and the keeper told me the story. Again he was a remnant bird, the last example of the local race. It was the spring spel, and he had taken a disliking to a passing hiker, no doubt in his frustration to attract a non-existent hen. The caper's aggressive display distressed the hiker so much that the moron killed it with his stick and that was that.

The reader may ask why is the capercaillie included in this book because it is now off the shooting list. In answer, I have included the caper for three reasons. The first is because Prichard included it in his original book, and the situation then and now shows some stark differences in the bird's fortunes. Secondly, those differences should be seen as a warning for what may become of our other sporting species such as the black grouse, and hopefully remove some of the blame incorrectly laid on the sportsman. Lastly, this prince of all gamebirds is an absolute delight to hunt. Yes, you will have to cross to the continent to take up the chase, but I assure you it will be worth it.

Prichard provides a good description on the way our continental cousins hunted caper at the turn of the last century. Stalking the displaying bird during its spel is still practised today in Russia and other countries. I have hunted this princely game bird in Norway, Sweden and Russia, I have seen it in Austria too, but I was about the chamois on both occasions I came upon one, and quietly gave them grace. However as exciting as the account he relates, Prichard doesn't mention shooting caper over pointers or – my preference – hunting them with tree barkers. Those delightful little Swedish spitz hounds flush and chase the birds in flight until they finally perch in some distant pine. Once the bird is marked, they set up some fuss and keep the caper actively engaged with their antics while the shooter stealthily stalks in.

Sweden is a beautiful country and, with a total population of less than that of the city of London, its great expanse is still relatively unspoilt. Indeed, Sweden's forests are described as one of the last two remaining wildernesses of Western Europe, the other being the central Scottish Highlands. It has been in Sweden where I have shot the majority of my caper, and the northern and western districts seem to hold a booming population.

Us British hunters are mostly a nation of bird shooters, and as such are bound by strict rules of etiquette that remain largely foreign to our conti-

Left: The author with a very wily and ancient capercaillie cock, stalked and shot after a long approach

nental cousins. Safety is paramount and any deviation from safe shooting practice wherever one is engaged in sport should not be tolerated, however, when hunting in other lands with their own unique set of traditions and customs, UK etiquette does not apply. As long as safety is not compromised, we as visiting shooters should remain open minded and not appear ignorant. When in Rome, do as the Romans do: a useful adage when shooting overseas.

Prichard tells us that some scorn was directed towards hunting displaying caper, and went to great pains to explain otherwise. I too have felt a similar contempt from sportsmen who have never engaged in branches of foreign sport alien to what we do in the UK. For the man who has experienced what he talks of I am all ears, but those who base their opinion on hearsay or prejudice I have no time. Let us visit a past hunt in Sweden and make up our own minds.

I had returned to Scandinavia with two friends to hunt that most majestic of game birds: the capercaillie. My two pals, Chris Beadle and Peter Kenworthy, are both stalkers and shotgunners; indeed, both are renowned driven game shots and are fortunate to enjoy a number of days each season double gunning on some of the UK's most prestigious estates. So it was with some trepidation that I booked the following hunt in Sweden, as the traditional Swedish way to hunt the caper is with rifle and a Swedish or Finnish spitz hound. The hound finds and flushes the bird, following it during its short flight until it is treed, whereby the hound begins barking madly, thus keeping the bird's attention and marking the correct tree for the hunter to approach.

Both Chris and Peter were experienced stalkers and also generally good sports; I therefore felt that the two of them would probably give the tree barkers a try. After much deliberation and counter argument, a compromise was decided – we would spend three days hunting with shotguns over pointers and three days hunting with the rifles and the tree barker. This would give Chris the opportunity to put into action his Heym 20 bore .222 drilling, which later proved to be a rather useful piece of weaponry indeed.

The weather was kind to us and the first three days' shooting over the pointers was productive, producing some excellent sport, putting three black cocks, four grey hens, six brace of willow grouse and one hazel hen in the game bag for both guns. However, although we had seen a number of capercaillie they had proved reluctant to hold a point, preferring to run on ahead and flush, well out of range if pressed by the pointer.

Thursday arrived with a change of tactics. Our guide, Roga, arrived with Odin the tree-barking spitz hound. The terrain was similar to some parts of Scotland not yet scarred by modern sitka spruce plantations; indeed one could almost imagine it was the ancient forest of Caledon. Underfoot the forest understory was a cushioned carpet of blueberry, cranberry and various heathers. The stately pines and firs were adorned with sprays of the silver stranded, silk-like moss that only grows in the purest of air. Everything here was fresh and vibrant, from the lichen-clad rocks and fallen timber to the numerous babbling brooks interlacing the landscape, teeming with small trout and grayling. The water was of the highest quality and I filled

Image: Peter Carr Collection

my flask, confident it wasn't a cocktail of polluted nitrates, pesticides or effluent.

The hunting had moved up a gear compared to the easy going of the previous three days. Hunting over the pointers had been civilised, taking turns walking up to the pointing dog, waiting for the flush on command, taking the shot and hopeful retrieve before leisurely moving on. With the Finnish spitz hound we were now playing catch up the whole time. The little dog was tireless,

Above: The author making friends with a Swedish spitz that provided him with a lot of sport

Left: The author with his first hen caper shot Swedish-style from the tree tops

covering the ground like a pointer but hunting with a spaniel-like action. It wasn't long before the spitz flushed a caper hen that launched itself skywards, crashing through the tree canopy like an exocet. The hound sped off in hot pursuit, disappearing into the forest giving voice much like a beagle.

Roga began to deploy the aerials on the direction finder to track the dog but paused as the distant yapping changed to a staccato barking. For the first time in four days, our bearded Viking guide's face contorted into a smile. "The dog does his work well, the bird is treed," croaked Roga in his mechanical-sounding English. We all moved cautiously forward in single file, mindful of the wet ground that threatened to invade my gaiters and swamp my boots. The late autumn sun was at its height and this had encouraged the black cock to engage in a bit of premature leking, their 'brrruuuwww brrruuuwww' calls echoing through the forest.

Soon the little hound was sighted, jumping forwards and backwards, barking furiously with its head held back at an awkward angle, its gaze fixed on the bird in the pine bough above. Roga motioned for Peter and I to sit before nodding Chris forward. I glassed the pine tree with the 7x50 Steiner binoculars as Chris patiently stalked toward the yapping spitz. It wasn't long before the mozzies found us, their high-pitched whining betraying their presence. With some difficulty I eventually found the hen bird in the glass, its russet and dun barred plumage camouflaging it perfectly against the tree bark. Chris executed the stalk perfectly, always keeping a tree between him and the targeted bird's probable position. However, he was now

having some difficulty in locating his hen caper in the canopy. Chris was well within range and close enough to disturb the bird, which was obviously irritating our Viking guide: it is bad for the hound if you don't shoot a bird they have treed for you. The spitz was now swapping its gaze from the caper to Chris as if to say 'well, go on then!' Fortunately Chris spied the bird as it changed position and swiftly mounted the Heym drilling. A sharp report cracked through the trees, silencing the leking black cock. The .222 solid bullet, used to ensure the bird wasn't damaged, found its mark. The caper rolled forward, falling off its perch lifeless, and Roga broke into a sprint in an attempt to prise the caper hen from the jaws of the spitz, who thought it was great fun to pluck his long awaited prize. The bird was successfully retrieved and Chris was all smiles having taken his first caper.

Moving on, we experienced a number of false alarms as the tree barker took a distinct liking to squirrels, infuriating its Viking handler. Roga had the ability to distinguish whether the dog was marking a bird or a squirrel: if it was the latter he would remark: "He lie," before charging after the dog. The spitz's barking was soon swapped to a high pitched yelp as Roga showed him the error of his ways with some booming Norse profanity and a well-aimed stick.

I got my turn as the afternoon began to fade into the evening. Heading back towards camp the dog had been missing in action for a half hour or more. Roga was cursing at the electronic receiver, trying unsuccessfully to get a signal from the dog's collar. A large cock caper came flitting through the tree tops like a crippled WWII Lancaster bomber

Left: A majesctic capercaillie cock bird mid-way through his spel song

– and following on in full cry at speed came the missing spitz. The cock caper had had enough and lit into a pine some 50 yards away, oblivious to our presence. We were then treated to a fine display of how things should be done as the tree barker began to mark the bird excitedly. The capercaillie crouched over in obvious anger, audibly grinding its bill at the dog, shifting from one feathered foot to the other. Keen to capitalise on my good fortune,

as I had hardly carried a gun all trip, I mounted the 6.5x55, drew a bead and squeezed off a round. It instantly ended the cock bird's displeasure.

Peter, meanwhile, had been off on a little jaunt of his own. Having got to grips with the area, he had taken his leave and decided on a little solitary hunting. He was alone apart from some canine company, a fox terrier belonging to one of Roga's friends that had taken a liking to him. Amazingly,

Image: Igor Timmermans Collection

the little tyro terrier worked like the best of cocker spaniels, and flushed a superb specimen cock caper. Peter clinically despatched it with a reflex shot of 36gm 4s before it escaped through the trees.

He was a handsome mature bird in perfect feather 'resplendent in varying green'; indeed it turned out to be the bird of the week, and is now proudly displayed in PK's living room alongside a hen taken later.

That night, sat round the campfire, the constellation Orion was as close as I have ever seen it due to the absence of light pollution in the Swedish wilderness. Out across Lake Tapmuktj, a loon began its mournful, eerie meowing. I threw on another log and watched the blue flames lick the fire back to life, listening contentedly to two happy hunters as they cheerfully chatted the night away, fully converted to hunting capercaillie the Scandinavian way.

The record bag for capercaillie shot in Britain is 69 birds that fell to seven guns on an un-named estate in Perthshire on 4 November 1910. Notable rights and lefts involving caper are: C. Mclean who shot a cock caper and a roebuck at Kildrummy Castle, Aberdeenshire, September 4 1906. Sir Alan Mclean managed a jack snipe and a caper at Littlewood Park, Aberdeenshire, in October 1923, but it wasn't quite a true right and left as the Baronet's gun was opened after the first shot but quickly closed to take the second bird without reloading. Finally, two capercaillie – both cocks – were killed with one shot from a 20 bore by D.C.H. McLean August 29 1936 at Hall Head Weed, Corse Aberdeenshire. The McLean brothers, like Prichard, were clearly capercaillie aficionados. **PC**

Image Igor Timmermans Collection

Prospecting *for* Roe

In Prichard's time the humble roebuck did not command the respect the animal now does. More often roe were killed on dedicated battues, and frequently just peppered by inferior shot from a shotgun on these hunts and as an incidental on driven pheasant days, rather than pursued purely with a rifle of a suitable calibre. This was the Edwardian order of the day, and had its origins going back to Norman times when the roe was considered more as a beast of warren (a classification rather than the earthworks of a rabbit, as the term is now used) than of forest, and as such commanded only minor protection on par with the hare, far less than was afforded to its larger cousins, the red and fallow deer.

Therefore in Prichard's original work – apart from the occasional reference expecting a roe coming through on a particular caper drive, or a number of roe included in the overall bag at

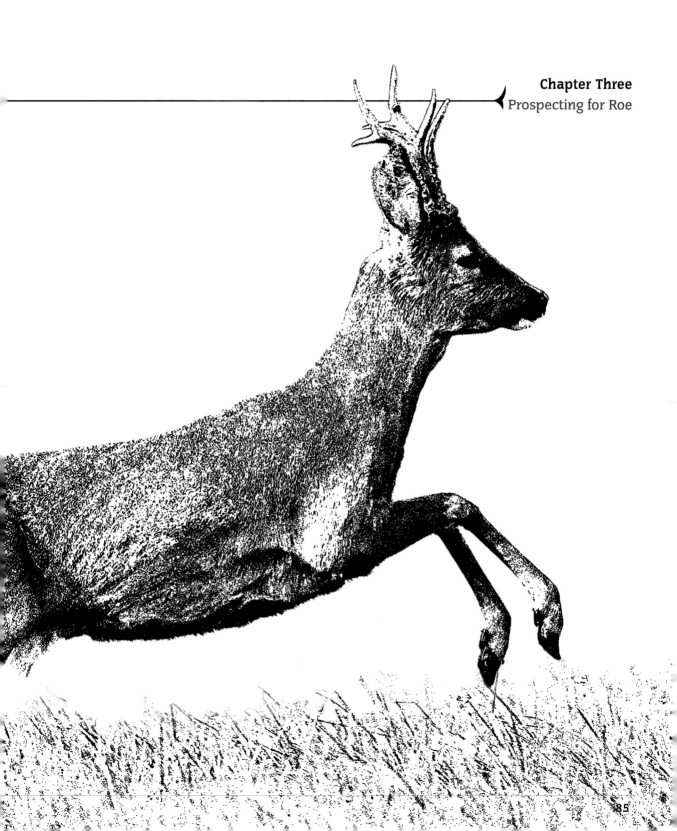

the day's end – roebuck are almost completely absent from his writings. That Prichard was expecting both caper and roe with the shotgun does offer some ethical comfort. As such, he would have at least been loaded with heavy shot (he prescribes such in his capercallie chapter), which is so much more suitable to kill a buck at moderate range than the standard 6 or 7 bird shot. Estimating range of course is a prerequisite for a successful sniper, and as Prichard had proved to be one of the best in the Great War, we need have no worries in that department.

The virtual omission of roe, never mind a dedicated chapter by Prichard in SIWB, is hardly surprising when one considers the authors he occasionally refers to. Indeed when I searched through his library and studied those books therein that included the pursuit of this species,

it was no surprise at all to find little regard shown towards the roe as a sporting beast to set out and stalk. John Colquhoun (pronounced Cohoon) in his masterful work *The Moor and the Loch*, seventh edition, published in 1885, is the most disdainful:

"The roe is occasionally stalked, and shot with the rifle, and I have heard it alleged that it is thus raised to the dignity of a deer, whereas the common method of buck-shot degrades it to the level of a hare. Having several times tried this experiment, I may safely pronounce it a most wretched burlesque upon deer-stalking. Roes almost always confine themselves to the woods; and although by peeping round corners and openings in the plantations, you may sometimes get a good rifle-shot, yet you are much more apt to come upon them quite within range of buck-

shot, especially if the cover is very thin, which when a good haunt of roes, it seldom is. They are thus almost sure to see and hear you, and steal away unperceived; but should you succeed in getting the shot, it is pretty certain to be a running one, and you will stand but a poor chance with a rifle at a roe bounding among thick plantations. The great excitement of deer-stalking consists in seeing your game from a distance without being yourself perceived, which affords ample scope for skill and tact in approaching it."

Strangely enough, John Colquhoun was an advocate of hunting roe alone with a buck-shot loaded shotgun and a very slow and deliberate foxhound. He hated taking part in bigger organised battues, when noisy beaters were employed to move the roe to a number of guns. He believed this disturbed the roe too much and was at best an ineffective method. However, his narrative delights at their solo pursuit, with just man and hound, particularly the way a roebuck would circle his territory at the trot, keeping slightly ahead of his canine pursuer. Eventually the buck would come within range of the waiting gun, who of course knew the local haunts and likely places the game would pass. By listening to the hound's progress, he could work the wind and change position at will to his best advantage. He clearly endorsed their pursuit, but loathed foot stalking roe deer as we know it today.

Similarly, another classic book of sport mentioning roe was found in the Prichard collection that subscribed to similar views as those expressed by Colquhoun, albeit more favourable to a team of beaters in the right circumstances. These were contained in the eighth edition of

Wild Sports & Natural History of the Highlands by Charles St John, published in 1878:

"In shooting roe, it depends so much on the cover and other local causes whether dogs or beaters should be used, that no rule can be laid down as to which is best. Nothing is more exciting than running roe with beagles, where the ground is suitable, and the covers so situated that the dogs and their game are frequently in sight. The hounds for roe-shooting should be small and slow. Dwarf harriers are the best, or good-sized, rabbit-beagles, where the ground is not too rough. The roe, when hunted by small dogs of this kind, does not make away, but runs generally in a circle, and is seldom above a couple of hundred yards ahead of the beagles, stopping every now and then to listen, and allowing them to come very near, before he goes off again; in this way, giving the sportsman a good chance of knowing where the deer is during most of the run. Many people use foxhounds for roe-shooting, but generally these dogs run too fast, and press the roebuck so much that he will not stand it, but leaves cover, and goes straightaway out of reach of the sportsman, who is left to cool himself without any hope of a shot."

When it came to shooting roe, St. John was certainly of similar mind to Colquhoun:

"In shooting roe, shot is at all times far preferable to ball [military term for a rifle bullet, not to be confused with a round ball fired from a smooth bore musket]. *The latter, though well aimed, frequently passes clean through the animal, apparently without injuring him, and the poor creature goes away to die in some hidden corner; whereas a charge of shot gives him such a shock that he drops more readily to it than a rifle ball, unless, indeed, the ball happens to strike the heart or spine. Having killed roe constantly with both rifle and gun, small shot and large, I am inclined to think that the most effective charge is an Eley's cartridge with No.2 shot in it. I have, when woodcock-shooting, frequently killed roe with No.6 shot, as when they are going across and are shot well forward, they are as easy to kill as a hare, though they will carry off a great deal of shot if hit too far behind. No one should ever shoot roe without some well-trained dog to follow them when wounded; as no animal is more often lost when mortally wounded."*

On the last point we are at least agreed, but the shooting of roe with a shotgun is thankfully today not the norm, other than for ethical dispatch. Strangely enough for reasons within the law, I too have actually shot a roe with a shotgun, loaded with No.6 shot on a woodcock shoot many years ago. I was waiting on a ride in a poplar plantation in the hardest of weather. The marshy woodland had become deep frozen, and I watched as four startled roe dashed onto some ice and fell about in a god awful fashion. Slipping

and sliding, they eventually gained firmer ground and made a bid for freedom. Unfortunately, the last of their number had broken a lower leg during the exercise, and was spinning about in an ugly manner. As the bevy passed close by my stand I executed the unfortunate doe with a close range charge to the heart – she was thrown back and died instantly – but let's not forget we are talking of singular feet distance.

Before we leave St John and his benchmark work on sport in the Highlands, I will record another short passage from the author of an event that will give all who pursue sport with gun and rifle cause to gasp in horror. It certainly reinforces the point of never putting the gun up to anything but a confirmed and desired target:

"A curious and melancholy accident happened in a parish situated in one of the eastern counties of Scotland a few years ago. Perhaps the most extraordinary part of the story is that it is perfectly true. Some idle fellows of the village near the place where the catastrophe happened having heard that the roe and deer from the neighbouring woods were in the habit of feeding in some fields of high corn, two of them repaired to the place at dusk of the evening with a loaded gun, to wait for the arrival of the deer at their nightly feeding ground. They had waited some time, and the evening shades were making all objects more and more indistinct every moment, when they heard a rustling in the standing corn at a short distance from them, and looking in the direction, they saw some large animal moving. Having no doubt that it was a deer that they saw, the man who had the gun took his aim, his

finger was on the trigger, and his eye along the barrel; he waited however, to get a clearer view, of the animal, which had ceased moving. At this instant, his companion, who was close to him, saw, to his astonishment, the flash of a gun from the spot where he supposed the deer was, and almost before he heard the report his companion fell back dead upon him, and with the same ball he himself received a mortal wound. The horror and astonishment of the author of this unlucky deed can scarcely be imagined when, on running up, he found, instead of a deer, one man lying dead and another senseless and mortally wounded. Luckily, as it happened, the wounded man lived long enough to declare before witnesses that his death was occasioned solely by accident, and that his companion, at the moment of his being killed, was aiming at the man who killed them. The latter did not long survive the affair. Struck with grief and sorrow at the mistake he had committed, his mind and health gave way, and he died soon afterwards."

However, if there is one book in Prichard's library that shows more evidence of use than the above two works, it is a wonderful book called *Autumns in Argyleshire* by Hon. A.E. Gathorne-Hardy. The author, with a little stretch, could be considered a contemporary of Prichard, albeit Gathorne-Hardy was a much older man. He was actually the father of Prichard's two companions that feature most in SIWB, namely Geoffrey Gathorne-Hardy and Alfred Gathorne-Hardy. Both brothers had also served with Prichard in the Great War. Indeed it was Alfred who crawled across no-man's land with Prichard one night

to successfully recover a sample of German bulletproof breast plates for sniper school testing. It is not recorded what happened to the Teutonic owners of said armour, but it would be a fair bet to say it was no doubt to their detriment. But I digress, the author of *Autumns in Argyleshire*'s actual attitude to the pursuit of roe for sport differed massively to others of his time, and indeed to those before:

"Opinions differ as to the merits of the roe from the point of view of the sportsman, but this, I think, is mainly owing to the fact that so many are killed in the course of the winter battues. No doubt they add an element of the picturesque to the bag as they are arranged in line before the door of the lodge, with blackgame, woodcocks, pheasants, hares, and rabbits, and perhaps a few odd capercailzie; but I for one would always prefer not to pull the trigger of a shotgun at an object like a calf, although I have had many an interesting and exciting day after them with the rifle. It is true that the "old masters" like Colquhoun and St. John agree in recommending shot as preferable to ball for roe-shooting, on the ground that fewer are wounded; but those who humanely take the advice of these writers do not sufficiently appreciate the great advance which has been made since their time in the manufacture of weapons of precision, of improved range, velocity, and accuracy, combined with lower elevation. I do not profess to be a first-rate shot with a rifle, but I do not remember losing a single wounded buck, although I have accounted for a very large number during the last twenty-five years. I believe that many (shot with the shotgun)

carry away a few pellets under such circumstances, and that if the roe could be consulted in the matter they would unhesitatingly express their preference for the bullet."

Amen to that, says I. However, though the Hon. Gathorne-Hardy favours the rifle, he certainly agrees with the old masters that slipping the hounds on roe is the most fun, whatever weapon is used:

"Perhaps the most amusing way of shooting roe, when the ground is suitable, is for the guns to take up positions on heights commanding fairly open glades in the woods, where the cover can be drawn by hounds. The scent is very strong, and almost any kind of dogs take to it kindly, but a scratch pack of otter-hounds, or old slow fox-hounds, are the best for the purpose. A really fast pack would drive the roe too quick and too far. The object should be to get together a few steady hounds with plenty of "tongue," resolute on the scent, with perhaps some bustling terriers to start the buck out of the thickets

and bracken. Unless too much pressed, roe are inclined to trust more to cunning than to speed, while their habit of running in a circle and their disinclination to break cover give the sportsmen every chance."

Interestingly, although this form of hunting roe has long since fallen out of favour, it is a specialist method used in Sweden with just one or, at most, a couple of hounds very similar to basset. The breed is known as a dreve, and they are low slung in confirmation and lemon and white in colour. I have seen these hounds work the roe round in circles to eventually come past the hunter or hunters who are most often placed in high seats with rifles – but alas not mine. Similarly employed for the same purpose in France is another basset-type breed, the blue roaned or ticked Bleu de Gascogne, with which much use could be made in British forestry to flush roe to waiting rifles.

Although the Hon. Gathorne-Hardy is the first of our notable sportsmen of Prichard's time to recommend foot stalking as a most enjoyable method of taking roe. It is the officer generation of his sons, which of course included Prichard, on returning from hostilities in France and Belgium, that really brought home the sport commonly only then practised on the continent.

This renaissance in roe stalking that began after the Great War really took off after World War Two. Many more returning officers from postwar deployment in Germany had sampled some traditional roe stalking and enjoyed the respectful practices shown towards this prince of hoofed game. A few dedicated enthusiasts eventually

Right: A Scottish border buck stands for the rifle on the forest edge

Above: The author proudly displays his buck, after the best stalk he has experienced to date

secured the species the status it now enjoys today, by respect, management and dedication. It may surprise some that this newfound respect is a relatively modern change in status. The roe's lesser status and subsequent persecution still continued well past Edwardian times, right up to the recent past in Scotland. Indeed shooting roe with shotguns was still commonplace even in my youth, although the rifle was really by then the norm. Thankfully, legislation eventually protected the species from being peppered, quite often with inadequate loads of inferior-sized shot. And that protection is solely sown to dedicated sportsmen who stalked their game with an adequate rifle, that understood deer, and their ethical pursuit.

I often wonder what those few early pioneers, long in their graves, would think of the many that now pursue roe by foot stalking today. It is their legacy we have in trust, and it is a responsibility we should enjoy, but not abuse, and pass on to the next generation of eager roe enthusiasts.

Hunting roe in wild places is the very pinnacle of the sport: the trophies may be inferior to the medals of Hampshire, Wilshire and Somerset, but it matters not. It is a different sport entirely, and every roe head is a worthy prize – that is, if it is an old beast towards the end of his prime, and has had ample opportunity to spread his DNA to better the species in his locale. I disagree vehemently with one of the "old masters" – Colquhoun in this instance – when he records that roe are inferior to the red on the hill.

On the contrary I find hill living roebuck every bit as sporting a prospect – if not more so – than the red stag. But perhaps readers will best be able to judge the sport if they come along with me as a rookie, and my old roe stalking mentor, to engage a buck in the Angus Glens.

It was Stuart that first taught me how to call up roebucks, with first the Buttolo call and then the Hubertus cherry wood call. And as head keeper on the Glen Moy estate, part of the Earl of Airlie's vast acreage, he presided over one of the best deer forests and grouse moors in the Angus Glens that contained a good head of roe too. Although I had already experienced some degree of success, self-taught with the help of Richard Prior's instructional cassette, I listened intently to Stuart's advice, initially on the operation of the Buttolo call, but actually being shown how to work the bulb helped me immensely in becoming a proficient caller. I was soon delivering the required 'fiep' at the right pitch that emulated

a distressed roe kid calling for the doe. These calling lessons took place at his house, nestled below the aptly named heather-clad Donald's Hill. Stuart was a hard taskmaster who wasn't short of a curse if I got it wrong – but the smell of a peat fire and a rapidly dwindling bottle of single malt still remain sharp in my memory, as does Stuart's wife Aileen, who must surely have been driven half-crazy by my noisy efforts. I remember vividly the joy I felt when I first lifted a doe in the long heather, followed by a buck, on my initial attempts with the Buttolo under Stuart's direction.

This was on a weekend that still remains the best two days of roe stalking I have ever experienced. It was late July in the early 1990s when we left the keeper's house in the small hours. We headed out in the 110 Land Rover, parallel to the Moy Burn, driving past the shoot bothy perched below the Shank Hill that lies in the shadow of a higher peak, called the Dog Hillock. It was on the Shank that I had enjoyed afternoons walking up rabbits over Stuart's springer spaniel, Misty, and also on the high ridge of the Dog that I'd stood in February, to receive driven mountain hares. Sadly, the white hares are now a shadow of their former number, probably due to climate change.

Stuart cut the engine as the Land Rover rolled quietly to a halt beside the West Glen Bridge, below the twin peaks of Finnbracks and Manywee. As we set off, I struggled to keep up with the Scottish superman as he strode out up the steep West Glen road until about half-way up the face of the next hill Manywee. He halted beside an outcrop that shielded us from view but gave us a good sight of the hill's face. Trying

not to look out of breath I peered through the binoculars, but my exertions hadn't escaped the keeper. "Out of breath are ye?" mocked Stuart as he deployed his three-draw Gray's telescope to scan the glen below us. "Just a tad," said I. "Aye, it's a fair pull upwards for a young loon like yer sel" he continued mockingly. Then, becoming all-serious he calmly directed my gaze towards a doe lying in the heather. "Ya ken yon white rock below the big peat hag, just below that there is a roe doe." I pointed the binos in the required direction and found the white rock, but couldn't see the doe. More urgently and with some annoyance Stuart repeated "Ya ken the doe Peter?" "Yep", I lied. "Good, because there's twa of them, she has a wee buckie tending her, and it's one to shoot", Stuart said, retracting the telescope with an air of finality, which didn't bode well for the buck – or me for that matter – if I messed things up.

I carefully slid my 6.5x55 Browning A-Bolt out of the canvas gunslip and deployed the bipod. Lying prone next to Stuart I cupped the Buttolo and gave the four fiep squeaks at five-second intervals, suppressing the two holes on the bulb. The result was instantaneous. The doe rose and cantered towards us with the buck following on. I fitted to the rifle and picked the buck up in the scope as the two deer closed fast. Stuart carefully exchanged the telescope for his Zeiss binoculars and let out a low whistle. The two deer instantly halted, which was what I needed. I ran the crosshairs up the front near leg of the buck and settled mid-shoulder and paused a breath before squeezing off a 169-grain Norma soft point. The buck was killed instantly, its legs kicking involuntarily.

Right: Glen Moy's former head keeper Stuart Donald in a happy mood as he takes over the gralloch

Image: Peter Carr Collection

Quickly, the doe realised this wasn't a great place to be and bolted off over the adjacent ridge. "Aye, now you've shot him you'd best go git him", instructed a smiling Stuart. I soon realised my folly in going out on the hill wearing Le Chameau wellingtons, a greenhorn mistake I have not since repeated. By the time I had retrieved, gralloched, and carried back that buck, my feet were both blistered and cooked.

Next day we again parked alongside the West Glen bridge, but this time would follow the West Moy Burn below the tops of Finnbracks. The early morning was a real pleasure to be on the hill; the 'gadow, gadow, gadow' calls of the cock grouse were a delight. A midsummer sun rose above Glen Ogle in a duck-egg blue sky. The heather-clad hill threatened to burst into a purple carpet within the next few days. Flushing a ring ouzel, it flew on ahead for a few yards and alighted, flicking his white bib towards us in an agitated fashion before flying on again to a repeat performance. I found the going easier now that I had swapped my wellingtons for hill boots, complete with the best gaiters that money could buy from Hamish Cromarty of the Black Islander Co.

As events unfolded I quickly found we wouldn't be needing the call today. Rounding the next bend in the burn, we put up a roe kid. The kid ran on and began 'fieping' in his own language. Slowly lowering ourselves to the prone position, both a buck and a doe appeared from nowhere. The doe was on our side of the burn and the buck was on the opposite bank, as was the distressed kid. I then witnessed roe behaviour that I have never seen since. The doe, obviously concerned about her offspring, stretched her neck forwards and puckered her lips to make a sound like a toddler pretending to drive a car: 'Brrrrmmm'. Her kid skipped up the burn away from us; it knew we were there and was alert. The doe trotted alongside, up the waterway. We waded into the burn half-crouched, and moved on in pursuit – but the buck saw us.

He began prancing slowly forward, raising his front legs high in an exaggerated fashion. The doe then caught his attention again and he too skipped after the kid. This game of cat and mouse carried on for a good two hours with the concerned doe calling in this unusual fashion, until finally the buck jumped over the burn. We came to rest on a small bump of turf and I unslipped the rifle as Stuart whispered: "You'll nae be quick enough, but mind the wee calfie as he's crossed the burn twa." Sure enough, the young roe was between me and the buck, which was now hot on the tail of the doe amid obvious foreplay.

Stuart let out a low whistle, which caused the buck to spin round and face us head on. The only presentable shot was at the base of the neck and I took it, flipping the buck over in spectacular fashion. We waited until the doe and kid were out of sight before approaching my second trophy of the weekend. When I made as if to gralloch the beast, Stuart berated: "Nae, nae, nae – we'll be here half the afternoon going on your performance yesterday. Move over and watch and learn." Stuart deftly eviscerated the buck in a professional fashion that would equal the best medical examiner's post mortem.

Right: This was the author's most productive morning ever, two medal heads, a screw buck, and another soon after this photo was taken

The second deer carried a poor, spindly head. Neither of the bucks that I'd shot that weekend were impressive by trophy standards – hill roe seldom are – but to me both were perfect. These two might be the least impressive heads in my collection, but the spindly-headed roe remains without doubt my personal favourite among some striking medals I have attained since those early days. Indeed the pursuit of those two roebuck still remain among my best ever stalking memories: of wild sport in wild places and in wild company.

Years later I had let a week on one of the Balmoral estate beats, mainly on the strength of Stuart Donald becoming the stalker. Stuart had left the employ of the Earl of Airlie, and become the interim stalker for Her Majesty the Queen on Glen Doll, before taking up a career change with the Forestry Commission. The week proved to be one of the best I had spent in the Highlands with like-minded friends, who all enjoyed similar sporting aspects and aspirations. It was late September, and we were up there for the red stag rut, but unfortunately it hadn't yet kicked off due to the mild weather. Despite this we would all manage to grass our stags, apart from publisher Wes Stanton, who grasped an opportune roebuck in desperation instead:

With molten lead coursing through my calves, ankles creaking, and an intense thirst taking hold, I reached the brig across a small burn at the head of the stone path up from Moulzie cottage. It had been a tough walk to the top with the rifle and rucksack, and I was ready to stop. A half-hearted signal to stop to the stalker, Stuart Donald, by waggling the walking pole was either misunderstood or ignored. Without a hint of irony, he looked at the struggling mess of a man behind him, and paused for a very brief moment before he spoke again: "And now we start the climb."

Earlier that morning, in the Land Rover, Stuart had opened up to me. It had now been seven weeks since the terrible mishap with his poor uncle. Here was a man sharing his inner emotions with a complete stranger. Clearly some-thing utterly terrible had happened to his relative and his face betrayed his near-physical pain. It was a poignant moment between two human beings, touched by real human empathy. Saying how sorry I was to hear about his relative, he shot me a look that said, "Oh god, I've got a right one here," and went on to explain how he had to use two walking poles owing to the pain. 'Ankle' sounds remarkably like 'uncle' if you're not used to the vernacular.

Yes, I really hadn't made a good impression on Stuart Donald. The rut had not yet started, which had clearly added to his concern that he'd be able to find me a suitable stag to shoot, and though we could see plenty of red deer on the hill on the way up the Glen it'd be a long walk back to get near one for a chance.

Another hour's climb and my physical pain was overtaken by the rousing imperative not to come across as a complete idiot any longer. I was on the Balmoral estate for goodness' sake.

The royal estate at Balmoral is breath-taking. An exquisite piece of the Highlands, the walk up to the first peak was overlooked by grey granite cliffs, dreadfully steep, with heather carpeting

Image: Peter Carr Collection

the rises, punctuated by bracken and short grass in places. Bachnagairn Wood at the foot of the first peak broke up the journey to the top, with ancient mountain ash in abundance along the burn, its berried silver branches betraying winter's proximity. Continue up, through the Scots pine understory and out towards the next hill Broad Cairn lying in the shadow of higher peak of Lochnagar, and the arduous climb is rewarded with views of mountainous hills in all their heather-clad glory. Reassured by the spare Twix in my pocket, I thought I'd stick to a sandwich for lunch and resort to chocolate in an emergency.

Working our way up a burn to the top of the next brae the mist thickened. With visibility dropping to fewer than forty yards at the top, we rested for twenty minutes to see whether the mist would subside, watched by two red grouse

wondering what we were up to. We pressed on towards Glen Doll itself, but with no visibility it would only have been luck to encounter a stag. The mist thickened, and our ghillie Shaun was beginning to look worried. Stuart pulled out a compass and pointed the way. After another check on the compass we made our way down the hill, disappointed our day was prematurely done. And if you think going up is tough, try coming down.

Peter Carr spends much of his day wrestling Cape buffalo or stags off hills with his bare hands. I spend much of my day behind a desk wrestling with spreadsheets. And Peter, who organised the trip, has a constitution able to deal with Scotch whisky with aplomb. I don't. Day two on the hill felt all the more difficult for too much Highland nectar, though I could have sworn that Stuart looked brighter when he saw the first big stag of our trip. The magnificent animal, a twelve-pointer and clearly north of twenty stone, had begun stocking his harem with suitable hinds – and the roars that had broken out the previous evening raised expectations. Stuart was clearly in a dither over whether we could take this magnificent beast or not. It was the right age and size of animal – but clearly the pressure of Stuart's short-term stalking contract on Balmoral was at the back of his mind and he wouldn't want it made any shorter by culling a beast that didn't meet royal approval. That and the knowledge that the Prince of Wales would be out on this same hill in a fortnight and would no doubt expect success. Looking like a man who had just signed his own death warrant, Stuart set off up the hill.

Following him we eventually closed on the stag to where we might get a shot. He was just shy of two hundred yards. But at an angle of thirty degrees downhill, Stuarts face was not filled with confidence. And his lack of confidence unnerved me. My thoughts of just how much a 105-grain bullet in .243 calibre might veer off its target in a wind of eighty miles an hour worried me too. Though the ghillie, Shaun, was keen for me to take the shot, it was Stuart's call and he decided to press on in search of another beast.

Our second stalk, not half a mile further on, would have been easy if we could have walked down the gully. But with beasts on both sides, one spooked deer could bring the whole thing to a premature halt. Stuart spotted another stag, this time a little over 150 yards, and before we could get into position for a shot, it moved round the hill to our left. Keeping low, we moved down quickly and Stuart, in his determination, pressed ahead of us. He hadn't seen three young stags back up the hill as we descended, and they spooked the shootable beast when we were not 80 yards from it. Painful ankle or not, Stuart hurled down his sticks in frustration amid a torrent of what I think may have been a prime selection of Gaelic expletives. Another stalk concluded without success.

That was my red stag stalking over; I'd been invited up on the Monday and Tuesday and had to make it back to Dundee airport late on Wednesday. Could I get another quick stalk in? The other guest, Fieldsports Channel presenter Charlie Jacoby, is a gracious chap, and let me take his morning's stalk. We'd seen a big stag

Left: The pursuit of hill roe is the author's favourite pastime with the rifle

near the start of our journey, and it would be quite a walk to get back for a shot. I repaid the graciousness by leaving Charlie a chance at the big stag (which he secured that afternoon), taking my chances with whatever we'd encounter on the hill.

On the approach to the wood, I spotted a chestnut blob up to our right. It was a roe doe, feeding on poor quality grass among the heather. And then Peter Carr spotted a tatty looking roe buck to her right. Still undetected, Stuart gave Pete and me the nod. Quickly we moved into action with Stuart watching events with some amusement. Crossing one of the South Esk feeder burns on precarious stepping stones, we narrowly avoided a wetting. Keeping a few fortuitous boulders between us and our quarry, we closed on the buck. A final crawl through the thick heather onto a grassy knoll would get us our shot.

Gently unzipping the Thompson-Center rifle from its slip, I slid forward as Pete confirmed the buck a shooter. He slid in alongside me, obviously pleased we had made it across the open without spooking the roe. I deployed the tiltable Harris bipod to bring the rifle to attention and carefully bolted home a round. Through the Zeiss scope, I could see that the roebuck was a good beast in the body, its tatty appearance only due to it starting to shuffle off its chestnut summer pelage in favour of a greyer winter coat.

I'd shot a nice neat group with the Thompson Center .243 on the target on the day of my arrival before setting out, as tradition demands. With the wind now diminished, I was confident of a positive shot. Lining the Zeiss centre dot just half-way up the roe buck's body in line with its front leg, I waited until his head was down feeding. Pete whispered "when you're ready" and I let the round loose. Knocked straight over, the roe buck appeared to strain its neck upwards momentarily, but a perfect shot had killed it immediately.

The doe seemed nonchalant, taking a good thirty seconds for her to realise something was up and bound away. After she had disappeared from view we scrambled up the heather bank; the range-finder showed that the roebuck lay just one hundred and seventy six yards from where I'd shot but it was a good five-minute climb up to the carcase. Handshakes all done, Pete reasoned that, as I had shot it, I should carry it down. And so it was I dragged the buck down and ferried it across the burn with a lot of moral encouragement from mine host whenever I stumbled.

Stuart looked at me. Then looked at the perfect shot placement. Then he looked at me again. "I should've let you shoot that stag yesterday," was, I think, his way of saying "good shot" and perhaps admitting that he'd talked himself out of shooting that red stag on the hill. He thought the roebuck to be a harder shot than the red stag – but I was very pleased with my trip to Balmoral. I was delighted to have added another special trophy to the office wall (part of our recruitment process is to sit prospective candidates in front of skulls and antlers and ask them what they think of fieldsports). It was more than a suitable replacement for my missed chances at a stag, and every time I glance at the trophy I think with a smile of Stuart's poor uncle and then wince.

Roe deer and their pursuit have brought me and most of my friends an enormous amount of pleasure, and in my mind there isn't a more sporting prospect than engaging a good buck on the hill. You have to work hard for your game. He isn't easily outwitted, and by the time you've hiked off the hill with a 40lb buck on your back you really do know about it, but for me anyway, it has always been well worth the effort. I'm so glad that our sporting reasoning has changed for the better towards the roe since Prichard's days. The following records are from those times that are now thankfully resigned to history, but nevertheless they still make interesting reading.

The record bag for roe taken with shotguns was 56 head on Monromon Moor, Angus, Scotland, on one day in 1849. An interesting right and left was scored by C. Mclean taking a roebuck and a cock caper on 4th September 1906 at Kildrummy Castle, Aberdeenshire. **PC**

Above: A silver medal from East Yorkshire shot by the author during the 2014 season

Curlew

on the **Moor** and **Marsh**

It is certain that the curlew has a place of its own in literature. Indeed, few birds have done such yeoman service – for the novelist at any rate. "As Hamish descended the Hill," one reads, "the curlews rose, calling plaintively from the little wood on the outskirts of which Jean was waiting for her lover." The habits of these curlews were, to say the least of it, out of the common. Indeed, it may be confessed that ornithological equipment of novelists (even the greatest) is not invariably accurate; but as long as they keep to the sea-shore or the moors they are fairly safe with the curlew, and probably to the end of time the bird will be used as a literary property by all and sundry.

On the other hand, it has inspired some great passages; among them the beautiful dedication of the *Stick it Minister* to "Robert Louis Stevenson, of Scotland and Samoa," in the words:

"... I dedicate these tales of that grey Galloway land, where about the graves of the martyrs the whaups are crying – his heart remembers how."

The cry of the curlew is, indeed, rarely absent from wildest Britain. It breeds from Cornwall to Caithness, and one of the things the British traveller first misses when camped beside an alien ocean is its questing and sorrowful note. Still, one has to travel far to leave it behind; for its range extends (apart from allied forms which cover Turkestan, India, China, and the Malays) from Greenland round every European coast. Sometimes, also, the African traveller comes across it in the interior of the land of Ethiopia, and the pilgrim to Mecca hears it as he recites the attributes of God. Yet it is also to be found all the year round upon our own coasts, even in the nesting season, when the young cock-

birds do not repair with the parents of the race to the high moors in order to undertake family cares, but live beside the tide edges where they are joined later by the vast flocks from the uplands.

The estimation in which curlew are held by individual shooters differs tremendously. Some place them amongst the highest of sporting birds: to others their name is anathema. "Those cursed curlew," says such a one, "they lost me a fine chance at the widgeon. I wish they were all killed off." So do not others. The curlew has given to some of us – at least – days or even weeks of interest, and has enlivened many a weary wait. He is a splendid bird on which to start the youthful sportsman; for there is exaggeration in the old saying that he who has bagged seven curlew is a master of the gun, yet the boy who stalks and kills a curlew with a pea-rifle deserves to be permitted to cope with the horned beasts of the mountain.

There is in Jersey, on the eastern coast, where the sun rises over the sea from behind the stones of Dol, a long, long bay with a curving pebble beach of perfect symmetry. Here is a sea-wall carried on more or less continuously until it merges into the golf-links. Standing almost on the wall are two or three Martello towers, formerly rented as dwelling-places to the island peasantry. Some of these are farmers, others labourers; but one and all seem to possess the inalienable right to gather "vraick" on the sea-edge opposite to their dwellings. This vraick, or seaweed, is dried in the sun and used for purposes of manure. A part of it is burnt as fuel – the ashes afterwards enriching the ground. One of the farmers, an old friend, told me that in a single year he had gathered eighteen pounds worth' of "vraick," and on eighteen pounds a year he and his wife (so strong is the thrifty Breton blood) were rich. I often went to see this old man in later years, for he was excellent company and had a considerable fund of dry humour.

Congratulating me one day, on my safe return from South America, he said: "I should like to travel too, me, ah, yes! *But not more than an hour from the land."* He had never left Jersey but once, when he had gone with his white capped, lean-faced old wife to Guernsey, where the two salient impressions he received were, first, that there were "bad peoples" in that island who asked him 2d. a pound too much for butter; and secondly, that one could ride "long ways" in the tram for a penny. Albeit, he was a very shrewd old fellow, crabbed to a degree; but having known me from a child was ever ready to further my youthful plans in any conceivable way – legal or illegal. Yet a more pig-headed antag-

onist than he habitually made to the world at large it would be quite impossible to conceive. He would certainly have died, pitchfork in hand, in defence of the least of his rights, and once, when a passing terrier chased his farm-cat (an animal which I know he loathed) on to the roof of his house, he ran after the carriage which the dog was accompanying almost into Gorey, three miles away. He is dead now, and let us hope the vraick-scented sand lies lightly on his bones. He never showed the least outward sign of affection for his wife, but he only survived her a few weeks, struck suddenly by her loss out of a hale old age.

In a neighbouring farm lived Phillip John Gaudin, who won the Queen's Prize for rifle shooting in the old days when the competition took place at Aldershot. He was not a sportsman, nor did he ever, to my knowledge, fire at a bird, though sometimes I used to persuade him to give me a les-

son with the rifle. Never shall I forget, or cease to be grateful for his words spoken when he met me at the age of twelve carrying my first gun. "Ah, young master!" said he. "Here you come carrying two deaths!" To this day, it is difficult to watch a wild shot without remembering that cogent remark. Evening after evening old Phillip and his three sons would lie with their rifles on the short grass outside the farm practising steadiness and position. For many years they were able to beat any other four that might essay to try conclusions with them. But (except when the brent geese came) none of them, nor of the other farmers, ever fired a shot on the shore; and this though in the interior of the island (where shooting is free) every lane was patrolled by local or French sportsmen in search of blackbirds and fieldfares. A few gunners from across the channel carried horns and blew them, but whether over the fallen thrush, who knows? Certainly there was

little else to blow them over, for the last red-legged partridge had been slain at Plémont in 1876; and though there was still in 1888 a legendary hare, I did not hear that it ever came out from the land of myth into any of those green-tasselled game-bags. On the other hand, the shore despised by the gunners of the island was not ill supplied with wading birds, and in the season with both widgeon and geese. At low tide a vast panorama of rock and sand was exposed, the tide receding to an immense distance. On the wide flats the curlew were naturally almost impossible of access; indeed, the place possessed certain disabilities that made curlew shooting really difficult. Thus, when the flocks (there were in August but two or three of them) flew down form the hills above Grouville at the hour when their feeding-grounds by the shore began to be exposed, they usually passed over too high to reach, and on the open flats a stalk was

out of the question. Something was to be done by lying for hours among the rocks – but not much, as the area was so wide that the flight was never concentrated. Each fortnight, however, brought two golden chances. These occurred when the tide reached its height just *before* dawn. Before dawn because the vraick-gatherers were terribly early people, and their appearance was, of course, always a signal for the curlew to seek the high lands in the interior of the island. But when high water heralded the dawn, the curlew gathered under the sea-wall in positions where they could be approached with every chance of success. Owing to the fact that the sea-wall was built into the dunes, there was no such thing – save here and there – as an easy approach. Every bird killed meant a crawl and a quick shot, if the weapon was a shot-gun; whereas one that fell to what Colonel Roosevelt calls "the weapon of the freed-man" – that is, the rifle – was in reality a more worthy trophy than is many an outwitted stag.

Glorious dawns were those spent lying face downwards among the diamonds of the dew on the short close-growing turf that bordered the shingle ridge, when a successful shot had power to brighten the whole world, and a failure to darken it. Quite alone, and without advice or aid, I was in the happy position of being able to work out my own salvation. At the age of thirteen I conceived and carried out the brilliant idea of hiring (*2s.* a day. or *7s. 6d.* the week) a huge single barrelled 8-bore. It was almost as tall as the bearer, and it was not in any way necessary or desirable for shooting at curlew in August; but pride in its huge proportions survived the bleeding nose and puffed-lip that resulted as five and a half drams of black powder (the gunmaker was a wise man and lessened the normal loads) made seven stone gasp and flinch. One morning, however, the huge hireling went off into a flock of curlew of which three remained behind on the shingle, to be gathered in the ecstasy of a joy never to be forgotten, and not since, I think, approached.

The main cause of the scarcity of curlew on the Les Marias beaches was probably the over-population of the island behind them. The curlew moves at sight of man sooner than other birds. Once I had a fine object-lesson of this. Coming over the crown of the downs (it was in Uist in the Hebrides) I saw along the length of a great bay below me a large quantity of fowl of various kinds. Quite close beside the tide edge were a flock of oyster-catchers and dunlins, beyond them a pair of great black-backed gulls; further, a number of sheldrake; and in the distance, by the other horn of the bay, a flock of about a hundred curlew. These were gathered on a rock surrounded by the tide. In the water near this rock floated an eider duck with a family of three, and some cormorants. Such was the scene that a careful survey with the telescope disclosed. On my rising against the skyline, the oyster-catchers, which were not a hundred yards away, were the first to fly – after them went the curlew, though a full mile distant. The black-backs let me come within a hundred and twenty yards, the sheldrake within three hundred. The only birds that I believe to be better able to take care of themselves than curlew are grey geese. They do not, it is true, fly when danger is as far off as do curlew; but their departure when the fowler is still 200 or

300 yards away is not (as is the curlew's at a mile) born of panic, but of reason – the sagacity of the super-bird. The goose is wise where the curlew is merely wild; yet this ultra-wildness renders the killing of curlew a matter of difficulty even when experience, knowledge of the ground and numbers are on the side of the "gun." Good bags with curlew are, of course, to be made; but success can never be guaranteed even to the limited extent which is possible with ducks. I have known evenings when a single gun could have shot twenty curlew – once, when flighting, I have killed ten in half an hour, and then stopped shooting because, combined with the morning's duck-shoot, we had as many birds as would supply the crofters.

Perhaps a drive is necessary in order to bring out to the full the possibilities of the curlew as marks for the gun, and when the birds come down-wind there must be good shooting to fill the bag. But it will be more satisfactory to illustrate with a concrete instance.

In one of the Outer Hebrides there is a spot where an arm of the tides runs far up into the dunes. On one side of this arm lie saltings which are a favourite resort of curlew, especially at high tide, when the ocean-surrounded rocks that form their sanctuaries are covered. The tide flows into the bay by a narrow channel of swift water which has cut its way through the dunes so that its silver beaches abut on jagged cliffs of sand some fifty feet in height. On the other side of the water, under slopes of green turf, lie the large saltings I have described; behind them, on the summit of the cliffs, extend in

their season many acres of stubble of barley and oats.

Here the curlew congregate; indeed, by driving the beaches and saltings, and choosing the hour when the tide is nearly at the full so that the rocks in the bay are submerged, hundreds of curlew can be moved on to the stubbles. The driving must, of course, be carried on with knowledge, and the birds moved in a skilful fashion from one feeding-ground to another. The guns then take their places under the high cliffs of sand facing the stubbles and dunes, while two men, sent round very carefully, move the curlew towards them. If this is gently and quietly done, the birds come in small companies and even singly, giving splendid shooting; so that it is quite conceivable that the most favoured gun may fire twenty or even thirty more shots. We never had much success when trying to drive

curlew up-wind; but with a gale behind them, which bore them forward and blew away the noise of the shooting in front, the sport was splendid. A few blue-rock pigeons often came over, as well as plover, both green and golden. The quickness with which the curlew turned on seeing the guns was remarkable. If one managed to shoot before the curlew discovered the presence of danger, the result was generally satisfactory; but when the flock broke and scattered, the dip made by the birds in that act was as quick as the twist of a snipe.

Curlew cannot be driven often, for no birds sooner abandon a line of flight upon which they meet with persecution. Drive them the same way twice in one week, and the third time the bag will be exceedingly small; it will probably consist of a single old bird which, as it were of contrariness, flies along a different line from his fellows.

Wild as curlew are, they occasionally give easy chances, and very occasionally they may be shot rising like snipe. Such opportunities occur when the gunner comes suddenly over the brow of a hill or rock; but this reference specially applies to birds rising from tussocks, and more particularly from among potatoes. A rising curlew is rather a clumsy, flurried bird, and always exceedingly vociferous. In the breeding season the curlew, then birds of the moors and mountains, find a courage as remarkable as is their timidity at other seasons. Let the human intruder wander near the nests and the outraged parents will fly screaming about him, so near that their expostulation is deafening; in this demonstration both sexes take part, for the cock is an excellent husband and bears his full share of domestic toil.

When the curlew are feeding in a flock, they do not seem to appoint one of their number to act as sentinel, as do wild geese, though sometimes a bird seems to sustain the part voluntarily; but, on the other hand, a dozen curlew may often be seen all feeding at the same time – a state of things that would never be permitted among geese or widgeon. Still, the curlew are so quick of sight and hearing, and so watchful by nature, that every member of the flock may be said to be a sentinel.

As far as my own experience goes, other birds dislike the neighbourhood of curlew. This does not refer to small waders, but rather to duck, geese, and widgeon. Cormorants and curlew seem to be good friends, at least to the extent of frequenting the same rocks. Large flocks of curlew and green and golden plover feed close together, but do not actually mix to any great extent.

The curlew spends a good deal of his time during the autumn in the cornfields, where great sport may be had. Half a dozen painted wooden decoys, and a secure and well-concealed hiding place among the stooks, are necessities, while the services of a ghillie, who may be told to keep the birds moving in any distant haunt they are known to frequent, will always add to the number of shots obtained.

One summer evening I was watching for curlew with a couple of painted wooden decoys set up, when an old bird flew noiselessly up and settled within a yard or two of the decoys. It was some moments before he discovered there was something wrong, but when he did he made off in a terrible state, continuing the shrillness of his clamour until he was out of hearing.

Curlew are birds of very regular habits, flying here and there at certain stages of the tide, and to a less extent at nightfall and dawn. It is when their favourite sea-feeding and resting grounds are uncovered about sunset that the full opportunity of the fowler comes. If he can hide himself behind some rock in their line of flight, he may shoot till his barrels are hot. Such a spot is to be found by a northern estuary, where a sandbank is uncovered within half an hour of the beginning of the ebb, and as it is some three-parts of a mile out in the water the birds on it are not, after dusk, much disturbed even by the continued banging of a gun on the shore. The curlew flocks, moreover, fly down a long string of marshes bounded by dunes, so that the main flight is of necessity concentrated. Evening after evening I have there awaited the coming of the curlew. On the first occasion they arrived quite early, flying comparatively high, perhaps fifty or more feet above ground; on the second evening only a few birds put in an appearance, but chancing to go out at a later hour I heard them calling on the sandbank. Therefore on the following night I remained longer. It was bright starlight, but the birds did not begin to appear till half-past eight; then for half an hour they were coming all the time, flying so low that it was impossible to see them against the dark background of rock and marsh. By changing my position and lying some yards down the side of the ridge I was able to get a momentary glimpse as they topped the skyline ahead, and never have I enjoyed shooting more. A good many plover came with the curlew, and the bag which fell to a great deal of powder and shot was fourteen head. It might have been much more, but it was necessary to send the dog at once whenever I thought that a bird was down, and as the dog was as black as the shadows and the night, the low-flying curlew could not be shot till he returned.

But of all sport that has ever fallen to my lot with curlew, far and away the best (because the conditions presented difficulties that seemed at first sight insuperable) was on the great stretch of sand in St. Ouen's Bay, Jersey. Here were plenty of curlew, a bay some miles in length, a beautiful strand, and actually not a particle of cover. The tide recedes to a good distance, and lying with a glass among the dunes, the watcher may count large flocks feeding on the sand-hoppers and running on the edge of the water. A few efforts made at high tide, when stalking was possible from behind the dunes, were not altogether unproductive of result; but the absolute immunity which the curlew enjoyed upon the open expanses at other times gave the birth to a strong desire to outwit them there.

So it came that one October day – when the sky and sea, the sun and gorse, made up the blue and gold colouring typical of the Channel Islands, and the hard sands were so white as to hurt the eye like the glare of a North African highway – I waited until the tide was nearly ebb, and then commenced to dig a series of pits in the sand about 200 yards apart, and each 100 yards nearer the shore than the last. Starting in the centre of the bay, I thus had a series of hiding-places to suit each stage of the incoming tide. The pits were rather inclined to hold more or less water, and at first the displaced sand was very obvious, but soon the sun bleached it to dry whiteness. An hour after the turn of the tide I occupied my first pit, while a companion went round and walked the beach towards me from the eastern end.

I have often thought that among the most delightful moments in the whole of one's shooting career are those when first one lies in ambush and contemplates the chances of success. Anyhow, the memory of those moments in the shallow pit on that glorious day of blue and gold, with the autumn sun boring a hole into my back, have not passed away.

There were several flocks of curlew, and the first of them rose while my companion was still a long way off, just as I had seen them rise a dozen times before my own advance. On and on they came, not ten feet off above the sand, and sailed right up within range without suspicion. And then,

as the two barrels went off, what a commotion, what a swerve out to sea! The same thing happened with other flocks at some of the other pits. We drove them east and we drove them west; a great day, and one which the unusual and almost sub-tropical weather marked out in unique relief.

There is a lot of fun to be had with curlew in a country with stone walls, where the birds are on the plough or in turnips and potatoes. If the walls are high and their building solid, the stalk is easy; but where they are storm-blown and tumbledown the skill of a true hunter is called forth.

I remember an occasion when a curlew feeding under such a wall proved too great a temptation to a schoolboy who was supposed to be shore-shooting along the tide edge of the Firth of Forth. In those

days a famous headmaster used to permit shore-shooting to chosen boys of his great school. One day I was walking on the road to Aberlady when two bareheaded boys with guns came charging out from behind a hedge. One of them held a dead curlew in his hand. They began to run at full speed along the road, checked and had an argument, one pointing one way and one the other; then they deliberately came up to me.

"I say, you won't give us away?" the spokesman said panting. "We're going to hide behind that wall. The keeper's is after us. The Head . . ." He paused, thinking perhaps he that he had given away too much to the casual stranger. We stayed, looking at each other.

"You'd better get behind the wall quickly," I said.

"Thank' awfully," came from two voices: and, with almost uncanny suddenness, I was alone in the road.

I strolled on a little, and soon heard the beat of rapid footsteps behind me, as a hard-featured old keeper ran up.

"Have you seen my two young gentlemen, sir?" he asked.

Cunning man! He wanted to give me the impression that the boys were under his charge and sent out to shoot with him by his master. His cunning, however, made my answer the easier.

"I have not!" I said definitely – my last scruple, if ever I had one, gone.

"They run down this way. They were after my partridges, shooting into a covey from behind the dyke."

We looked at each other and I swear he reddened.

"This has been a very good partridge year up here?" I asked.

He stared, "Not good not bad." There was something in his eye as he said this that told me how best I could serve the young sinners who were quaking within fifty yards behind the wall.

"Do you see many pintail about here?" I asked. "I read in last week's *Field* that the Firth of Forth. . ."

But he thought I was delaying him on purpose.

"Good afternoon, sir, good afternoon," he said testily. "I must be getting on." He walked till he was round the corner, and then I heard the plunk of his boots in the mud as he started again at the double. A few minutes later and the boys climbed over the wall.

"Thanks awfully," they said a again, and set off running in the opposite direction to that the keeper had taken.

I met them, by chance, later that evening, waiting for the same train. They greeted me shyly, but with evident friendship. I asked for news.

"It was all right. We didn't see him again. He's an awful liar," one said. "We never touched his rotten partridges. It was a curlew quite close to the wall. We crept up, and . . . You see, we couldn't get near to them on the shore, and . . . and . . . It's a ripping bird, isn't it?" The boy had the bird wound up in his jersey. He produced it. "I'm . . . we're going to have it stuffed," he ended.

I never learned the boys' names, but I have sometimes wondered if either of them was an embryo Selous[1], and if somewhere a battered curlew on a stand may recall an early adventure and an escape from the tempestuous and roaring wrath of one of the greatest of headmasters.

Many people debar themselves from curlew shooting because the curlew, they say, is no bird for the table; and it is true that, while I have eaten some good curlew, others have needed the seasoning of hunger; but all through the Western Isles, where the greater part of my curlew-shooting

has been done, the native relishes curlew almost as much as duck. He likes cormorant better than either, in which he approaches the standard of taste in vogue amongst the Eskimo, to whom the bird that enjoys a diet of fish or sea-lice forms flesh that most rejoices the palate of the squat *gourmet* of the Arctic.

Although the curlew is more essentially, perhaps, than any other bird a denizen of the wild, yet sometimes he may be seen near the centres of civilisation. In the evening, flocks often fly by Ravelston Dykes over Edinburgh, and we may believe that Alan Breck heard them as he waited for David Balfour at Rest-and-be Thankful, that spot which is nowadays the Mecca of the Writer to the signet's Sunday constitutional. The curlew is not out of place there, nor out of the picture which includes the high Corstorphine Woods, as well as from another vantage point, that view which drew out the word-picture: "I saw all the country fall away before me down to the sea, and I the midst of this descent, on a long ridge, the City of Edinburgh smoking like a kiln . . . and ships moving or lying anchored in the Firth."

But the curlew occasionally appears in other places; at the heart of populous cities where one would scarcely expect to see him, or on wharf-surrounded expanses of black mud in the shadow of giant houses of merchandise. Once, near Glasgow, a single bird rose from a pool of slime in the vicinity of a huge gasometer – he rose and headed away for the Clyde; let him reach it and pass over the tossing water, flying above giant liners until, far away, his sharp eyes discern the Kyles of Bute. **HP**

[1] Capt. Frederick Courteney Selous DSO, the famous big game hunter and close friend of Prichard

When I initially took on the commission to write a modern perspective of Prichard's SIWB I set out to shoot a curlew, as it is one species that has evaded my gun in our isles. Of course in Britain we had long lost the curlew as a legitimate quarry species some thirty years before, and it looked like Ireland was about to remove the wader from their list too, so time was of the essence.

Alas, despite a number of attempts, the time ran out, and legislation finished the endeavour. Therefore it saddens me to say that I shall never be able to claim a curlew by sporting pursuit. As a boy I came very close to securing a curlew on the foreshore, and I shall relate the tale here as it remains strong in the memory as one of extreme frustration and ultimately abject failure.

Every opportunity to be out with the gun was taken back then, usually under the advice or direction of Joe or old Joss, but occasionally I would steal away before dawn and do business with the gulls on the cliffs, or the redshanks on the tide edge. It pains me to say, but crawling between the bladder wrack shrouded scars and skerries, in the half-light one could often make a good bag of redshank. The sporting considerations mostly came second place to a "bag". In one particular place the limestone formations would enable the young gunner to lie parallel to a long strip of sand beloved by the redshank.

Trips of the noisy little wader would begin to alight as dawn turned the shadowy foreshore into a mosaic of wrack, rock and sand. Covered as I was with handfuls of bladder wrack, and pressed low between the skerries, the vocal waders paid me

Right: The loss of the curlew to the shore shooter was made on a whim

no heed and their numbers would build up into a good congregation.

It was a case of picking one's moment, and not letting the excitement (which banished cramp, dampness, and all other discomforts that such an endeavour entailed) get the better of the eager gunner who knew his game. The hypnotic rhythm of the incoming tide wished and washed, back and forth, with the waders running in at the water's edge to pick morsels turned over by the relentless wave action.

I wince now when I think of how I'd wait for the redshanks to make a good bunch, pull back both hammers of the Henry Clarke 12 bore and let 'em have two barrels of Eley Alphamax by pulling the triggers simultaneously. Let's just say that it was effective, and I hasten to add all birds were eaten – quite good they were too. How that old gun never suffered a barrel burst I don't know, but the action as described sometimes resulted in a thick lip, bruised cheek and, on one occasion due to poor gun mount, a black eye and a bleeding nose. But it all seemed worth it in those days.

However, the reader must now have a good idea of the morals of an impetuous youth who loved to be out on the saltings, roaming the woods and fields, or tramping through the heather. And I'm sure one could understand the young gunner's dilemma when he lay in his favoured cleft of limestone, hammers back, contemplating the stands of piping redshank running hither and thither along the tide's edge when a respectful herd of curlew (for that is the correct collective noun), came into view, followed the foreshore and on towards the hidden tyro. What a dilemma! The congregation

of redshank before him promised to be the biggest bunch ever to grace the game bag, and the incoming squadron of curlew flying fast afore the wind, low above the spindrift-foamed skerries would be a far harder mark, but to bag a curlew would be really something.

The decision was done, and the bladder wrack apparition that rose up in front of the great congregation of redshanks sent them into a cloud of apoplectic piping panic. A crescendo of alarmed "chipe, chipe, chipes" drowned out even the wind and the waves but the curlew were even now

banking out to sea. A fast-reaching swing saw one barrel discharged and then another at the leading bird, but it wasn't enough. Or was it? A bird in the rear of the formation began to peel away and loose height. Then the slightest of splashes in the wind-lashed swell confirmed the bird down. I was fleet of foot and cared not for the consequence of skipping across wet rocks, made greasy by the flora of the sea. It was an incoming tide, and an onshore wind, but the junctions formed by the scars and skerries were many. Try as I did for four long hours the bird remained lost. Any one of the multitude of rocks,

Below: A foreshore-foraging curlew was often the difference between a blank foray and getting something in the game bag

their bladder wrack curtains washed in and out by the suction of the tide, could have hidden the prized bird. As the anxious minutes turned into hours, my despair was replaced by remorse, and I promised never to risk losing a bird again if I could at all avoid it, and I believe I became a better gun for it.

For the keeper the curlew is a friend. He ranks alongside the blackbird and the wren as an effective early warning system of vermin being about. On one occasion I was sitting in one of the grouse butts above Collier Gill, Farndale, in late spring spying for a fox. We knew there was a litter in the sand holes over at Oak Cragg, and my position was a good one from which to watch for the comings and goings of the vixen and dog. The head keeper was away and I was keen to prove my worth and his trust in me with such a responsibility. It was a curlew and her mocking cries that brought my attention to the vulpine marauder. Coming in from behind me she had no doubt been doing great harm among the nesting grouse. Mobbed as she was by the alarmed wader, her direction and probable route was easy to work out. I intercepted her and put an end to her mischief with the 12 bore and a charge of AAAs, all thanks to that alert curlew.

But let's get back to more recent shenanigans. There was no solid scientific reason to deprive our Irish cousins the pursuit of such a worthy quarry as the curlew on the marsh. Here on the mainland, we regrettably lost the curlew during the debate leading up to the Wildlife and Countryside Act, which was passed in 1981. MPs voted to remove the curlew from the list of quarry species, justified by one MP because: "the curlew has such a lovely call." I ask you! No one would doubt the bird's musical prowess, but because it sings sweet is no justification to stop shooting a sustainable quarry species. Curlews have never been in any danger from over-shooting, and to lose it was tragic. The main threat to this species, as to so many others on the foreshore, lies in the loss of habitat; it should not go unnoticed that wildfowling clubs are very good at both retaining habitat and its subsequent restoration. Just why a fight was not put up to keep the curlew in the early 80s remains a mystery to me. But again we have digressed to the past.

More recently, the last bastion of the curlew shooter was Ireland, but that door too has now been closed with hardly a fight. Irish legislation has effectively deprived the wildfowler forevermore of the chance to engage this most sporting and wary of waders.

The curlew was given protection on the basis of a whim rather than on considered judgement and that should be a lesson learned, we have lost it twice by inaction. And perhaps it is time we should be lobbying this species to be reinstated to the quarry list, and why not consider others as well, such as the redshank and Brent goose? Now that is a thought worth some consideration.

No less than 60 curlew have been killed with one shot from a punt gun by the Rev. Mr Close of Kilkeel Rectory in Carlingford Lough, Co. Louth, date not recorded. Captain K. Dover got 47 with another punt gun shot in the Moy estuary, Co. Mayo, and the record with shoulder guns seems to be 56 shot on one tide by two unknown fowlers, at a place and a time now lost to history. **PC**

Black Geese

To touch for a moment on a personal note. In an experience of a sport which has extended over varied portions of the world – some of them in its wildest and most remote regions – I frankly own that the sight and chase of no beast in plain, forest, or mountain has raised in my consciousness a more vivid sense of romance and delight than has the sight of geese flying out of, or into, the cloud-wrack of our British skies. The sound of the wind about the dunes and that most arresting clamour of geese, grey or black, flying over sea-girt isles, drowning the piping of lesser fowl, seem to have virtue to stir some nerve of recollection which pulsates with an almost poignant sense of pleasure. No doubt the cause of this is to be found partly in heredity, in the descent of the spirit of some woad-clad marshman or estuary-dweller, as partly in the fact that a first wild goose shot at fifteen marks a far more notable epoch in one's life than a first bear slain in early manhood.

There are still in these British Isles, or rather in the seas around them, many small islands, generally an outcrop of the dunes of the mainland, which the bernicle geese have used, some as resting-places, some as feeding-grounds, for

such time as the memory of man runneth not
to the contrary. From their arrival in October or
November, right up to an early Easter, the gaggles
haunt these isles, arriving regularly to the clock
each evening, departing to the minute in the
morning, for in spots – and fortunately there
are many – where the geese are not disturbed,
the premature darkness of a stormy evening does
not much affect their time-table of flight.

One spring, I camped for a week upon an
islet perhaps an acre and a half in extent, and
situated a few miles from the western Irish coast.
Upon the Atlantic side, no land broke the force

of the gales until, two thousand miles away, the grim headlands of Labrador, Capes Harrison and Harrigan, frown down upon the frozen sea. I have gone to this islet to try and get a specimen of *Halichoerus grypus*, but on the first night a storm arose and blew away the roof of the earthen hut in which I was sleeping, so that I awoke with a mouthful of peaty dust and got up to have a look round outside. Never shall I forget the surprise I received – and gave. I had slept for several hours, my fire was long since out, I had no companion, not even a dog, the hut was merely a kennel or a place tunnelled in a mound by some fisherman, and years previously used by him as an occasional summer residence. Doubtless the isle had appeared untenanted to a vast flock of bernicle geese, some three or four hundred strong, which were standing and sleeping up to within five yards of the door when I stepped out among them. In the moonlight, I could see the eyes of the nearer geese in that infinitesimal portion of a second before the air was rent with the noise of wings and tongues. The geese circled once and

pitched upon the farthest rocky margin of the isle, where I could hear them talking and complaining until, having concluded thorough repairs to my roof, I once more went to ground. In the morning they had all collected upon a strip of grass at the extreme north-west corner of the island, and there they stayed within a hundred and fifty yards of the hut until nearly eight o'clock, when they departed north. That evening, and upon all subsequent evenings while I remained upon the isle, they returned, but never again did they venture upon the central plateau of grass, but always stuck to their quarters upon the north-west spur. I never molested them, but I had my reward, for I could take a good look at them through the glass before emerging from the hut; but the moment I put in an appearance they flew off.

It is worthy of note that they never had a definite sentinel, though generally not more than half the flock were heads down feeding or sleeping at the same time. Probably they had not been shot at on this island at any time, and had come to regard it as a sanctuary; and there is no bird more conservative than the wild goose – black or grey.

A point which I first noticed on this occasion, and which the weighing-machine has since confirmed, was the extraordinary difference in the size of individual bernicles. Many old birds weigh 5½ or even 6 lbs., while others, also full-grown, scale as low as 3 and 3¼ lbs. This disparity is very apparent when one watches bernicle geese feeding at close range.

There can be very little question that bernicle are more easily driven away from a particular haunt than are either greylags or pink-footed geese. I have had reason to draw this conclusion at times when I have had the good fortune to shoot over ground where both bernicles and greylags were to be found. During one February week we visited such a spot three times. On the first occasion we saw over four hundred bernicles, on the second not half that number, and on the third a single bird, while the numbers of grey geese remained approximately the same.

Some days of the finest goose-shooting I ever enjoyed I owe to the kindness of Mr. J. D. Beveredge, who owns an estate in North Uist. The first day that I went over, I was accompanied only by an attendant, John, the ghillie of a shooting where I was staying, in another part of the island. We spent a very pleasant day spying out the land, and, apart from an abortive stalk after a gaggle of some seventy graylag geese, were content to do no more than use the glass.

The island of North Uist, of which the interior is dotted with innumerable lochs, large and small, comes at this its north-western extremity to the headland of Griminish Point. Following the coastline to the east, the land recedes, forming the deep bight of Vallay Sound. Vallay itself is the largest of the islands in this Sound. There is a small loch upon it, but for the rest it is made up of the knolls and hollows of sandy dunes. On the day in question we did not cross the Sound, a strand not unlike that of Holy Island, and passable only at certain stages of the tide. We spent our time among the heather of the mainland, where a couple of lochs gave safe harbourage to companies of widgeon. At these no shot was fired for fear of disturbing the greater game, and after the failure of our solitary stalk, undertaken among the ruins of a deserted croft, the only geese we saw winged their way to the safety of Gaskeir, and as evening fell we drove our seven miles home through the curlew-haunted dusk, while once, somewhere beneath the stars, a flight of wild swans passed over us.

It was a few days later before my friend, the laird, again drove me over. On the way, we saw many widgeon and seven whopper swans, besides, on the strand at Vallay, widgeon, mallard, and innumerable representatives of the wader family. On arrival at Vallay, we had but a hundred yards to drive up to the house of the factor. This house overlooks the strand, and near it there is a hollow in the downs, perhaps eight hundred yards by six hundred in size. Never in Britain have I seen such a sight as this area presented on that February day. To the north of it, not half a mile away, five grey geese were feeding on the short grass, and perhaps eighty yards from them eleven bernicles were intent upon the same purpose, on a stubble. At some distance farther on another flock of bernicles, over a hundred strong, formed but an outlying party to a vast body of three or four hundred. As we watched them, John remarked: "There was a minute when I was thinking it was sheep."

We descended from the trap and shook hands with the factor. The laird explained the purpose of our visit, for, owing to the tide, the letter announcing our coming had not arrived.

"There are the geese," said the factor; "they have been there this three weeks." Whereupon he introduced me to the ghillie, Norman McClennan, and forthwith we made our plan of campaign.

Of all the geese within sight on the landscape, only the eleven bernicles were in a stalkable place. McClennan said that the best way would be for one of us to go with him and stalk these, while John and the other made a detour to a high point nearer the eatern end of the island over which the geese, when disturbed, would probably fly. The laird, with his usual generosity, insisted that I should take the stalk, and then set off with John for the spot which McClennan had pointed out, while the latter and I incongruously started our stalk by creeping along under a wall of the farmyard and passing through a cowhouse. After this, the ground hid us from the geese, and a detour of a few hundred yards brought us in at the back of the amphitheatre of downs where they were feeding. Here a depression ran up between two knolls, and up this McClennan signed me to creep. I did so, and then very carefully raised my head, expecting to find myself within easy shot. A cautious spy, however, revealed no birds, so I crept back and then forward again along another similar depression, which ran parallel to the first, until

I was able to peer through the bents at the eleven geese, now within fifteen yards of me. They were all together, and a shot in the middle of them, even with a 12-bore such as I was carrying, would have been very killing. As I showed my head, the eleven rose and bunched together. I picked two outside birds and scored a very easy right and left. Had I fired into the brown, I might have done twice or thrice as well. All the geese within hearing rose at once, but to the great surprise of McClennan and myself, pitched again very quickly. They had no idea where the shot had come from – that is, except the eleven – and from their four or five hundred throats rose a babel of sound as they discussed matters in their feathered parliament. I was very much astonished to observe that the five grey geese pitched among the bernicles, for never before had I seen these wildest of all British birds take so short a flight. Norman now suggested that I should go down and conceal myself under a bank of turf on the far side of the new position taken up by the geese, which he pointed out to me. By doing this, he said, I should probably get a shot at the geese when he drove them over, as he would try to do as soon as I reached my place. He said also that I should probably flank them in, and increase the laird's chances of a shot. I now crept back upon the line of my stalk, and, once safely below the skyline, ran as hard as I could back to the farm, where the factor very kindly took me to my place for the drive, and there left me. The geese were now within three hundred yards of me, and as soon as Norman showed himself, they rose and crossed about forty yards wide. My first barrel, which was loaded with No. 4, produced

nothing but a rattle of shot upon the feathers of an enormous gander, but the No. 1 in the second knocked him out of time. The others flew on, but passed wide of the laird on the hilltop. We watched them grow less as they winged their way towards the mainland, and then spent the rest of the day upon the western end of the island, where a seaweed-gatherer had reported several flocks of grey geese. We saw them, but were unable to come to terms at all, and finally drove away, after promising to return two or three days later for a second trial of cunning.

This we did, but I will spare the reader an account of the day. It will be enough to say that it was most successful, and remains a joy in retrospect. We secured two grey geese and seven bernicles, once stalking right up to the latter and killing five with four barrels. Nine wild geese to two guns is a good day for the Hebrides, or indeed anywhere else in the British Isles. Larger bags have been made, the record for North Uist being, as I was given to understand, eleven to one gun. These included six brent geese, and the gun was an 8-bore. In South Uist twenty-one have been killed in a day by two guns.

Personally, I have never used anything larger

than a 12-bore, an ordinary game-gun, with which to shoot wild geese, and as long as my sport is undertaken for pleasure – and for what other purpose can it be undertaken within the limits of civilisation? – I shall certainly not use anything heavier than a 12-bore, though, were I to do much goose-shooting, I should use the long-chambered variety. The essence of sport is surely enjoyment, and the satisfaction of a successful flock shot with an 8-bore is rather mathematical than artistic. Of course, one has killed two, three, or even eight ducks or plover with one barrel, but not often. Again, I have fired occasional shots at the central bird of a flock and with the inevitable result, which is cruel. No doubt, fair sport entitles hunter and hunted to equal chances, and there is also little doubt that wild geese usually have ninety per cent. of the odds in their favour. But as I grow older, the more strongly do I feel that the fair right and left at geese, as at lesser fowl, is the ideal to which the well-armed modern shooter should strive. Bags will be small perhaps, but there are places where even so they will not be always empty.

Of the power of a 12-bore to kill a goose cleanly and fairly at thirty yards, I have no doubt at all; but at forty your shot must be large, unless you hit him right in front. A bernicle also will succumb to a blow that would merely hasten the departure of a graylag. The upland goose of South America is a bird of about the same size as the bernicle, and an ordinary 12-bore and No. 4 shot was most satisfactory in bringing him to bag.

There are, of course, wide flats where the chances in favour of the fowl are ninety-nine to one, and this fact of heavy odds led to the introduction of the punt-gun. Shooting afloat is, in some of its aspects, perhaps the highest form of sport pursued in the British Isles, and, where the fowl are approachable in no other way, it is legitimate. Yet, after a successful shot, there must necessarily be a number of birds hit which are never picked up and never recover; not more, however, even after the most successful cruise afloat, than in a day's pheasant-shooting or grouse-driving. The shot-gun is cruel – we cannot avoid that conclusion; it remains with sportsmen to make it as little so as may be. But apart from these ethical considerations, my idea of sport does not consist in carting about an 8- or 4-bore and seeking with it the family shot.

Less is probably known of the bernicle than of other geese. On the east coast it is very rare in most parts, loving as it does the grassy isles of the west. It is in fact a bird remembrance of which is inseparable from the wetting rains and vivid greens of the wild Atlantic shore. The gaggles often rest, or when disturbed seek safety on the wide strands of estuaries, but, where the bernicle is unmolested, it loves the dunes. This preference, which it shares with the graylag, makes it the delight of the shore-gunner; for what is more fascinating than the splendid walking and stalking afforded by the dunes? I remember once, when stalking geese with a friend, hearing him remark: "What a glorious spot this would be if it were golf links!" A horrible thought! But on a windy day it would certainly be possible for the driver of a ball over that scented earth to land it among an outlying flock of startled bernicles. But with golf would arise the concomitant hotel, and the geese would vanish from the land, only to be seen flying high on their way to some Avalon, some far island of the waves. In March and early April, the bernicle becomes a tamer bird. In these months there are certain cattlefolds in the Hebrides which they frequent regularly.

Very different from the bernicle, those true friends of the modestly armed wildfowler, is the other variety of black geese – the brent. They are to the shoulder-gun enthusiast infinitely the least approachable of all the goose tribe. Their habitat is the margin of the tide, where they find the *Zostera maritima*, in which their anserine palates delight. They are our latest arrivals; January is their month, and from then onwards till April they are usually, if not always, to be seen in favoured localities, a black line or phalanx well out, a mile or more from any cover. The brent never comes inland; rarely does he desert the area washed by the tides. The sandbank and the tide-rim form his kingdom and thither must the fowler go to seek him. He is a small, wideawake, and most interesting goose; but so far as the game-gun fowler is concerned, his habits make him completely master of the situation. To stalk him is usually impossible, to drive him is to court failure; the only way in which the 12-bore can bring him to bag is to make use of the infrequent occasion when he sits beneath the shelter of some reef or isle, and even then nine stalks in ten prove abortive. The occasions are few and far between when he makes an error of judgment and pays the penalty, but such errors are sometimes made owing to the formation of the ground, and the presence of suitable cover for his enemy. For the most part, he can count on immunity save from the punt-gun.

Few sea-fowl or water-fowl will fly over the land if they can by any means reach their destination by flying over water, but a careful study of the lines of flight adopted by brent does sometimes result in success of a kind – a thin success, and one where the payment is as sure as retribution. The brent may die, but the fowler will pay for it in rheumatism, and when the fires of youth are quenched, most gunners will vote the price of mastery too high. Still, he is a worthy quarry, this little black-headed fellow with the slaty wings, who breeds up within the Arctic circle and is only chased thence by Kabibonokka, the mighty Wind of the North. Not one, of the many thousands that come to these shores, falls to the shoulder-gun; and of all the tens of thousands I have seen, fourteen only have been prevented by me from returning to those solitudes of Nova Zembla and Siberia, which are the cradle of their race.

Nevertheless, occasional successes remain most pleasant memories, though none so much as the first, attained twenty years ago while still a schoolboy. It was totally unforeseen, when one January afternoon I waded out through a quarter of a mile of cold English Channel to a skerry, over which the curlew often flew. The change of tide was right, and I had fired several resultless shots at these birds. I know now that I had moved too soon and taken the birds too far out. They saw me and twisted, as only a scared curlew can twist, and then winged on their way, making the bay re-echo with their loud complaints. The tide had almost left the skerry on which I lay, when I

saw a flock of a dozen birds flying low towards me. They passed a hundred yards wide, but I was quick to speculate as to whether they might not be geese. Turning, I watched them pass on until, as they faded against the winter background, another lot, hitherto unobserved, passed a little wider. My disappointment soon faded and was replaced by wild eagerness, as I became aware of two more birds heading, as it seemed, straight for me. I ground my face against the rock, my heart beating with a fury of hope. They came on, but, seeing the skerry, swung to pass wide of it. They were flying almost together, quite low and perhaps fifty yards wide, when, deliberately swinging a suitable distance in front, I fired both barrels. One brent flew on, the other fell. I leaped to my feet, mad with delight, only to see the goose, which was winged, head seaward. Gun in hand, I waded in, firing as soon as I could re-load.

The goose dived, rose farther out, and we went on in this way until the water was up to my middle, and most of my cartridges, save those I had in my gun and one in my breast-pocket, were wet. The sea became gradually too deep; the brent ceased to dive and paddled slowly out. I returned to shore and watched him till he was shut in by some rocks, then ran home, a distance of about a mile and a quarter, for a dog. I do not know how long it took to cover the ground, but it was all too long for me, divided between hope and fear, for to secure that goose seemed to me to be the one great event likely ever to happen in my whole life. The dog – I did not think so then – was a bad dog. He was a handsome spaniel, and on land he would lift no bird though he would bite a rabbit, but from water he would retrieve. The tide had receded a great way, and, studying the wind and set of the currents, I was soon upon a rock searching. The suspense was not long. Almost at once I saw something floating far out, and I knew it for my goose, and, glorious fact, it was floating belly-up and dead. It was near a quarter of a mile away, but, running round to the nearest skerry, I was within two hundred yards. I now urged the dog to take the water, which he did, but after swimming fifty yards or so he came back. Urged on afresh, he again went in, and up to the limit of my powers I guided him with stones, but he returned once more, barking as he came, while I cursed him with all my schoolboy gods.

During this time the goose was drifting slowly out. So, tearing off my coat and waistcoat, I caught the dog to my bosom, and carrying him thus plunged in. The water grew deeper by degrees, and it was probably very cold, but I never felt that. Within a hundred yards of the goose, the sea was up to my shoulders, and from here I expelled the dog towards it, as a man-o'-war launches a torpedo. He swam a little way, turned and made for shore. He was neither sulky nor unwilling, only obtuse and bored. Having retrieved the dog, I expelled him once more and then groped on the bottom for a stone. It was my one chance. The dog would swim to where I threw a stone. I had to duck deeply for it, and then, wringing the seawater from my eyes and nose, I waited while the dog swam half-heartedly and pessimistically forward until, just as I thought he was going to turn, I threw the stone. With an access of slightly renewed interest, he swam on. He was now within fifty yards of the goose. I ducked for another stone and failed to find one. I was aware of the miserable dog in the act of

turning. I plunged my hand into my pocket and pulled out a two-shilling piece and a heavy metal cartridge extractor. I hurled the latter towards the goose; the dog turned and swam a little forward, and then suddenly he saw the goose itself. A moment or two more and his mouth had closed on it, and not many more beyond that before I had taken it reverently from his jaws. In the cold early dusk I walked home, my whole soul flooded with that peaceful satisfaction which we know not too often. As I went, I remember I praised the dog, but in the back of my mind I foresaw dogs of the future which would be worthy of picking up geese. As I write, the dogs are lying beside me, and they have retrieved geese and strange fowl beyond my wildest dreams, but the feeling that long ago flooded my soul has never again quite reached that first tide-mark. Youth has its own wisdom – a wisdom that can see but one thing, and see it so largely that it covers the horizon; but we lose that wisdom as the years go on, and however keen the joy of sport may remain in a man's mind, we think also of politics or the Stock Exchange or love or ambition, and the height of early feeling is never touched again. Well, here is a lot of talk about a very ordinary incident.

There is another opportunity that the brent geese give to the resident fowler, but which is of little interest to the sportsman. In my own small experience I have only known the eastern coast of the island of Jersey, where there is a fine stretch of *Zostera maritima*. In two occasions there, newly arrived brent allowed me to approach within shot under conditions which in ordinary circumstances would have been condemned to

certain failure. These birds seemed utterly weary after a long flight; and on another occasion a farmer, with a fifty-shilling 12-bore gun loaded with five drams of black powder and large shot, killed five geese at a shot. This man was a friend of my youth, and I remember the gun well. It had skelp or "sham-dam" barrels, its maker preserved a beautiful anonymity, for nowhere was there engraved upon it any hint of its origin or his responsibility. Its mere possession would, even when loaded with ordinary charges, have put up any one's life insurance premium to a high percentage. How it ever got rid of the ten drams of powder without killing more than the geese is hard to say. However, it did so, and the fame of the shot reached Gorey upon the north, and Pontac upon the south.

There is a method of shooting brent geese which is not much followed save by the truly keen, but which, if any man even occasionally adopts it, stamps him at once as a true sports-man – that is, using the word in its sense of a confirmed lover of lonely pursuits when the odds are vastly, almost absurdly, in favour of the quarry. This method consists in sinking a tub in some mudbank, and, after ensconcing oneself in it, either shooting the geese if they fly over it or near it, or, more exciting far, remaining therein while the geese come in upon the edge of the advancing tide.

It is lonely work, of course, but the shooter to whom loneliness is not refreshing, who does not feel exalted and uplifted by contact with desolation, had better stick to the company of his kind upon moor and stubble. How many men are there of cheery disposition, the good fellows of clubs, talkers at breakfast, who, when faced by such conditions, change into magnets of silence and gloom! Once, on a shooting expedition in Canada, a man, having left the last house where it is possible to obtain an illicit glass of beer and plunged into the green and spuce-scented, but nevertheless curiously massive, silence of the Canadian forests, exclaimed, "Never would I go into the woods alone! It is like stepping into an icy bath. Even with pals it is oppressive, but, alone, it makes me shiver!" How different it is with the lover of desolate places! To pass into the lonely woods, to feel the silence enclose and enfold him, to face the wind and smell the rain, raise him in a sense of physical well-being and of mental tonic that has no reaction.

However, we are wandering rather far from the barrel sunk in the mud and the sand of the estuary, where the brent geese feed beside the tide bubbles. Come with me and we will visit it. First, be it understood that the barrel, if it lies in dry sand, must be sunk two or three days before it is used, else the newness of the upturned sand stands out in advertisement of something not as usual, and the geese regard the unusual as the to-be-avoided, and will certainly give it a wide berth. But let us imagine that all is as it should be, and that we are walking, gun in hand, over the dunes. We wear tweeds, rubber boots with at least two pairs of stockings in them, and in a sealskin bag we carry our woolies, for it will be very cold. A light oilskin is usually quite necessary, but this afternoon we have left it behind. The wind is in

the north, the sky is covered with patches of light cloud, but no rain will fall, and if it snows the snow will be hard and will not cling. Our clothes are not very thick because if the feet be warm there are colder places than a barrel, however fiercely the north-east wind may blow.

We arrive above the estuary. Let us sit a moment upon this hillock and spy out the flats with our telescope. You see that sandbank three-quarters of a mile from shore? It is upon the western face of that bank that our barrel is buried. Yes, just within a few yards of those oyster-catchers, or seapies. Let us sweep the flats. There are twenty curlew or so off the skerry, and at least fifty widgeon there by the tide, and out farther, nearly two miles to seaward, a black line like a causeway of attenuated stepping-stones. Those are our quarry – brent geese, about a couple of score of them. They will be joined by others later. Come on! The sooner we get into our hiding-place the better.

We walk over the flats, the curlew move away with their alarming outcry, the widgeon are too far off to care – we may see them again later. We must not forget to shut out our movements from the geese; it would never do for them to see us suddenly disappear into the sand. Here we can get out of their sight naturally enough behind this rock. Now to the left! Here is our bank. We must approach it from the landward side; geese do not like footprints.

Ah! there is the barrel. No one would have suspected its presence, would they? In you get. Sit on that crossbar. It's a tight fit, so in the body I will leave you, though I'll remain in spirit. Your cap, fortunately, is a good colour. At its highest

point, too, it is a few inches below the rim of the barrel. Already four o'clock! The tide has just turned, and the February evening is imperceptibly closing in; the wind has hardened to a gale, it drives little spurts of sand into your skin – you will do well to anoint your face with oil before you sleep to-night. Hullo! What's that? A mallard passed over within easy shot. You were quite right not to shoot. *Aut anser, aut nullus*, is the motto, though if the widgeon come in nicely, you'll need all your self-control. And now for an hour you watch the sights and hear the sounds of the winter shore. Many birds you see, and at closer range than you have seen them before. Oyster-catchers, curlew with their Sherlock Holmes noses, peewits, golden plover, and in flocks and companies the waders, which almost at all seasons touch these solemn sands with life.

And now let me explain the plan of campaign, such as it is, upon which your chances of a shot rest. You see the geese? Very well. They are almost on their last legs on that bank; in a minute or two now the advancing tide will cause them to rise. There are several banks to which they may fly, but usually they come here or go to that bank over there. You see it? It would have been worth while to erect some scarecrow on it, a handkerchief on a stick, but it is too late to think of that now. Look! Look through the glass! They are beginning to be uneasy, and two fresh lots have joined them. They're up, by Jove! and heading this way. They've pitched. No, they have not. See, what luck! They're coming – coming right in! Now they're down – down right in front of us and only a hundred and twenty or a hundred and thirty yards away. Now the fun begins, and it is fun, isn't it? This bank is never quite covered in these tides, and if luck looks our way the geese will move up with the rising water until they are within easy shot. You see that white pebble? That is just forty yards away. You must let them pass that, and then –

Hullo! hullo! a little lot of a dozen widgeon have come in. There are four cocks among them, chestnut-headed beauties, the dandies of the tide. And now the water creeps up, the geese are within a hundred and twenty – a hundred yards. They look nearer? Yes, but they will seem to be right on top of you before you must fire. Close quarters with geese means dead birds. Five more minutes. Surely you will have your reward. Get ready! Oh, what is that? From overhead a hard, discordant break of laughter – arrogant, insolent laughter. It is the old black-backed gull, one of a pair that patrol the coast. He has seen you – the wretch – and is now informing the beach of his discovery. Up go the necks of the geese. Shoot? No, no! They are ninety yards away. There! They are off, and the old gull, the spoil-sport, is laughing like a villain in a melodrama. Well, well! Better luck next time. I told you your chance of success was about one in a hundred. The gull was one of the ninety-nine chances against you. We had better go; the twilight is falling fast, and far out at sea the first flash of the new lighthouse shines like sheet-lightning though the dusk.

Another goose whose visit to our shores has been recorded is the Canada goose, a splendid bird. I have never seen him in British waters save in the semi-domesticated state; but elsewhere,

in Canada, in Newfoundland, and in Labrador he has many times rejoiced my eyes.

There was an occasion when a very curious incident befell me in which a Canada goose played a part. I was, at the time, in camp by the Terra Nova river in Newfoundland, up which I was about to start on a trip into the interior, and during the day I had seen many Canada geese. Night fell, as wet and stormy as it can only be in England's oldest colony, and I was about to turn in when a voice boomed through the darkness: "Is this my friend Prichard's camp?" A moment later, that most remarkable and able man, the late Judge Prowse, K.C., C.M.G., advanced into the circle of light. He was at the time between seventy and eighty years of ages, but as vigorous as many a youngster would wish to be. He was clad in a thin butter-coloured suit, his neck and chest were bare, and his feet were thrust into a pair of easy slippers. The spot where I was encamped was on the river, and the Judge informed me that he had been down-stream looking after some salmon-poachers in the interests of the Government, and had not eaten for fifteen hours. It was ten at night, the day had been drenching wet, and he was soaked through. I and the woodsmen with me marveled at the strength and stamina that enabled him to undergo such hardships. He was a man whose bodily gifts were only exceeded by his mental powers; and had his role in life been cast upon some larger stage, his natural energy and force would have had a wider scope, and he must have left his impress upon his generation.

Soon he was sitting before a roaring fire, clad in my "extra change" and eating a meal of trout

and bacon. While we were talking together, I was suddenly aware of a curious noise behind me among the spruces. It sounded at first as if some animal were beating itself against the ground. "What is it?" I said.

"A fox or a lynx," was the Judge's suggestion.

I caught up a log of wood and hurled it in the direction of the sound. It ceased at once, and, picking up a brand from the fire, I went towards the place and presently came upon a young Canada goose. The log hurled at a venture had struck it on the head. I carried it back to the fire.

"A goose! a Canada goose!" cried the Judge. "It must have been attracted by the light of the fire. This is most interesting! I will write a letter to the papers telling the facts, and will send on a copy to the London *Field* at the moment I get back to St. John's."

Later in the night the Judge departed, taking the train which passes through Terra Nova station, rather higher up the river. I went to sleep.

I awoke just after dawn to find a red-haired man regarding my camp with gloom.

"Have you seen my tame goose?" said he.

I explained exactly what had occurred, and, with many apologies, invited the red-haired man to dinner.

He accepted. At the end of dinner I said, "The Judge intends to write to the papers in St. John's and London about the singular attraction possessed by fire for wild geese."

The red-haired man smiled sadly. "It was a good goose," said he. "It would follow me about like a dog. Pass the whiskey."

The letter of the Judge to the papers was providentially never written. When, on my return to St. John's, I asked him what he had done, he said: "I forgot all about it, my boy, but I'll write it to-night. You can take home a copy with you on the boat for the London *Field*."

Then I revealed the true story. The Judge was convulsed with laughter. "I'll tell that story against you in the Cornhill. It will please my friend, the Editor," said he.

But that letter also was never written. And now even his iron strength has not availed, and he has passed on through those changes which he never dreaded, for I believe he was one of the few men whose faith knew no fear. **HP**

Of course the brent goose is one of our wildfowl that was lost to the shooting list decades ago, although the burgeoning wintering numbers we have in Britain today should qualify the species' reinstatement. The Barnacle too is now lost to the shore shooter. In fact, the only black goose that is available to the British sportsman nowadays is the alien Canada goose, which has colonised our isles so well it has been relegated to the ranks of vermin, and can, if certain conditions are met, be shot the whole year round in England and Wales, a very sad state of affairs for such noble a creature.

When my thoughts are drawn to brent geese, it always brings to mind the only close encounter I have had with this bird. I shall relate it here as the memory is one of those that is as vivid now as if it had happened only yesterday.

It was on the opening day of the buck season in the early 90s, when I was about the cliffs and dunes of the Holderness coast, looking for a buck I had spied a week earlier. I had been digging in some iron stakes on the foreshore to anchor my T and J net, used when commitments allowed, for netting the shoals of sea trout that run this stretch of coast at varying times of the spring and summer. During my exertions I noticed a buck working among the dunes, thrashing away at the old rosebay willowherb or bomb-weed stalks, probably in frustration at the lack of suitable saplings to fray. I earmarked him there and then as a suitable buck for the rifle.

A few days later I was couched down out of the wind in a natural trough in the cliff top. Formed by coastal erosion the fissure I was ensconced in would eventually become a landslip, but on this occasion it was firm enough, and ideal for my requirements. The new dawn haemorrhaged its terracotta ochres and amethyst mauves to slowly spread along the horizon that separated sky from sea. Although a recent easterly gale had now abated, the wind was still strong enough to make my mission debateable at best. However, the keenness of youth had

Image: Wikimedia/Tim Bowman

overridden sensible thought and the ambush was set. As the half-light grew into a brand new day, I watched my net anchor floats bob and disappear in the short swells, whooshing relentlessly, in and out against a barren beach. The usual waders were noted by their absence, banished by the onshore wind. Only gulls, both herring and black back, braved the wind-scoured sands. Flocked like defiant sentinels among the spindrift, their occasional raucous cry was lost to the breakers' roar and whistling wind.

Hidden in the lee of some dunes below me, something dark caught my attention. Leaning over the edge of my clifftop eyrie, my face and eyes were immediately stung by the salt-stained sand. Whipped along by a gusting wind, the sharp particles welted the cheeks and forced tears to well in one's eyes. I brought the binoculars to

Above: The lone brent gander adopted an aggressive stance towards the crow

Above: The Canadas set their wings and whiffled in to the decoys unawares

bear on a handsome goose that proved to be a brent, picking away at the dune grasses.

Although he looked unharmed and full in feather, I knew something was wrong for him to be alone and so far from the foreshore, and even farther from the great beds of zostera grass that is the goose's primary diet. The closest of these beds was miles away on the southern shores of the Humber estuary. April was quite late for this bird to be still about, as most of his kind should now be well on the way north to procreate.

No doubt the recent gale had battered the brent inshore, and separated it from its late-departing brethren to end up marooned beneath the dunes and low cliffs of the Holderness coast.

As I watched on through the binoculars, a little melodrama unfolded. The brent's neck suddenly straightened at the "craw, craw" of an approaching crow. That aerial hyena dressed in Satan's garb, patrolling the dunes for possible carrion, was not averse to hastening some unfortunate living creature towards that state of the past tense. The lone gander didn't escape the corvid's ever-watchful eye, and the black marauder angled over towards the luckless goose.

Alighting close to, but just out of range of the brent's extended neck, held now in the horizontal and no doubt hissing like an aggrieved snake, the crow tested the gander's constitution. Hopping in quickly and "crawing" all the while he dodged the brent's thrusts. It was an obvious attempt to stake his claim over the gander's future existence. However, the brent was in better shape than expected by both me and the crow. With wings arched to exaggerate his size, and portray as much presence as possible, the gander advanced menacingly towards his would-be assassin. The duel was quickly won by the goose, and the villain of the bird world made a final half hop toward the gander in feint. Opening his wings, the wind caught his ebony-feathered ailerons and he was swept away by the airstream, the plucky goose already forgotten. Searching now for easier prey at the tide edge, the crow soars on. His jet-jewelled eyes seek out razor fish, clam, lobster, or some other unfortunate sea creature, dislodged by nature's recent tempest, and now destined to end up as crow or gull fodder among the flotsam and jetsam being washed back and forth on the expansive sands.

A sudden squall forced me to duck down out of the wind and hellish rain, but as soon as it came it had passed and I turned my attention back to the brent. Stirred by the wind action, and probably an overriding desire to head north, the goose began his take-off run. With wings outstretched and flapping like a windjammer in a storm, he headed for the sea. His ungainly webbed feet pattered rapidly along, creating little 'phuft's of disturbed sand, which were instantly whipped away by the wind. Then at last he was airborne. Banking round, the black goose straightened and headed away on a north-easterly course. His wing beats less laborious now, as he settled in to a cruising speed, I wished

him well, and wondered whether he would be heading to Svalbard, Greenland, or even further still. I guess the bird thought his strength had sufficiently recovered, and I hoped he survived the daunting journey to catch up with his kind, and bring off a brood that would return to Britain.

But it is the Canada goose, a cousin of the brent, and the only black goose available to the shore shooter on the British shooting list today, that I have mostly hunted. Indeed, his "ahonk, ahonk, ahonk" as he approaches has stirred my blood on many occasions. I have crossed the Atlantic and engaged him and his smaller cousin, the lesser Canada, in the country that bears their name. Saskatchewan really is the mecca for this species, but Britain now hosts a staggering number of Canada geese as non-migratory residents (albeit with some local movement). The British population is now in excess of a 100,000 birds.

The reader may well question this bird's inclusion in SIWB, as it is mostly classed as an alien, and often more as a feral bird rather than a 'wild goose'. I admit to having had a moment's hesitation myself, but it was soon dispelled.

Firstly, the wild birds I have engaged close to the sea and on the foreshore itself have been as wild as those pursued in their homeland. Secondly, not all our Canada goose populations have their origins in feral waterfowl collection escapees. It has been proved by ringed bird recovery that some have crossed the Atlantic on their own accord. That, in my mind, makes these geese just as wild a British sporting prospect as a migratory woodcock or widgeon. The difference between the parkland feral Canadas and their wilder brethren is much the same as that between hand-reared mallard, and the true wild mallard. Mostly the tamer ones of each species are reluctant to leave their pampered surroundings, while the wilder ones are those averse to human approach and flight between feeding and resting areas in a more natural manner. It is then they become a sporting prospect and earn their place in these pages. And finally, they are the only black geese we can now shoot, and I didn't want to leave Prichard's chapter without looking at the only modern alternative.

I guess it would be the Solway that has the wildest of these local populations, and shooting this species of goose on the foreshore in this environment is about as wild as it gets. Indeed the population here may well be based on genuine Atlantic crossers who have stayed on to breed. The west coast of Scotland or Ireland would of course be their first landfall.

During my teenage years a group of local commercial fisherman that were colleagues of my father's made an annual pilgrimage up to the Solway for the start of the season to bag a September Canada. This was the best chance to get your goose, because after the opening salvos the black geese became extremely wary, and almost impossible to get under on the foreshore after that. Sadly, I never ever made it on the first of September, though I have bagged a few later buglers on the stubbles over decoys. All of the said company agreed that the Canadas were as wild as the wildest of geese once they'd been fired at.

Although I have taken a number of Canadas in Cumbria and south west Scotland, it has been on the Holderness coast where I have harvested a good number of these large black geese.

Hornsea Mere is home to a resident population of Canadas that owe much of its origins to the Hull and District Wildfowlers Association. In the 1963 the association introduced 12 birds to the mere, forming the nucleus of the present stock. These were added to over time by incoming feral birds, and possibly but less likely by rare trans-Atlantic migrants. The mere itself is the largest natural freshwater lake in Yorkshire. It is situated just a mile from the North Sea and as such is a useful stop-over, or wintering point, for many varied species of wildfowl. The wilder members of this population flight out to the stubbles in September and visit the fields of winter wheat later on in the season. I have enjoyed some excellent sport shooting them on the stubbles, but put me on the cliff top, in inclement conditions, waiting for these feathered bombers beating into the wind every time. A Canada's lumbering-looking flight is deceptive, as strong wings send them along at a rapid rate and missing behind is a commonly made mistake.

One of the most enjoyable morning flights at this species I have taken part in happened many years ago in the company of good friends. At the time I was keepering at Sproately Grange, and I'd invited a few of my patient and understanding beaters, Les, Dave, Graeme, the two Col Clixbys (father and son), and neighbouring keeper Victor Coates would join me. As far as shoot staff goes these guys couldn't be beaten, and it was my way of a thank you to offer them a spot of goose shooting.

The shooting ground was winter wheat very close to the coast, only a couple of fields away from the sea. Geese in excessive numbers on a vulnerable arable crop are a disaster. These huge geese do as much damage with their webbed feet as they do grazing. The farmer in question was almost rabid at the destruction caused by the Canadas, and after a quick survey I soon understood why. His precious shoots had been grazed short, and the area paddled, with numerous green spiralled piles of goose guano. Clearly a hefty number of geese had started in a waterlogged section a hundred yards or so away from an overgrown ditch, and worked their way towards the field headland. This had worked to our advantage as the ditch would

do perfectly to hide a team of guns. Furthermore, the edge of the feeding strip was now only sixty yards from where the shooters would be hidden, so a few well-placed decoys in between this and the ditch should hopefully bring the black geese into ethical shooting range.

We were in position well before dawn the following morning. After a bit of a barrack room debate, I set up the decoys were I wanted them. The wind was quite strong and blowing at angle from right to left but slightly in towards our position. This I guessed would mean the geese would be angled crossers for those on the right of our gun line and almost straight incomers for those on the left. Hedging my bets, I'd overrid-

Above: A brace of the big birds is enough for any fowler but aging them isn't easy

141

Above: A two to one shot ratio isn't perfect but is certainly acceptable at geese

den the protests at spacing the guns out more than I would do normally. As decoys were short in number I opted to spread them out at the most windward end of the line. Why this episode stands out in my memory is mostly because of its uniqueness. It is the only shooting excursion I can remember when everything has gone totally to plan.

My guests were busy with the rose shears, carving out a hidey hole in the briars that swamped the ditch, as I kicked the decoys about and eventually pushed them into the ground, roughly head to wind. The game plan was simple; we would let the first skein come right in, to give us an idea of their flight route. If all went well we would take the second detachment as soon as they were in range, and the other guns may get a shot at the first lot taking to wing. Hopefully this would spread the shooting out, and maximise what was really a crop protection exercise.

A quick draught from the flask and a run through of the instructions to ensure the safety aspects were understood, and we all retired to our hides as the amber grey dawn quickly paled into a perfect but blustery mid-winter's day. Wildlife was virtually absent, apart from a clattering of jackdaws heralded by their harsh "chack, chack" call that gives them their group term. The cold wind cut through the briars and found the gaps in our clothing, but all thoughts of discomfort were banished by the distant bugling of geese on the move. Our quarry was both airborne and inbound, their "ahonk, ink, ahonk, ink, ahonk ink" increasing in volume as they drew nearer to our position. Expectant hands gripped blued steel and battered walnut, and I steadied my springer spaniel Gem with a hissed "sit".

Then the geese entered the scene beautifully, skimming over the tops of an ash belt, and rapidly losing altitude as they came directly into the decoys. Their clamour rose to a crescendo as the skein splayed their wings and landed less than deftly, some way short of our replica geese, but opposite the left-hand end of our line. Quiet now, apart from a few mutterings, they set to the wheat with gusto, shaving off the nutritious stalks without mercy. It was interesting to watch the dozen or so birds intermittently scanning for danger in between mouthfuls. There was never a moment when fewer than at least three birds held their heads erect, even for just a few seconds, before returning to the feast, as others in their group checked round for danger.

Soon after, another skein's bugling alerted us to their approaching presence, and this time we are allowed to shoot. I imagined my companions hunkering down as one, when the next flight of feathered bombers veered into view over the leafless ash trees. Swinging clumsily left and right, almost as if they would crash land, the geese plummeted and strove to settle between the first feeding gaggle and the decoys. Any second now, upturned paddles beneath billowing wings as they tried to shed speed, would give us the signal to fire. I picked my bird, but an adjacent gun beat me to him, the big gander turned turtle in mortal surprise as I heard the bang. He thumped into the wet ground dead, and I swung on to another of his companions. This time I had my bird, and I followed through deliberately towards his 'head end' and loosed a barrel. The Canada snapped his neck back, folded his wings and joined the fallen. More geese were tumbling from the sky, crumpled by the heavy 42gm BB loads. I took the last bird of the surprised first gaggle as they made a rapid retreat. It had been a perfectly executed broadside. All my comrades had their goose and most had two.

I cast Gem off with a "git on", and raced out with Graeme to retrieve the fallen before the next incomers arrived. The honking of approaching geese spurred on the effort, and I decided to turn over the reaming birds that had fallen belly-up to save time. Gem had kept my hands full, and two thirds of the bag now filled my section of the ditch. I just managed to curl up round the spaniel on top of the dead geese, as the next skein soared in overhead. This time I was effectively ruled out of the proceedings in my precarious position. However, I could tell by their different call that these were greylags and not Canadas. The collective reports from either side of me told of more success, though I couldn't see any of the action face down as I was. More honking said Canadas were also inbound, and these too were dealt with in a similar manner, but then the flight was over.

Rolling back towards the action I watched the last skein as it gained altitude and headed back towards the mere. One of them caught my eye almost at the same moment life left it, the goose plummeting earthwards on the edge of town. This was something of a concern; a twelve pound goose falling from the sky is a dangerous prospect. Furthermore, the goose had fallen on or near to a new housing development on the outskirts of town, all of which sported spacious conservatories. I shuddered at the thought of the deceased goose crashing through a conservatory roof onto some poor unfortunate. It was time to be off.

Besides my immediate concern, the sound of shooting had alerted the main flight proper. Two big wings of collective Canada squadrons flew on past at a great height to find sustenance elsewhere. No doubt alerted by the sound of the shooting, the sight of their fallen brethren had probably put them off too. With haste, we gathered up the birds between us and headed for a breakfast.

A few readers may say that this exercise

lacked something of the sporting aspect. However, I would disagree. Everyone had picked their birds and shot well. Fieldcraft and close attention to detail had drawn the geese to where we wanted them, and everything had worked perfectly – apart from the towering goose that chose to expire while airborne. We had shot well, and done the farmer a great service. All in all, it had been an exciting and fulfilling experience at the black geese. I'm pleased to say nothing more was ever heard of the goose we listed as missing in action, although it was a nervous time for few days afterwards.

I cannot leave the great Canada geese without a mention of my loyal cocker spaniel named Annie. It was earlier on in my keepering career and I had been beating on the Burton Constable Estate for the then-keeper Paul Barratt. We had just done the Lake drive, whereby all the guns ring the lake and the keeper and a few selected beaters put the ducks and geese off the water and hopefully over the guns. This was only done once or twice a season, and generally yielded good results.

This occasion was no exception, and after the whistle was blown to cease shooting we began picking the fallen fowl. I was a young keeper then and often in envy of some of the pickers ups' marvellous retrievers. My own spaniels worked well in the line and I was proud of them, but the questing dogs never got the glory of those retrievers that pulled off a difficult retrieve on a bird given up for lost. However, on this day a big Canada gander had fallen way out into the lake and the labs had failed to find it, despite it being in full view from the bank. Annie had marked the bird and was itching for a go but I didn't want to upset the more experienced handlers and fall foul of Mr Barratt. Therefore I picked my moment when the labs were heading once more for the lake side, goose-less, and cast the black cocker off. She paddled out past her more prestigious canine colleagues towards the floating goose. Circling beside the big bird she considered the best place to get a grip, and then took hold of the gander by the base of its neck and headed for shore. The return leg was clearly a slog for her, but she eventually made it to gasps of approval from the gathered guns. Stopping to shake her waterlogged coat, she put the goose down and, taking a different grip, brought the bird back to hand with a perfect delivery. It was indeed a proud moment, and it was a very sad day to lose that wonderful cocker spaniel two years later. **PC**

Image: iStock

With *Widgeon* and *Mallard*

The widgeon is a bird which offers a better challenge to the fowler than any of his kind. He is, of course, by far the most common of the sea-living or shore-living ducks, and he is never easy of approach; the rising shot when you see his grey back is very rare. He is, therefore, the king of all ducks, not even excepting the mallard.

Shooting widgeon, like shooting geese, has in it much of the elements beloved of the big-game hunter. Especially is this the case when the shooting is done upon lochs. Here you have the true pursuit of the wild creature undertaken in the proper conditions.

Imagine that we are driving along a road in one of the Outer Hebrides, and slowly coming to the head of a steep incline. On one side are the telegraph wires through which the wind, laden with the scent and sting of the At-lantic, blows its thin note. Beyond this and the road is no sign of life at all; but on the north, where the country falls away to a lower level, vast areas of heather, long unburned and now giving harbourage to an ever-lessening stock of grouse, stretch to the chiaroscuro of the hills.

Before we reach the top of the incline we stop the trap, and leaving the horse in charge of our single companion, walk over the hill. As we do so, a vast prospect unfolds itself, the dark heather merges into the silver sand, and beyond that the ocean lies like a floor of winking steel. But between us and it, three miles away, a dozen lochs lie embosomed in the dark heather.

We sit down upon a milestone and care-fully examine the nearer and then the farther surfaces. The nearest is tenantless, but on two

of the others we find the little dark-looking dots we desire. On the first they are well out in the centre, a hundred and fifty yards from shore; but on the next they have collected in a narrow neck, and the bulk of them are not thirty yards from land, while some are even nearer. We return to the trap and explain the situation. The faithful henchman departs to put up at a fishing village on the back-trail, while we and a dog go forward to try the widgeon.

The dog is well used to the procedure, and has been taught long ago on summer evenings when stalking rabbits to lie down and wait while a stalk is in progress. Nor does he come to gunfire, but to a waved handkerchief. Soon he is left to lie down, and we proceed on a long wet crawl. For two hundred yards all goes well, but then comes the crux of the problem, an open space to cross. Five or six of the widgeon are in full view, and we lie still and wait to see if they will not join their fellows under the bank. At length two of them do, but the other four remain obstinately within sight. Then they are joined by others, until finally all the widgeon are out in the middle again. We crawl away, and, going back to where the dog lies, are joined by Farquhar the ghillie. "I thocht ye'd got intae them," said he; but now he agrees that there is nothing for it but to move them. We know this loch well and their line of flight. If Farquhar shows himself on the far shore, the widgeon will rise and fly up the centre of the loch, and their exit to the sea will very likely be made over a couple of small islands. We carry out our plans on this assumption. Farquhar shows himself, I hide behind the larger island, the widgeon rise, but they do not pass over the twin islands at all. Instead they swing back and go out about a hundred and twenty yards wide of Farquhar. They have caused us to lose just fifty-five minutes of the short winter day.

But we will not continue. Suffice it to say that widgeon-shooting on Highland lochs is a very difficult pursuit in which to attain much success. I can conceive it boring the expert marksman, who is no more than marksman, positively to death. "Fun!" remarks such a one – "Fun! I have lain on my stomach in soaking heather and stared at distant ducks through a screen of grass and heather till my eyes ached. I have crawled down a burn and covered my best Purdey gun with moss and grit and scratches. I have fired eight cartridges at an average range of over fifty yards and I have shot two widgeon – as you call them. Let us go home. It has already been raining for three hours."

Although widgeon are very early movers, often leaving their night feeding-grounds just before any sign of dawn, yet they will sometimes remain resting on lochs until quite late in the day. Why they choose one loch to rest upon and never visit another it is impossible to say, as their choice is often to all appearance quite arbitrary. There are lochs teeming with food and lying between other lochs much favoured by widgeon into which no widgeon will ever come. These are things which no man can explain to the satisfaction of any other man, though he may nurse a theory of his own.

When widgeon arrive, which is in the first week of September, little parties of five or six sometimes go to the inland lochs. I have seen such parties two years running on the first of September on a loch in North Uist. Nor did these birds go to the shore at all during the first few days.

Widgeon are one of the most hopeless of all kinds of ducks to shoot at flight time with any success. They come in very late and go out very early. Often as late as ten o'clock at night the widgeon are still coming in, and in such cases almost the only hope of the shooter is moonlight; and even then, when everything is in the gunner's favour, only an added measure of good fortune can bring him much success.

Sitting out on the flats in some roughly improvised hiding-place for hours at a stretch is cold work in mid-winter, but if the feeding-grounds of the widgeon are at all concentrated, it is well worth a trial. As a rule, however, widgeon feed over wide areas, and though the night-shooter may see fifty and hear two thousand, he may not have occasion to fire four times. Yet night-shooting is glorious fun. The sights and the sounds, the swish of wings, the stars, the moonlight, and the excitement are delightful to the lover of Nature. What is not so delightful is the rheumatism which too much indulgence in these things brings in later years.

The same may be said in a somewhat lesser degree of another method of widgeon-shooting, and one which offers chances of success less uncertain. This is lying out on promontories.

My mind's eye sees at once an island containing five deep bays. At its western end a long headland juts out toward the mainland, here divided by a channel not half a mile in width at full tide, and much less at neap tide. The tide also as it goes back exposes splendid feeding-grounds, and at all stages widgeon are to be seen there floating on the quiet water, or sitting on the margin of that sleepy western sea.

Given a really rough day, no fowler could ask more than to be ensconced behind the ultimate rock of that promontory, while an attendant or other gunner advancing from the island's eastern end moves all the widgeon up the narrow channel. The persecuted widgeon has the instinct to seek the open sea, and hardly a bird that rises but will fly within a hundred yards of the hiding-place upon the promontory; a good proportion will fly over it. For half an hour there will be probable chances, and for five minutes a hot corner! You may have a dozen or fifteen down before the dog can go to do his part, and then, if only the sea be rough enough outside, the widgeon will come back in little parties and big, higher this time, sometimes so high that a well-killed bird will crash into the water two hundred yards

beyond the gun that wrought his downfall. This is the "poetry of sport."

In the days of my youth, having read Colonel Hawker's *Instructions to Young Sportsmen*, I was much struck by the crawling-carriage which is figured on page 394 of the sixth edition of that classic book. I had at the time been outwitted during all my earlier Christmas holidays by ever-present but unapproachable companies of widgeon, after which I had carried a huge hired eight-bore until everything but hope had flagged. The hiring of the eight-bore, the ammunition for it, and other incidental expenses had more than made away with my Christmas tips, so that it took time and eloquence to persuade a carpenter, who

had allied himself to one of the servants of the house, to form a partnership; he to construct the crawling-carriage for five shillings, to be paid at Easter, and to receive half the bag of ducks and geese which should accrue during the remainder of the holidays. So the carriage was made, and I wheeled it away myself after dark one evening in the rain. Before dawn on the following morning I wheeled it through the sleeping town to the little railway station, and it was not clear light before it stood on the sands. But it needs description. It was shaped like a wheelbarrow and had in all five wheels – one in front as in a wheelbarrow, the four others where the legs of the wheelbarrow are. It stood a foot from the ground, and its walls stood another foot. These walls were of narrow slats of wood. The system of progression was to lie on one's chest in it and kick it along with one's feet, which extended behind. In the garden of the carpenter it had worked, but now I found it very hard to make the seaweed which I hung about the walls stay on; but at length I had tied up my dog on the shore, and set out kicking myself along towards the distant widgeon. The sand was hard, but even then the narrow sheaths of the wheels sank in, and when I was two hundred yards or so away I was joined by my abominable dog, who had bitten himself free and came to me rejoicing. I had, therefore, to rise from the gun-carriage and take the dog back to a farm on the shore, where he was shut into a stable. Then once more to the shore, hot, ruffled, but full of hope. I was half a mile from the widgeon when my gun fell into the sand, and perhaps half that distance when the near wheel came off. But the final debacle was in some soft sand fifty yards or so farther on, where the crawling-carriage stuck hopelessly. There I lay, hoping that the widgeon would feed in with the tide. Instead of that they went out to a sandbank, and, all hope gone, I fired the eight-bore at two oyster-catchers and killed one sitting. I gave the oyster-catcher to the carpenter and demanded wider wheels. He inquired when I was returning to school, and made various difficulties, such as the cost of wheels and the uncertainty of getting them in time. Five shillings would have saved the situation, but the five shillings were not to be come by. At Easter I saw the body of the crawling-carriage in the carpenter's garden. It was inverted, and a hen was sitting beneath it among some gooseberry bushes. I never saw it again, nor have I since experimented with a crawling-carriage, though I would do so if I had a favourable opportunity. Geese, I think, could be killed in this way, and it would be easy to propel the carriage over the grassy lawns they love. But after one or two shots geese would not allow the carriage within a quarter of a mile.

Another system of approach, sometimes though rarely tried in Britain, is taking cover behind a horse. I have seen this successfully carried out in Spain; but there the *marismas*, which are the haunt of duck and widgeon, are also covered with fighting bulls, horses, and cattle, whereas the spots in Britain where a horse is a common object to wildfowl, though

existent, are not so plentiful. Still, even curlew will let a cart approach in districts where year in, year out, the crofters gather the harvest of seaweed, and in such places something might be done; but wildfowl become easily sophisticated and success would not last long, nor would it be worthy or even interesting save as an experiment, though the opportunities of watching bird-life would be splendid.

After the widgeon comes the mallard, though many will reverse that order, especially as the mallard, or common wild duck, is the duck of inland waters as well as a duck of the coast. Personally, I put the widgeon first, although, like other people, I have probably shot ten wild ducks to one widgeon. Far be it from me, therefore, to uphold the widgeon too strenuously.

Some of the finest sport in Britain is to be had with mallard, provided, of course, they are really wild and not the tame birds which swim towards the keeper's wife and refuse to rise and fly, even when the keeper waves his hat among them, shouting. Perhaps they rise and take a short and uneasy flight over the guns, and when fired at seek sanctuary upon the lake by the cottage. These things will happen, but how different is the true wild duck at whom, after the first fortnight in August, you can hardly ever get an easy chance except by skilful manoevring.

There are many ways in which the mallard may be brought to bag, so many that on a good duck-shoot all of them could not be put into practice on a single day. There is, of

course, the morning flight and the evening flight, the ordinary stalk in the reeds, the stalk in the loch, the drive and the waiting, when they fly into the corn. In addition, in stormy weather the mallard often comes to the shore of bays and spends his day upon some pond or pool of brackish water left by the receding tide among the rocks of the coast.

There is a scene which the sight of a mallard often recalls.

It is after breakfast, and two guns are walking beside a stone dyke overlooking a field which, in its turn, abuts upon a loch. Last night, from that loch seven fine trout were taken, and the fisherman as it grew later heard the quacking of mallards in the large area of reeds, an acre or two in extent. It is late August, almost September, and all the month this loch and that patch of reeds have been left as a sanctuary in which the moulting fathers of the race have spent the first week of the month when they cannot fly, and since have hurried to it from all parts of the moor and marsh surrounding. And now this morning the time has come for them to pay toll for that security.

It is a lovely day, pale blue is the sky, pale green is the turf, dark green the reeds, and dark, dark blue the peaty water which lashes the stony shores driven by the soft wind of the Atlantic. At one end of our loch is the hut of a crofter, its thatched roof surrounded with a necklace of huge stones attached by a rope, and hung there to hold on the thatch when the winter wind raves over the desolate moors. Such a necklace of granite might Ymir, the giant of Niffelheim, have worn and flung as a sign upon this human habitation. At the other end of the loch, and a couple of fields away, the white face of the shooting-

lodge is discernible. The ground rises sharply from the loch-side and we two guns take our places, I near the wall, and the other gun behind a hummock opposite the reeds. Then Donald, the ghillie, appears on the farther shore, and untying the boat from its moorings goes aboard. An oar creaks, up gets an old mallard. Straight over the other gun he goes. Bang! It is as if some one had smitten him sharply under the chin; he dies in the air. At the report several ducks rise, seven in all, and four snipe. We fire four barrels, a snipe and a duck bite the dust, both the other gun's. And now Donald reaches the reed-patch. Two drakes come straight to me, low as low grouse. Both fall. They are easy shots. And now the mallards rise in dozens and go over the other gun. Would I were fifty yards on either side of him, for, except that now and

then a snipe breaks back, nothing comes my way. But I have the fun of watching. The other gun is shooting quite brilliantly. The ducks rise and pass towering high above him, and in mid-air receive an instantaneous death. At the end I pick up my two mallards, and count six cartridges that spent their charges in the wake of various high snipe without result, while the other gun has ten mallards, a duck, and two snipe. The old birds have paid for their sanctuary.

Next we move on, and passing under the shoulder of the mound, open out a loch surrounded with reeds and indented with bays. At its far end a wall of reeds shows the vicinity of the Big Bog, one of the best wildfowling grounds in the British Isles. We shall come to it later. At the moment we toss for sides, and it is the other gun who has to cross over, while I remain where I am. He has a full half-mile to go, and while he is walking let us sit down and take in the prospect. On my side wild tussock-covered land rises from the loch-side to a stone dyke, from which two other stone dykes run down at right angles to the water. Many a time have those dykes screened the approach of the gunner. In winter this side of the loch is not very good snipe ground, as the reeds are covered with water, and only here and there a few snipe sit in the open on the margin of the loch. But now, in the early autumn, one ought to get a duck or two and some snipe. The farther side, to which my comrade has gone, contains the best snipe ground on the shooting. There, by that low wall, I well remember seeing seven snipe fall ere the gun who wrought their downfall moved from the spot where his first cartridge was fired. Beyond that again is an island, and behind it again the ruins of the old kirk crown a hill, and against the sky one can discern the tombstones of the last century. About it and on the hither side of the hillock are crops of corn in stook, and of potatoes; a flock of plover are sweeping over it, and the air resounds with the shrilling of curlew, of which I can see a flock some five hundred strong sitting on the island below the old kirk. The waters of the loch are lazy with weed, and only here and there does a clear pool show a winking eye to blue heaven. In these pools lie good trout. In fact, one year the score of fish taken from them averaged within an ounce of two pounds apiece.

The other gun, with the attendant figure of the ghillie, has now got round the loch and has begun to walk the outlying snipe ground. He fires two shots and bags the snipe; the first shot puts up a lot of six widgeon from the far end of the loch. They circle back to Dunscaur, the loch of reeds. It is at this moment that a large flight of peewits, and with them fifteen or a dozen golden plover, swing over and settle on the island. I rise and make signs to the other gun, who waves his hand in reply and begins to approach in the direction I indicate. I take out a glass and watch him. I can see the crested heads of the lapwings, but no sign of the golden plover, which are over on the other side of the rise. The other gun crawls up, and I hear both barrels, but it is impossible to see the result or results of the shot. And now we begin to walk our different shores. Here there is a wisp of snipe, there a duck, and a dozen times one sinks down behind the nearest stone or tuft when a curlew or a flock of plover seems to be approaching. Thus we come to the Big Bog. The Big Bog is a place of memories, thick as currants on a stalk. It was here that Donald, the ghillie of a bygone day, informed one unfortunate sportsman, by whom he was not attracted, but who had rented the place with gold of Glasgow, that "you just went straight forward and it wasna vera deep." History tells how he of Glasgow was hauled out later with ropes.

Indeed, when all is said and done, the Big Bog is a spot where it behoves one to be careful. Into certain parts of it you cannot go; in others you have to pay the price, which means reeking mud to the waist. In the days of my youth I was wont to go straight through it, since at that period of life it is hard to recognise that in snipe and duck shooting, as in other things, physical effort is not everything. How many times, how many hundreds of times, have I not found the air above me torn with complaining snipe, while a dozen mallard and teal sprang from the pools around, just as I sank to my middle in the mud and reeds, and from a hopeless position, one foot perhaps buried twelve or eighteen inches deeper than the other, I fired the hopeless, or almost hopeless, shot, which was often more in the nature of a salute than anything else. Now we rarely walk the Big Bog, but line up instead along the reedy loch shore beneath the old kirk, while David and John, armed with clappers made of packing-case boards, drive the birds over us. By this manoeuvre the old peppering or plastering of rising duck is done away with, and though we do not get as many snipe, we often get some "butterflies" – that is, snipe killed literally thirty-five or forty yards up, which come down with wings still spread.

It was in the Big Bog that David the valet, a good sportsman, always ready to get up before daylight to drive geese or to take his chance in the Big Bog, once found himself in a very bad place, the mud up to his shoulders and with a good chance of sinking farther. At his cries I ran to his assistance, and approaching through the reeds saw him striving to lift himself from the clinging mud; and when he failed and paused for breath, I heard the ghillie, who was squatting on his haunches in safety near by, say with an air of finality: "Ay, David man, ye'll never lay a tea again!"

Such is the Big Bog in early autumn when the reeds are green and high, and save for the stream which flows through the centre of it there are but a dozen pools or so. In these pools the mallard, the teal, and the shoveler, of which last there are a good sprinkling, congregate, and stirred from thence by a pair of clappers and a hoarse voice they fly straight down for the loch, and each time the place is driven they fly higher. Later in the year there is no cover, the reeds are brown and beaten by the raving island winds, the bog is flooded, it is deserted by the ducks, but day and night is the home and sanctuary of some hundreds of grey geese, sometimes of bernicle, more rarely of a few white-fronts. At this time of year very few ducks are killed on the Big Bog. He who would be successful there must do his work before the sun is far over the hills, or after it has sunk in the angry sea.

But enough of the Big Bog, and I shall not describe any shooting done there. In an arm of it I remember a very handsome dog belonging to one of my guests being drowned. He swallowed some of the black mud, and, though we got him out, he died. But hitherto the bog has been no murderer, nor has it sucked down a human life.

Very different to the cold long waits when flighting by the pool of the bog are the lovely September evenings spent in the stooks, or better yet in the still standing corn. Here is the perfection of duck-shooting of the contemplative sort. In this kind of shooting I have never, as far as mallard are concerned, pushed an advantage home, though it is different with teal, which all leave later in the year – at least, they certainly do desert the Big Bog.

It is easy enough to recognise when and where ducks are coming into the corn. Feather droppings and the ears destroyed are a certain guide. Give the ducks a week, and then go and sit *back to wind* in the high corn near by. As soon as the crofter or labourer "homeward wends his weary way" the ducks will begin to come in. It is wiser not to fire at the first two parties. Let them pitch. During the whole sunset hour the ducks will continue to come in, and you can make the shooting as easy or as difficult (both within limits) as you will. The birds will, however much they circle, settle finally against the wind. This is the moment at

which to kill all wild birds if a big bag be your object. The huge bags of wood-pigeons are ninety per cent. filled within twenty yards of the branch or spot on which they had determined to alight. But with ducks, if you want difficult shooting, turn the other way and face up-wind. The ducks will come in very fast, will sweep in, in fact, ere they turn into the wind

to steady themselves, and from your cramped position you will need all the quick swing you can command to bring them down. It is glorious sport. A blue evening sky, the rippling, waving corn, the gloom that precedes night makes a dusk upon the shores of the loch, the swish of wings, the solid face and deep-brown eyes of the old dog, about whom you have no illusions, or the brighter eyes of the young one, concerning whom you perchance have many, and when the sun is long gone and the ducks become dark cloves against the patches of fading brightness. And now that it is dark, you can hear the ducks, you can see them no longer. You rise; you have fifteen gathered, and two you think are down, which were too far off to send the dog for during the flight. You send him now. He succeeds and retrieves both. Then, heavily laden, but ballasted with a great content, you walk off to the Lodge. Long lies the way, for you have to skirt great areas of marsh.

Once, after a late September corn-shoot, a thick fog came down, and it took two hours of feeling and touching to find the path; but tonight it is clear, the stars are out, the smoke of peat redolent of many memories arises from the cottages, and presently a hot bath and a glass of sherry complete the perfection of content. At dinner you discuss the morrow's plans. Shall we have the boat and go to Deasker or Causamull, or even distant Haskeir, where dwell the mighty seals, or shall we try the inland heather country, or the geese upon the promontory ponds? Shall we get up at four, or shall we leave it till after breakfast? These are the discussions over the coffee. And then a pipe in the moonlight among the midges, and so to bed to dream until we arise on the morrow.

Forgotten is London and the smell of asphalt, the desk is a far-off memory, the newspaper comes like a message from a forgotten state of things. It is rarely necessary to write a letter, and hands hardened with gun and sail and oar close clumsily upon the pen. All this is good, and in it we forget the day when the collars will be put on the dogs and the luggage on the cart, while we, mounting the trap, shall drive through the plover-haunted land past the isle of Kirkibost, the isle of geese, and then, turning, leave behind the open sandy lands and plunge into the dark hills, and so steering by the grim Mount Eval come to Lochmaddy, a kind of Venice of the Hebrides, in that men and women visit it by boat, and there, after hearing who has caught what at the hotel, aboard the steamer for eighteen hours of the Minch and ocean. It has its uses, even this journey, for it takes the mind from what one is leaving. Late the next night, perchance, as one drives through the lighted streets and sees the placards of London and the white faces, the hum, the roar, the ten thousand solicitations of shop and theatre, one goes back in thought – the Lodge is dark, the little round grass patch in front is soaked in dew, the loch reflects the stars. Far up, far up beneath them the grey geese are flighting from Cuirheara. **HP**

Above: A good sized flight of widgeon returning from night time feeding to their daytime roost

Denys Watkins-Pitchford MBE better known to most as 'BB', referred to the cock widgeon as the "dandy of the tide" in one of his excellent books on wildfowling. I have always thought this a very fitting description of this bird – the most handsome of all waterfowl. He is something of an anomaly in duck terms as he is a saw-bill and built as a grazer, foraging rather more like a goose than a duck. However, he will revert to the dabbling duck method of feeding if it is worth his while and this can often be his undoing. Also, like both ducks and geese, widgeon delight in frosted potatoes when they become soft and provide easy sustenance. A keen eye in the daytime, or indeed a keen ear after dark, may locate their foraging visitations to the potato crop, and a suitable ambush set. My first encounter with this bird was in just such a scenario. I was then but a teenager and a trawlerman colleague of my father, who knew of my interest in all things shooting, had invited me along for a widgeon flight on the Leven potato fields.

I could hardly contain my excitement, and I must have bored Frank Powell to death on the half-hour journey from Bridlington to Leven, battering him as I was with myriad questions. Turning right at the Hare and Hounds pub, we were nearing our destination and the conversation grew more serious as Frank went through the safety aspects of the evening. I listened intently, and though I had been brought up well with re-

Image: iStock

them like a ramrod pressing home a musket ball to subdue the unwelcome noise, but it was all to no avail. Suddenly Frank stopped at the edge of the un-harvested rows, and me being somewhat engaged with my ammunition portage, clumsily walked right into the back of him. Demeanour now in complete tatters I offered a lame "sorry". Even more amused, Frank just raised an eyebrow as he turned back to the half-flooded rows, and studied them for a while. Taking account of the wind he placed me in a delve between two boggy rows, and said firmly "let them come in, they may come round once or twice as there isn't much wind but leave em' until they're right in." What breeze there was came from behind me, and I knew enough to know the ducks would come into the wind, so I hunkered down and watched Frank take a similar position parallel to me some forty yards away. We covered a slightly raised point of land that jutted out into small shallow flood water, no doubt the reason why this end of the field had been left un-harvested.

Daylight was fading fast and I had to hold all my resolve as the snipe started to flit past temptingly. I'm not sure how many passed by but I wished I'd ask my host the rules concerning snipe. However, as Frank let them alone, I figured they were off-limits for this evening's sortie. A two barrel salute from my companion concentrated my thoughts from those little waders to the duck. Two thuds followed his barrage and a brace of mallard opened up proceedings, but little else followed. We finished soon after, with me missing two opportunities at the teal and Frank wiping my eye by securing one of them, which turned

gards to gun safety, I carefully absorbed what he said, and assured him I understood completely.

The tarmac road turned into a cobbled lane, and soon after we pulled off into a passing place and parked. Frank let out his black Labrador, and the two of us quietly gathered our guns and game bags. Filling my capacious pockets with box after box of cartridges seemed to be a source of some amusement to mine host. Frank was now smiling wryly, "We'll not be defending Rorke's Drift tonight Carr'ie, lad" said he before turning about. Leaving the battered old Sierra estate behind, I struggled to keep up with Frank striding out across the half harvested tattie field. Conscious of the cartridges rattling away in my pockets, I tried stuffing my cap and gloves down on top of

out to be a beautifully marked drake. I had only secured what I thought was a duck mallard with a snap shot at last light. However when I picked it, the duck turned out to be a cock widgeon. As pretty as the teal was in the torchlight, he paled in comparison to that first ever widgeon. It had definitely been a quiet flight by later standards; indeed it would have made a better snipe flight. But back then, it was the best flight ever; I had secured my first "dandy of the tide". Strangely, the bird had slipped in without warning; it was nothing more than a fleeting shadow slanting into to the tatties with a barely audible 'whish', but my swing and pattern had found him.

Nonetheless, as we tramped away the widgeon let us know they were now on the move. Time constraints, and a lack of suitable shooting light necessitated our departure. But the piping "whee-oo" whistles of the flighting widgeon overhead captivated me. That first outrider had been silent on arrival, but his brethren were extremely vocal, and they seemed to fill the night sky. "Couldn't we wait for the moon?" I inquired, but Frank had other game to chase that night.

I never said so at the time, but I was heartbroken twice on that occasion. Firstly, to leave the flighting widgeon seemed a sin beyond all comprehension (despite the duck mostly alighting out of reach on a flooded grass over the boundary). And secondly, when on the way home, Frank stopped at Lisset village to give the ducks – including my cock widgeon – to the parents of a pretty young lady he had his eye on. Delightful though Sally undoubtedly was, I sorely lamented the loss of that debut bird. I'm happy to report

Right: Jumping the dykes and drains of Holderness often produced duck for the author

that Frank eventually won his girl, they moved in together, and are still in that happy state of accord today, but it took me a long time to get over that prized widgeon.

Getting on terms with this wonderful fowl is no easy matter. Prichard is certainly correct when he labels the widgeon as both unpredictable and an erratic latecomer. The latter point however, I have oft used to my advantage, especially when waiting for them at flight ponds. Widgeon are the most difficult of ducks to keep returning to a fed pond, certainly much harder than mallard and teal. Indeed, they are a faddy duck to attract to any pond unless it's a flooded pasture. Shallow pools on winter drilling are a better bet than a pond in woodland or one surrounded by high hedges. In short, the widgeon like open spaces, similar to the estuary mudflats or large reservoirs that they chose to roost on during daylight hours. More often than not the widgeon are the last birds coming in at flight time, if indeed they turn up at all. Building up a good flight of widgeon is, as I've said, no easy matter; there is always something to tempt these choosy and wary ducks elsewhere. However if the moon phase is favourable, this is one species where it often pays to wait on after the dusk flight until the moon rises. This is especially so if that lunar advantage is accompanied by or promises fleecy cloud. The cloud increases one's success rate tenfold, by providing a suitable illuminated backdrop to nicely silhouette the incoming birds. It goes almost without saying that a windy night is better than a still night. Wind stirs the duck up, roughens the seawater to wash the birds off the mudflats, and

Image: iStock

Above: A trio of drakes take advantage of some unfrozen water during a hard winter spell of weather

a natural draw for duck, close to the Humber estuary, Burton Constable Lakes, and Hornsea Mere. As such it was perfectly placed for foraging duck. Split by a narrow banked drain, the south side was overgrown with reed mace, but the north part of the pond was shallow around its entire margin, ideal for dabbling duck. It was deep enough in the middle to hold rainbow trout, a fact not overlooked by one youngster in the village who quickly relieved the pond of its stocked occupants – but that's another story. Along the drain banks that separated the two halves, four equally spaced hides had been built.

Part of my duties was to keep this pond well fed to attract the duck and, crucially, make sure I flushed any remaining birds off in the early morning. The rationale behind this was to encourage eagerness in the duck to return at evening flight, rather than fill their crops at leisure during the day. As this pond is in a reasonably quiet and secluded area, ducks were apt to use it as a daytime roost, which had adverse effects on the dusk shooting. Therefore it was essential to discourage any daytime lingering by the fowl. My day would often start by flushing any ducks off the pond, and this task was always a priority when we would be shooting the water. On this day I had done just that, soon after dawn, and was surprised to see a great company of widgeon depart as one.

That evening I harboured big hopes as the boss and another gentleman farmer arrived at the Grange to shoot. I would be shooting too, and Les Curtis, one of my best beaters, had also been asked along. We all climbed into the Land Rover

prevents them from 'stacking' up, that is, circling high above their feeding areas, suspiciously searching for hidden shooters below. In these conditions it isn't just the feeding opportunities that the duck are looking to exploit, it's fresh water and shelter too.

I recollect one particular flight when the required conditions as set out above came together nicely, and the result for two guns was really quite exceptional. It was during my keepering days at Sproately Grange. Every second Sunday evening the squire, Richard Beadle, would invite two or three guests to shoot the duck on a superb flight pond at Glebeland's Farm. This pond was

with old Ray acting as chauffeur. Both Les and I had our respective spaniels, Les a springer and I a cocker. The boss had a big burly chocolate lab called Cad (short for Cadbury, but his interest in bitches certainly qualified him for his moniker's other definition). Cad exceled at quickly retrieving shot duck, and the boss was justifiably proud of his ability, so Les and I were always careful to let him do most of the retrieving.

A good, stiff south west wind disturbed the reeds and rippled the pond's surface as we took to our respective hides. Pallet affairs stuffed with straw, the wooden blinds covered one enough for the ducks to pay us no heed in the shadows. We watched the Land Rover depart in the amber grey hue of the day's end, and readied for action. And it wasn't long in coming. Snipe whirled into the reeds behind us, fair marks if Les and I had been alone, but with the boss there, we wouldn't dare risk putting off the greater fowl's imminent arrival by popping at them. A couple of plump mallard were the first arrivals, beating straight into the wind and stooping toward the pond, and the boss and his guest claimed both birds neatly between them. An encore followed suit, and then five mallard presently angled in, four immediately paying the penalty for their indiscretion, and the going away singleton was neatly folded by Les.

I was always very conservative with my own shooting, indifferent as it was, when the boss had guests. It was different if we were alone – then it was every man for himself – but he was always quick off the draw, and a far better shot than I. The guns continued to shoot well until the teal tested them to their limit. Giving us no warning, their pips unheard in the wind, the tiny duck whizzed in at all angles, pairs, trios and occasional packs, but no widgeon. More mallard were similarly dealt with, and then darkness came proper. We had achieved a respectable bag of twenty or more ducks, mostly mallard and a few teal. The boss called up Ray to take us back to the Grange, and onto the pub for the traditional pint. Personally I was disappointed at the non-compliance of the widgeon, and politely asked if Les and I could stay on and wait for the moon. Assent was duly given, though I'm sure the boss thought I'd taken leave of my senses, as the frost had already started to bite.

Too dark to shoot, Les and I huddled together with two shivering spaniels as steaming wet sources of heat in the best (most wind-proof) of the four hides. It would be another hour before the moon would show itself, so we chatted away, and shared a chocolate bar. I used to hate Caramac chocolate as a kid, but I remember it tasting divine on that chilly December night.

There was still a good flight of mallard coming in unseen. The wind was certainly easing because we could hear the approaching birds' "quork, queck, queck, queck" greetings as the incomers conversed to those already floating on the inky blackness. A series of landing splashes told of a sizable troop arriving followed by an upswing in tempo of duck vocals as the massed fowl grew in number. We listened on intently to what must have been a hundred or more mallard taking full advantage of the barley I had spread for them in the shallows.

Eventually a silver sheen seemed to envelope

the landscape, the moon was on its way, and with it came the "whee-oo" whistles of the widgeon. The saw-bills were abroad at last, and looking for food and shelter. The land became brighter in the growing luminosity. Shadows lengthened, dark, gnarled twisted fingers extended over the field behind us, thrown by an ancient twisted ash tree, which stood silhouetted against the rising moon.

I made to move into the next hide and this caused an instant silence among the hordes of gathered mallard still on the water. The great flush erupted a half second later, with a whirr of wings the like I'd never experienced before, to melt away into the moonlit sky. We weren't worried at their departure, quite the contrary; we knew they would be the nucleus to maintain a good flight into the pond at dusking time. It was their estuary-living cousins we were most interested in, and tonight they would not disappoint.

Squadrons of our mysterious but beautiful quarry were clearly on the wing in numbers, but would they come in? I remember doubt forming as flight after flight passed over, perfectly visible against the racing clouds and serenaded all the while by their charming "whee-oo" chimes. I needn't have worried, as my misgivings were soon proved erroneous. A soft hissing of wings accompanied by that fairy-like cheeping squeak of approaching widgeon told of an inbound flight soaring in. Six shadows sped into range and the guns swung and discharged to bring down the first five widgeon of the night in one salvo. Another larger flight 'whished' in as cartridges were ejected and hastily reloaded. Yet another flight of five or more birds joined the company on the water, but the snap of barrels closed against lock caused the fowl to flush, with three of their number falling to another fusillade.

The shooting seemed relentless, and it felt like it went on for some considerable time, but in reality it probably lasted no more than twenty minutes until we ran out of cartridges. Looking back now I can still see Les illuminated by the bright moon in a silvery light. His expectant bearded face set with his head cocked, listening for the 'whish' of wings, indicating the next incoming flight.

Cartridge bags and belts empty, the spaniels were cast off to hoover up. We talked excitedly in between taking delivery of the fallen widgeon. What a bag we'd made! spirits were high and the fluting whistles still sounded around us as we tramped back over the fields to the Grange. It was time to part company and return home, to the silent house, lights long extinguished for it was now well into the wee hours. A little girl talked in her slumber upstairs, as I carefully locked the gun away, towelled down Annie the spaniel, and hastened to my pillow.

Whenever Les and I met after that, this ducking night would always come into conversation. These meetings were increasingly infrequent, because two months after this terrific flight, I took up another position to work with grouse on a North Yorkshire moor. Sadly, not many years later, Les ascended to the happy hunting grounds. He died suddenly in the prime of life with heart failure. I was saddened to hear of his death, and he will always be fondly remembered; nothing was ever too much to ask of him on a shoot day.

He would willingly turn up as a stop before dawn broke to help my head beater, Simbo, keep the pheasants in, and Les was always the one on the far wing I could rely on to bring the end of the beating line round sharply whenever needed during partridge driving.

Purists among my readers may cough at the liberty Les and I took that evening, as a good head of duck should be left to come in and build up another good flight. But in our defence I shall say this. The opportunities to do such a thing as detailed above are few and far between. It was

widgeon we sought, and the tail end of the mallard flight was allowed to come in unmolested. Yes, we had disturbed them when I put them off to resume shooting, but they had two hours or so of feeding before this disturbance so little harm was done, and the shoot that followed a fortnight later was a successful one. The point here is widgeon are unpredictable, but in the right circumstances they can be outwitted, though it takes a lot of factors to come together. Therefore by its very difficulty it can never be deemed unsporting, save in cases of extreme weather.

Above: The author after an excellent Holderness duck flight in 2012

Image: Shutterstock

I have enjoyed many a night's ducking alone or with various companions over the years. From high moorland ponds at Glen Moy and at Farndale, to gutters, creeks and flashes that crisscross the Holderness plain. One memory of a small pond near Roos stands out for its uniqueness. Vic Coates was a neighbouring keeper who often invited me for an evening flight. He had a number of ponds and as he worked no dogs, I'm sure the proficiency of my spaniels had more to do with the repeat invites than my mediocre shooting. This particular pond was unique because it always produced the plumpest, sweetest-tasting mallard on a regular basis. The surprising thing was it had never, under Vic's care, been fed by the hand of man. What it did have was two crab apple trees very close to its edge, and the ducks went crazy for the mushy fruit as it rotted. The amount of fruit these two trees produced was phenomenal, and being on a slanted bank overhanging the water the trees self-fed the pond until the hard frosts had ruined the fallen fruit. Occasionally Vic would kick away the tiny heaped green apples to allow them to continue rolling into the pond, but no other interference was given until shoot nights, when a few of the fat ducks and drakes paid their toll. Sadly, Vic ascended Valhalla around the same time as Les, and that particular pond drained, and put under the plough.

Micky Mires Planting was another water that produced duck without feeding it, although when we did so some great flights could be built up. This was a place that could be flighted in the morning as the returning ducks used it as a roost.

Left: A duck mallard makes excellent eating and provides fine sport

Evening flight worked too, but it was a marshy place of willows and islands, and the ducks had plenty of places to hide. That said, I have enjoyed some great flights there at both ends of the day. Situated in the centre of the Flambourgh Headland, it too is perfectly placed to draw in wild duck, migrating geese and waders.

Flighting on moorland ponds can be as wild and as exciting as on the foreshore. The evening sounds of the hill are so different from those on the low ground and coast. Though a little tail corn is needed to tempt the mallard, it is amazing what results can be had in these desolate places were one would be forgiven for thinking there wasn't a duck in residence for miles. I have had enjoyed one or two good flights at Glen Moy when Stuart Donald was keeper, but that pond is now no longer looked after, with the caring hand that kept it long moved on to pastures new.

Perhaps the best pond flighting I have ever enjoyed was, and still is, at the Demming Farm with the landowner Graeme Shephard. This farm has a number of excellent flight ponds, one of which I will relate to in the teal chapter of this book. However, the pond we are concerned with in this passage is the widgeon pond. The farm is situated close to the east Yorkshire coast, and as such is another one with a good natural draw for duck. In the centre of a large field there lies a depression forty yards square that never dries out, thanks to one of the land drains being deliberately blocked. It is an open area fringed by short cropped grasses and is favoured by widgeon. In fact, the pond is favoured by a variety of ducks, not just the grazing and dabbling kind, but diving ducks too. Shep feeds all over the pond – not just around the edge – by flicking out corn from a scoop, and that is why I think he attracts the diving ducks. The widgeon are hit and miss here, and they are always the late arrivals but when they come, they really come, and offer very exciting sport. Despite the unpredictable nature of the widgeon, this is the most consistent pond I have ever had the pleasure to shoot. Carefully fed with barley and wheat, the shooting is strictly controlled, with a bag in the twenties region considered enough for any two guns. Furthermore, it produces a variety of wildfowl each season, with a sprinkling of diving ducks, pochard, and tufted, the odd shoveler and pintail, but mostly mallard, widgeon, and teal in that order. It is a pond that proves that regular feeding in small quantities, alongside limited shooting, will make the sport last throughout the season.

The foreshore of course is the wildest place to engage true wildfowl, and it is here on the coast that the privations, ever present danger and the fickle balance of luck will occasionally reward the fowler with an occasion to remember evermore. Being there alone is often enough, to experience that wonderful solitude where no phone rings, or daily chore intrudes into one's own enjoyment. But the foreshore isn't a place to dally, dream or venture alone. My fondest memories of foreshore shooting are with my old mate Tony Megson. He keepers a shoot on a part-time basis, but somehow manages to balance this with the responsibilities of his other job saving lives as a paramedic. Situated right on the Humber estuary his southern boundary butts up to, and actually includes, some of the foreshore.

We have spent many an hour trying to outwit the stands of golden plover that congregate on his shoot, and even more time in the creeks waiting for the tide to wash the widgeon off the mudflats and put them on the wing. On crazy wild nights with driven rain and a singing gale we have enjoyed success at both widgeon and wild mallard. But we have had just as many nights when the duck have crossed over far too high or too wide to shoot, and disappeared inland without a shot being fired. But each foray has always been an adventure and an absolute pleasure to take part in.

Snaking across the marsh in the half-light

with a good chance of going over one's boot, or, worse still, ending up waist-deep in the mire that infiltrated everything, always had, for some reason, its own peculiar attraction. To stare along the shore as the Hull ferry thumped past, and wonder what the curlew and plover thought to the great terminal opposite or the huge suspension bridge that spanned the estuary a few miles further on. Despite man's obvious progress and industrial blight on the landscape; it was always a wild place. Unspoilt even by captains of industry, who governed the relentless international shipping that defied its sandbanks and wrecks to supply the terminals or ply their merchant trade. Civilisation and progress seemed to be halted on the tide

Below: A company of widgeon find both solace and shelter in a Humber Estuary creek

Image: iStock

edge and allowed to carry on only at nature's will. Sometimes in hard weather and big tides we would get the geese, but most sport involved the widgeon and wild mallard. I don't believe in all the times I shot there with Mego a single teal ever put in an appearance. It was a place one wished the curlew was still on the list as herd after herd of this bird would pass over on occasion, well

within shot, but safe in the knowledge that they were no longer in danger of the shotgunner.

For centuries man must have been fowling on this great estuary, as Iron Age dugout canoes have recently been found and excavated, after being hidden and preserved throughout the ages in all that enveloping Humber mud. I would wager the primitive owners of those boats also felt the familiar pang of Nimrod's tug, as they pursued the same fowl with sling and snare, as fowlers do today but with more effective engines of destruction.

Great punt gunners of yesteryear used to stalk the sand bars and mudflats afloat for that effective flock shot that was not so easy to come by, and took great skill to secure. But tonight we have driven up to the Humber bank and crossed from the manicured world of modern farming to the wild estuarine meadow and turf of the foreshore. A respectable troop of mallard lift off the nearest creek, startled by our heads showing above the bank. They had been sheltering from the whining wind that now bends the dune grass double. There are three of us tonight plus Mego's constant attendant, Jazz his springer spaniel. Normally there are just the usual two, but accompanying us tonight is a halfling. The next generation has already felt the call of Diana, and spent many mornings stalking roebucks with her elder. Tonight, the eight year-old will make her first trip wildfowling proper. Mego and I mutter to ourselves, and concur that the mallard will probably return. The decoys are cast into the creek, on their swivelled anchor lines, and we take our station pressed into a purpose built,

timber framed trench built by Mego's own hand with Jazz at our feet. This hide is invisible to most except the privileged few, and is only covered on the highest of tides.

The two of us often sit together as I am mostly a left-hand shooter, and therefore we can quite easily share the arc of fire. Guns are loaded with steel shells, as required by law, and Sienna sitting between us takes out one of the hot water bottles from her rucksack, and sits on it. Another is soon stuffed up her camouflaged jacket, hat pulled down, ear protection on, and gloves donned. Making herself comfortable, she casually inquiries of our guide "when are the ducks due Mr. Megson?" Mego then carefully explains about the rising tide, and accompanying moon phases, as I soak up the salt air and watch the redshank and shelduck flit up and down the Humber in the twilight. A deceit of lapwing whirls its way past, their mournful mewing cry capturing the young-ster's wide-eyed interest. Then come the curlew, and I shake my head at what sport could have been enjoyed already if the clock could be turned back fifty years.

It is almost too dark to shoot, the mallard haven't returned, and we are considering our departure when a single widgeon comes in like an arrow with a 'whoosh' on arched wings, to settle on the flooding creek before us. He is a cock bird and immediately pipes out his distinctive whistles "whee-oo, whee-oo, whee-oo". I can sense the youngster's excitement, no doubt marvelling at this close encounter with one of our shyest fowl. Another rush of wings indicates more of birds coming in, attracted by the deeks and the

Image: Peter Carr Collection

providential whistle of their kind. Mego and I rise in union, our three shots are answered by two satisfying thumps and Jazz is away to sweep up our precious birds before they are claimed by the flooding tide. Two mallard follow their cousins into the game bag, and another cock widgeon joins the fallen. We are shooting the ducks now against the light of the terminal, but the flight naturally draws to a close as the tide begins lapping at our feet. We wind our way carefully

Above: The author after a successful widgeon flight on the Humber foreshore with Tony Megson

Left: A couple of mallard drakes angle in at flight time

back across the marsh, but not before Sienna insists on carrying her share of the ducks. Mego passes her a handsome cock widgeon from his game bag, and I think to myself the force is strong with this one as she gratefully receives the bird. Reaching the bank, I pause a while before stepping from the wild foreshore into civilisation and the stress and responsibilities of modern life. Redshanks pipe away to each other, the raucous call of a patrolling herring gull is carried on the wind, somewhere way out on the mudflats geese are murmuring, and a rush of unseen wings tells of duck still on the move, a "whee-oo" confirms them as widgeon, and I turn away for home.

I cannot leave the widgeon without telling of an amusing incident that befell me a couple of summers ago in the Lake District. I was working the shoreline that surrounded Beacon Tarn (the setting for Arthur Ransome's book *Swallows and Amazons*), trying to tempt a trout or a mythical charr from its depths when a duck widgeon burst from the heather at my feet. Stood as I was in the shallows the smooth, rounded

Image: Shutterstock

departed and left her to it. The soaking had been worth it though, for that rare, albeit brief, window into the life of a widgeon.

My best search of shooting records shows that the biggest bag of widgeon shot with shoulder guns was 93, taken at Skipwith Common, Escrick, North Yorkshire, on 22nd Novemeber 1920 by five guns on morning flight, the bag also included 3 mallard, 57 teal, 9 shoveler, 1 tufted duck, 1 pochard, 3 pintail, and 10 snipe. The guns were Messers. Leopold Paget, C. McLean, P.H. Wormald, J. Wormald, and Hugh Wormald.

However, I know of a similar bag of widgeon shot on a pond near the Humber in the early 1990s by three guns. And Sir Joesph Nickerson shooting alone shot an undisclosed amount of widgeon, mallard and teal to his own guns (with a loader), on Reads Island in the River Humber on 2nd December 1983. Remarkably he was using 28 bores.

The record number shot by a punt gun is 96, shot by Captain Nugent on the River Shannon in 1879. Sir Ralph Payne-Gallwey shot 70 widgeon with one shot on the west coast of England, and on 18th January 1881, in a terrific blizzard, he bagged 139 but this is thought to have been more than one shot, a rare feat with a punt gun.

Accurate bags of truly wild mallard are difficult to ascertain, but Prichard's friend and colleague J.G. Millais with another gun Mr. P. D. Malloch shot 108 and teal on Loch Leven in a gale on 13th December 1885. And again two guns Messers A.H.E. Wood and Frank Greenfield killed 76 mallard, 16 widgeon, 10 teal and 1 snipe and 4 various on 8th February 1913. **PC**

and heavily weeded stones were as could be expected – somewhat slippery. The shock of this unexpected feathered eruption caused a temporary loss of balance, with a subsequent slip, followed by a loud splash and a very sodden angler who'd now drowned his third mobile phone of the trout season. This was the first and only widgeon nest I have discovered. There were eight creamy coloured eggs with an apricot tinge, surrounded by down in a perfectly hidden nest. They must have been close to hatching because the agitated duck kept close by. I quickly

Left: A flush of mallard rapidly depart from a field drain

Causamull Ducks

Causamull is an island which lies some three miles west of one of the outer Hebridies. Beyond it, the foaming reefs round the gaunt rock, Desker, can glow like molten gold in the sunset, and from them a venturesome prow may sail onwards and see no shore until the cliffs of England's oldest colony, Newfoundland, rise from the fog.

Causamull, in a word, is queen of a hundred skerries; Sgeirleir and Lagan Maskeir are in her court, since upon her alone is set a crown of vegetation – rank grass and weed, it is true, but which, none the less, after a shower shines like an emerald in the sunshine. The island itself at spring-tide is not half an acre in extent, but at low water an expanse of perhaps a quarter of a mile of black boulders exposed; among those lurk pools of water which grow salt after high tide, but in the neaps brackish with the rain that

rarely fails to fall some time during each four and twenty hours. In addition to the pools at the mercy of the tide is one greater pool beside which two or three grey seals give birth to their young every October.

But all this information was gathered at a later date. The first time we heard the name Causamull was on an occasion when two barrels had brought down a single mallard, and his seven comrades flying over the shoulder of the hill were suddenly lost to sight.

"Where'll they have gone to, Donald?"

The ghillie answered, "Causamull."

"Let us follow them there."

That was before the gunner knew that Causamull was an island. The fact became duly impressed on him in the days which followed. Teal and ducks rose wild from the big bog.

"Have they gone to the ponds on the North

Point, Donald."

"I'm feared no. They've carried on over to Causamull, I'm thinking," replied the ghillie from the brow of the ridge, then continued as in mediation, "Yon Causamull is a regular sanctuary, A' the big old burly ducks and teals is there. A mon can tell Causamull duck most times by the puir size of him."

And so was coined the term "Causamull ducks," meaning not only a duck from that island, but a "burly" duck. We enjoyed the shooting of many lochs and bogs upon the mainland and shore where were killed a goodly number of wildfowl, notwithstanding which our hearts were sore because the wind was contrary, and the only boatmen within reach were by no means either well equipped or eager to attempt the landing on Causamull in anything approaching "weather", or to desert for any such hazard

ous employment the lobster-fishing by which they won their daily bread. So, day after day, we watched our mallards and teal rise and make for the distant rock, round which they seemed to circle ere they pitched.

Only twice in that season did we succeed in landing on Causamull. The first time the ducks were unheeded, greater game being in view, to wit, the grey seal, a fair-sized old bull; the second time we killed two teal, almost every living thing except these and the terns, which swooped and stooped over the heads of the intruders, having left the island as we approached it, owing to a difference of opinion amongst our lobster-catchers as to the channel we must choose to reach the rock, a dispute which they carried on in Gaelic at the top of their voices. They were very soulless hunters.

A dozen years passed before, on a certain 2nd of August, two of us stalked a large lot of fourteen or fifteen mallards on Na Roe, the loch on the peninsula which lies opposite to Causamull. On this occasion we accounted for three; the rest rose up in straight and purposeful flight and passed over to the island.

During the whole of that August and September Causamull remained a thorn in our sides. It was a wild season, the wind rarely dropped, and although the lobster-fishers of old days were departed, their great unwieldy boat had passed into the hands of a new firm, who certainly

showed no more pronounced love of risk or adventure than their predecessors. But they met our overtures mildly. They would shake their heads, and gabble in Gaelic; then the spokesman, a long-faced man in a khaki coat, would say, gently, "We couldna do it the nicht." Once they landed us in the daytime and we killed three teal, but at the first discharge the island was naturally left bare of ducks. Many of them flew towards the shore and went down in our own Big Bog, but we returned too late to take any advantage of their very temporary presence there.

It was at this time that we heard the story of Causamull, which may or may not have its bearing upon the dislike with which the island is regarded. It appears that some years ago a family set sail from Houghhary in Uist for the Monach Isles, taking with them their worldly goods and beeves. The distance is some seven or eight miles, and the course they sailed past Causamull. As they came abreast of it, a squall struck and overturned the boat – one man, the father, alone fought his way ashore. Some say that a boat passing between the islands reported the non-arrival on the Monachs of the migrating family; others, that a long-sighted crofter working at tangle-burning on the Uist dunes caught sight of the solitary figure of a man standing upon Causamull, outlined against the glow in the sky. With whichever story the truth may lie, the fact remains that a boat was sent off to the island, but stress of weather forced it to sail away leaving the unfortunate man upon that lonely rock, stretching out his hands in vain. As soon as the storm abated the boat returned and took him off, but not before he had spent several days upon the rock. Providentially, one of his drowned cows had been washed up by the tide, and from this he cut the tongue with a sharp stone and devoured it.

At length there came a night when the wind dropped away all together, the ghillie was sent down to the hamlet, and in due time returned, bringing the promise of the lobster-fishers to meet us at Scolpaig Point at 1.30 A.M. That evening the usual rubber of bridge was eliminated and premature sleep attempted. Such attempts are not always successful, and to one of us at least it seemed that he had hardly closed his eyes when David was knocking at the door. Some coffee and a sandwich, and then we shouldered our guns and give the cartridge bags to John and go out into the night. A walk of about a mile over the dunes, among scurrying rabbits frisking on the night-wet turf, while above our heads an occasional green plover wings over half seen with his peculiar cry. Soon we are able to hear the light plash of the sea upon the hard

sands; a flock of curlew rise with their shrill complaining, just as we move out across the base of the Scolpaig promontory. John whistles. There is no reply.

The lighthouse upon Heiskeir[1] reveals and hides it brightness, the tide sucks at the weed-hung seal haunted skerries. We wait half an hour and then one of us suggests that the lobster-fishers are not going to fulfil their bargain. But the words are hardly spoken when John hears the boat. He jumps up, whistles again, and this time is answered.

By the light of a lantern we descend the rocks and get aboard. Last of all to leave the land is the Labrador dog, Sinbad. He is ill-named, he is the worst of sailors, and in consequence hates all boats. For a moment, love of the gun and hatred of seafaring struggle in his heart, then the ruling passion, strong in worse than death, prevails, and he jumps and lies upon the ballast amidships. John receives his final orders. "As soon as it is light, John, you go and stir up the teal-pool and both ponds on the North Point. And try and

[1] *Heiskeir, the skerry with a lighthouse, must not be confounded with the double island of Haskeir, where the great grey seals breed.*

see where the
ducks we put off
Causamull go to." "All
right, sir," says John; and we lose
sight of him as we push out from between the
rocks.

It is very dark upon the water, and though
there is no wind there is a very perceptible swell
over which we blunder propelled by a pair of
immense sweeps. The low black boat struggles
on like some gigantic crippled beetle, her pace
seems one of infinite sloth, for dawn we know
comes early and we must be hidden among the
boulders of Causamull and the boat well away
before the east begins to grow white. We point
out these things to the long-faced helmsman. He
executes the usual Gaelic jabber with the crew,
assures us that "it can be all right still."

An hour later, an hour filled with the creaking of oars and the troubles of Sinbad, and at
last we see the dark outline of the island with
its cairn of stones, a cairn popularly supposed
to have been raised by the shipwrecked crofter
whose story has been told, but in reality built
by the far less romantic hands of a Government
surveyor in the performance of his ordinary
routine. There is still no hint of dawn as the boat

is piloted towards the rock. This is fortunate,
since the entry to the tiny harbourage is made
the occasion of advisings from all crew, a
continuous fusillade of Gaelic which, though
spoken in a series of raucous whispers and with
admirable intentions, puts every bird upon the
rock to wing. But this matters not, for the birds
are only curlew, terns, and cormorants. The
ducks are still feeding and plashing in the pools
and lochs of the mainland whither they fly at
sunset. That much we know for certain, for we
have seen them coming in so high over the land
that it brings to mind the words of the American
sportsman and poet anent Canada geese:

"And the baffled fowler watches,
Hopeless till they fade from sight."

At length a leap and we are ashore; we hear
the boat put out again and soon she is lost to
hearing as well as to sight. Causamull is shrouded in darkness; still as is the night, the breakers
are thundering on the western reefs. We are a
full half hour too soon. So after choosing each
a pool, we come together and chat, till, warned

by a real or fancied whitening in the east, we go finally to our places.

Causamull is covered with vast boulders among which is easy hiding. I stand behind one facing the mainland and the east. In front of me are two pools of brackish water, all the island around is dark, but these two pools begin to turn from black to grey, and then more slowly from grey to white. "Whish! whish!" Those ducks have passed over! "Whish! whish!" again. How curious! Where can that lot have gone to? I wait in expectation. Surely they are only circling round, but alas! I wait in vain. Then "Swish! Swish!" once more. This time I swing up the gun and fire. A great body falls from the sky, so great that I have my fears. I send Sinbad to find out. He takes a long time, longer than he should. At length he returns dragging a huge fowl scart by the tip of its wings. He has scarcely got to cover when three teal come straight in very low. They are all bunched together, and the three fall to the discharge of two barrels.

And now my companion shoots in his turn. He has made no mistake, for I hear two thuds upon the rocks. I think from the distinctness of the sound they must be mallards which have fallen, but in that I am mistaken, for they turn out to be teal. Meantime, the east has grown so bright that the sun cannot be far below the horizon. It is to be a red sunrise, for the pink takes a ruddier hue, which presently extends over half the sky. It is time now that John should be putting something off the mainland ponds. Ah, here they come!

Nineteen ducks flying swiftly from the land but high, high above the surface of the sea, so high that although they pass clean over me I do not fire, as surely they will circle round again. I watch them; on and on they fly into the dark west until they are lost to sight. Next come a really big flock of teal; there are more than thirty birds in that flock, but they are, if anything, flying higher than the mallards which precede them. They too, pass above me, and this time I swing two guns' length ahead of the leader and fire both barrels. The teal jump into the air, shooting straight upwards as they will when fired at, but this is the only result that my shot produces, and they also wing their way into the last of the vanishing night-cloud. Now a single teal pitches in the pool right in front of me. I did not see him arrive, and just as I am about to flush him he is joined by a second. They swim rapidly out of sight. I step from behind my rock and have a rising shot, but kill only one bird and miss the other. I have not time to get back to shelter again before four ducks come wide and high only to pass on in the wake of the others towards the Monach Islands.

It is a full day now, but the beautiful night has been succeeded by a grey sky; a light rain is beginning to fall, and as the sun has risen red it is pretty certain that the morning at any rate will develop badly.

I now go to pick up the first three teal, only to discover to my disgust that the rising tide has swept them from the pool in which they fell, and by now they are no doubt twisting in the currents that foam and rush between the rocks. I gather one that fell in the pool and re-join my companion. He has killed three and gathered two, the third has fallen in some hole among the rocks; indeed so jagged and full of crannies is the Causamull formation that twenty-five per cent of the birds shot can never be recovered.

We were both, as we laid out our bag, grievously disappointed at its very meagre proportions. We had dreamed of thirty ducks and behold three! And the curious part of it is that we had seen the ducks and the teal, seen them clearly and distinctly ere they vanished into that black night-cloud which has now lifted completely, leaving in its place the pale dunes of the Monachs. What has prevented the ducks coming into the ponds that we were watching? Ourselves, we are sure, they had not seen. Could it have been the boat? We know well enough that the present of the boat would cause every duck to sheer off, but in the steady purposeful flight there has been no sheering. We climb to the cairn. No, it is not the boat. There she lies, well away, quite far enough away to make it impossible for the sight of her to have affected the duck's destination. We wave the men to come for us and row sorrowfully back to the mainland.

The boatmen, when questioned, acknowledged that they had never seen ducks behave in such a fashion. Where could they be making for? Out to sea, they thought, for there are few pools in the Monachs. Finally the boatmen rather fancied that the ducks must have sighted us, but receded from this opinion when we pointed out that various curlew had passed over us without suspicion.

It was about seven o'clock when we disembarked once more upon Scolpaig. John was there to meet us. He had seen few ducks and thought perhaps it was rather early in the season for the ducks to pitch upon Causamull. Further speculation was interrupted by the spying of a large gaggle of grey geese in the amphitheatre of the dunes. These we tried to circumvent by driving, but luck was dead against us that morning, and the fine birds went away unshot at by one of the many unguarded points.

A good solid rain was falling long ere we reached the house. Our expedition was over and the anticipations of several days had ended in blank failure. If all the ducks we had seen had pitched upon Causamull, or had circled round it or even had flown over it, we should have got ten or fifteen brace, and the fact remains that one of us, watching in the early morning, had several times seen the ducks fly out and circle and drop. Why had they failed to do so on this occasion? We learnt the answer that night. Higher up the coast lies a certain village where at the time there was but a single, and that a not very seaworthy, boat. The owners of this craft, tempted by the fair weather, had upon the evening previous to our visit to Causamull put to sea. About five or six o'clock, finding themselves in the vicinity of Causamull, they had landed upon it in search of driftwood, and had even fired at a family party of ducks upon one of the pools. No wonder the ducks flew high when we waited so patiently for them just ten hours later!

We were not, of course, so much cast down at our ill-luck once that ill-luck was satisfactorily explained. We knew that could we but land upon Causamull any time after the middle of September our reward would be a rich one, for soon the ducks would forget the visit of the fisherman and return to their natural haunts. During six whole weeks we were ready each and every night to put to sea, but not once did the weather give us an opportunity. Wild storms and stiff breezes with hardly a lull or an interlude ruled all those weeks, nor in that year were we able to get a return match with the ducks of Causamull upon their own ground. Upon ours the case was different, for by dint of lying out at flighting time and waiting on the stubbles in the dunes, we occasionally got back a little of our own.

Once, for instance, the gardener's boy came with a story that each day as he walked over the hill in the early morning he saw a large flock of mallard rise from the reeds of a certain loch and head straight out to sea. We had often shot this loch after breakfast, usually driving it, and grand sport had we had there. In one stand alone mallard, teal, snipe, golden plover, curlew, pigeon and peewit had been shot, but never had we caught the Causamull ducks lurking in its reeds.

The morning after the news of the gar-

dener's boy had been received two guns and a ghillie were at the loch-side soon after daylight. One gun took up his position behind an in-habited hen-house on the farther side of the loch, while the ghillie and the second gun went in the boat. Hardly had they started before a flock of some forty mallards rose out of the reeds. The hen-house gun, surrounded as he was by indignant fowls, succeeded in getting a right and a left in front and a single snap behind before the flock were out of shot – all three that fell were the very fathers of ducks. The rest headed straight away for Causamull, nor did they ever, to our knowledge, visit that loch again.

Once, indeed, one of the guns had a most trying experience. He was waiting in the evening among the stooks at the edge of some barley, which the ducks had been visiting very freely, when a gaggle of about sixty grey geese came bugling down the wind to pitch within two hundred yards of him. There was every prospect that they would feed into the corn and give the gunner such a shot as would cause the occasion to be marked forever with red in his sporting diary. After lying watching the birds, which were slowly approaching, for a quarter of an hour, the gunner became aware that a party of ducks were flying in from the sea. Causamull ducks, undoubtedly! They flew over within nice shot and were followed by several other lots, which were, of course, permitted to pass. But there was not, alas, any reward for abstinence, as darkness fell with the geese still a hundred yards away, and a hurried stalk in the fading light ended in complete failure.

In that year, indeed, the ducks of Causamull met with but one even moderately severe reverse. This was a windy evening when they antedated their shoreward evening flight into the barley by a quarter of an hour. The casualty list showed thirteen.

Causamull, as has been said, lies three miles from the mainland. As a breeding-place for ducks it is impossible, and this for a variety of reasons. First there is no food; secondly, the sprays of ocean fly over the entire surface of the rock; thirdly, the place is haunted by great black-backed gulls, besides being the nesting station for numbers of sea-birds of various kinds, with whom the wild ducks would not be permitted to dwell in any amity. The ducks, therefore, certainly breed upon the marshes and loch-sides of the mainland. This being so it is wonderful how soon they find their way out to their sanctuary and the sea. Young flappers fly there in earliest August. On one occasion an exceedingly thin moulting mallard was found in the highest pool in the island on the 19th of the same month. Doubtless it had flown across just before it lost the use of its wings and had remained an involuntary prisoner. So thin was it that its breast-bone was nearly breaking through its skin.

And now another year has passed away, and once more the ducks are beginning to gather upon Causamull; once more we have stolen ashore there before the dawn, but this time a great many birds have carried on out of shot over us to Deasker. This constitutes one of the many difficulties that make a good "flight" on Causamull early in the season so rare. Many factors must work together to ensure it. First, the weather must permit a landing; secondly, the tide must not be too high or there will be no pools for the ducks to pitch upon; lastly, it must not be too low, or half, and more than half, the ducks will fly over Causamull to the attractions of Deasker, four miles seaward.

Why not, you may say, have one gun on Deasker and two on Causamull and circumvent the ducks that way? We discussed that plan and longed to be able to carry it out. But if the nights when one can land upon Causamull are few, those upon which a landing may be effected on Deasker – in the local judgements by which we are bound – almost reach vanishing point.

Deasker is simply a reef; at spring tides it is covered by the sea. It is so small that half the birds one shot would fall into the water, and even in calm weather their masters would not lightly venture Sinbad or Gambler in the Atlantic swell. Nevertheless, but for the boatmen who, after all, little as we may like to acknowledge it, ruled our schemes, we should ere this have flighted Deasker. Some day in the future we may yet do so.

But for the moment we have another plan, and that is to reverse the order of things and "stir up" Causamull by daylight. Two guns will go in the boat to the island, and one will wait on the north point upon the mainland. The latter will get some shots at the ducks as they fly in top the ponds; more important still, he will be able to observe where the birds, which go beyond the Big Bog, pitch, and afterwards, joined by his companions, will pursue them.

It is a perfect day as the North Point gun walks to his post upon the promontory. On the way he puts up a gaggle of at least a 150 grey geese, which wing their way towards the dark hills that look so grand and so gloomy in contrast to the turquoise sea and sands bright as a silver bar.

At length he arrives at his appointed post beside the larger of the promontory ponds. He finds five ducks upon it, but in quite an unstalkable position, and at once they are up and away – off to Causamull.

And now lying on the fragrant dune beside a little island in the pond, whereon wild flowers blow, and while the boat with its dark sails – they are really dirty, but here, as elsewhere, "distance lends enchantment" – creeps out towards Causamull, let us look round. We have a glass; we examine the skerries, the Monachs, the lighthouse, even grim and distant Haskeir, that vast rock in whose bowels the Atlantic plays thunder-music. There it lies, robbed of half its savage gauntness by the haze.

An hour passes – the boat is quite close to Causamull. Down come the sails; now they are landing. Bang! bang! and from far away the ducks and teal begin to appear. Few of them come to the ponds on the North Point, but many go down in the Big Bog, some on Dunscaur, and others continue their flight till the eye loses them against the inland hills.

Presently our comrades re-embark. We gather up our two teal, all we have secured, and all meet for lunch at Seal Point. Afterwards we pursue the ducks, and by the time we knock off to go fishing we have bagged twenty. Not a great day, but a pleasant one. A day the results of which may cause a smile, yet to us who have participated in it a day of real sport, to be underlined perhaps more heavily than many another when the panniers groaned with their loads of grouse, or the game cart carved deep ruts in the drive.

Well, that is the best to date, but we often picture the glorious twenty minutes about dawn when the ducks fly in to Causamull, and a desire, which is never quite at rest, strengthens a desire to return and try to wipe out in fair and honourable victory the many defeats we have experienced in our too rare encounters with those gallant adversaries, "Causamull ducks".

Note. – Since the above was written, two of us succeeded in landing on Causamull in February. We picked up twenty-four ducks and widgeon, and seven various at morning flight. The number might easily have been more than half as many again, but the tide was high and rushed between the various rocks of the Causamull formation with such force as to be very dangerous for the Labrador dog. It was therefore useless to shoot unless we could make fairly certain of dropping the bird on the rocks, and consequently many a splendid chance had to be forgone. **HP**

Monarch
of the Glen

For whatever reason, Prichard chose to omit red stag stalking from his selected sporting species in the original edition of SIWB. This I found extremely surprising, as the red stag has to be the most iconic of all sporting species found in the very wildest parts of Britain. If we look at all of his writings as a whole, we may find the bare thread of an explanation. It is clear beyond question that the pursuit of geese was Prichard's favoured winged quarry with the shotgun. Equally, the Barren-Land caribou had to be his rifle's counterpart (if we exclude his time in the trenches of course). It is then, perhaps, his obsession with the greater game of the polar north, which he sought and shot in Newfoundland and Labrador that made the pursuit of the red stag inferior by comparison. Also, the tradition of being led by a stalker into your stag was perhaps not to his liking.

Prichard was a leader of men, and a very experienced hunter. Being forced into a backseat 'guest' role, with almost all decisions of the chase made by another, can tarnish the experience of one who normally leads. Much depends on the stalker of course, as some are better at it than others, and making the guest feel he is contributing his part to the 'campaign' can actually enhance a day on the hill. Conjecture or not we shall never know – the real reason is forever interred with the author's ashes in the family vault at St Michael's Church, St Albans.

Prichard certainly pursued red stags on many different estates during his sporting lifetime, and although he left little in relation to his Scottish red stag stalking experiences, I did find during my research an interesting extract published in the *Queenslander* (9th March 1933 edition). It was taken from a letter written by Miss Diana Hesketh-Prichard, the daughter of the famous author, published in the *Field* the previous year. Her words show that the Nimrod gene was passed on to not only Prichard's two sons Alfgar and Michael, but to his daughter too.

I got up on the morning of my first stalk so thrilled that I hardly knew what to do: far too excited, in fact, to take any notice of breakfast, and then I went out and had a little target practice with a stalker named David Cameron. At about 8.45 we started off. We had to go about twelve miles, and on the way we picked up the stalker and an old gillie who waits with a pony. We crossed the loch in a boat at the far end, walked about a mile or two, saw some hinds.

Then the stalker David Cameron, had a spy, and the stalk began. We saw two or three stags, nothing very big. Our stag was about half way up, and looked a fair sized beast.

We went downhill to a river, where we spied again. Then we crossed it and started up the other side. Heavens! It was steep, and when David stopped for another spy I was more thankful than I can say. But I soon recovered.

Presently we began to crawl, sometimes we crept, lying flat on the side of the hill, upwards and ever upwards. At last we were level with our beast, but very far away still. We paused in a hollow. David Cameron, the stalker, had been going first, myself second, and a young gillie – also a Cameron – following. We left him in the hollow, as higher up it was even barer, and with him we left our sticks and my spy glass and everything we could spare. It got more thrilling every moment. David had stopped dozens of times already, and we had to retrace our steps. Now we went on, lying flat, on the face of the hill in full view of all the deer. There were lots of others to complicate matters.

It was incredibly thrilling. We had made half a semi-circle round our quarry, and were looking down on him, but not straight down. We had a long way to go to do that, and some beasts above us started to move. We lay quite flat till they were reassured, then we went on. Now and then we came to the very rocky bed of a tiny burn, up which we could crawl on all fours. I was terrified of dislodging a stone. Then we would take to the bare hill side again. It was bright and sunny most of the time, though a fine rain fell for a short time and we got very wet.

At the end of the stalk:

At last we came to some big rocks, almost directly above the stag. He was not suspicious, though he looked round every now and then. One or two of the hinds were lying down. We crept cautiously forward from behind the rocks on to a grass promontory. The deer were hidden for a bit and then came into view again. We were on a smooth, steeply jutting out place, above them; I could just see the stag's antlers. We went on, coming more and more into view as we got nearer on the sloping ground. Then it fell steeply, almost sheer about 20ft. to a nearly level place, where the deer were feeding. We stopped at the very edge and I took the rifle.

The stag got up and looked round. He

was quite a nice eight-pointer, straight below me, about 80 yards away. I was so excited that I shut the wrong eye. Then I pulled myself together and sighted the rifle on him. He turned away. My arms began to ache. He turned broadside again and Cameron whispered, "Sight it very fine." I did so. "Ye can fire any time now," he said, and I pulled the trigger.

They galloped away to the left in sudden panic at the report, and I quickly got ready to fire again if necessary. But it was not. The stag faltered and stopped, the hinds looked at him in surprise. David got out his glass. He had been crying excitedly, "You've got him, you've got him. He'll not go very far. You must have got him!" He looked through the spy-glass and announced that he could see the shot.

The hinds fled away to the right, up wind; and the stag lay down. I had hit him a trifle high, through the lungs, but shooting downwards. He got up again, sagging, as we started down the hill, went on a few steps and fell dead. We rushed down, Cameron crept up and touched him. "Quite dead," he said. He cut his throat and then came up to where I was standing.

"I have to paint you," he said, and there and then I was blooded on the forehead and both cheeks. Then he gralloched him and the boy come up with a rope and sticks, and our lunch. It was then 3.30, and we had started the stalk at about 10.30 and began to crawl soon after 12.30. David said we had crawled nearly three-quarters of a mile, and we had made a complete semi-circle round the stag. One of my stockings was no more as a result of it all.

So this is how, on the. first day of October, after her first stalk, Hesketh Prichard's daughter Diana killed her first stag with her first shot, an eight-pointer, with a "nice wee head," weighing 16st. 11lb. **DP**

My first stag was shot on the heights of Manywee, that majestic ling and stone sentinel that divides Rottal from Glen Moy, ringed by a large distinctive neckerchief of short tight heather, the result of a fire that had 'gotten away' during muirburn operations on a day long forgotten. I'd shot hinds and countless roe under the direction of famed stalker Stuart Donald. We'd both had a good stalk into the stag, when on the final approach the big Scotsman said "on yer go, tak yon beast yersel." Pride flooded through me on receipt of this rare honour, and I was determined not to make a hash of it. A careful crawl along the ridge, with the mist swirling in and out around me, did eventually, after more yards than I can care to remember, put me into a suitable position for the shot.

My beast was the highest one of a good group, which had settled below the ridge, out of the wind, with a commanding view of the glen. Inching round the side of the smallest of hummocks, indeed it was a mountain version of a molehill, I fitted to the rifle and viewed him in all his glory. His eyes were squinted into the wind, but his nose worked constantly, testing for danger. Then without warning he lifted his hind quarters out of a peaty bed, and rose up on to his hooves. I had the wind, and was equally well hidden, but the beast's early warning senses had clearly kicked in. It would do him no good however, because the bullet was on its way before his head had finished turning in my direction. He collapsed instantly where he stood. I'd placed the bullet a little high and forward, taking the stag through the shoulder, but had still killed him instantly. I knew Stuart would give me something of a berating for damaging the shoulder venison, but I could take that safe in the thought I'd secured my first stag.

Years later I'd be stalking other stags with Prichard's great-grandson Charlie Jacoby, under the direction of the same stalker Stuart Donald, on Her Majesty's estate Balmoral situated in the area of Aberdeenshire known as Royal Deeside. As an estate it has gradually expanded to more than 65,000 acres, employing 50 full time staff and 50 to 100 part time. It is so much bigger than all of us. You can see why even Tony Blair's ego was once dented when he came to stay here.

The Balmoral estate has had a blueblooded pedigree of ownership. It began as a home built by Sir William Drummond in 1390. The estate was formerly owned by King Robert II (1316–1390), who had a hunting lodge in the area. After Drummond, the estate was sold to Alexander Gordon, the third Earl of Huntly, in the 15th century. It remained in the family's hands until it was sold in 1662 to the Farquharsons of Invery, who sold it again in 1798 to the second Earl of Fife. The estate formed part of the coronation activities of King George IV in 1822. The foundation stone for Balmoral Castle was laid by Queen Victoria in 1853. This was

after a protracted purchase by Prince Albert after the Empress had sub-leased the estate for a number of years from the Earl of Aberdeen.

The estate comprises 45,000 acres owned between Balmoral, Birkhall and Glen Doll, 7,300 acres of grouse moor at Corgarff and 11,500 acres of sporting rights rented from a neighbour. Some 7,500 acres are forested. There are seven Munros (mountains over 3,000ft) and most of the land lies more than 1,000ft above sea level. A team of dedicated keepers preserve and manage a great variety of wild game species including red and roe deer, capercaillie, black game, red grouse, ptarmigan, and miles of excellent salmon fishing on the River Dee.

Charlie, as always, could only squeeze a day or two into his hectic schedule to head north, for yet another sporting episode in the Highlands. I shall leave it to him to relate his version of the events.

The burns are clearer, the weed in the burns is greener, the hillsides are set at the most aesthetically-pleasing angle (did Queen Victoria hire the artist Turner to install them?), and you get free soldiers of all things to handle the ponies and ghillie at Balmoral.

We spend the first day on the hill just spying. On this beat, in this wind, the best way on to the animals is to walk up the steep hillsides where the beasts are browsing and drop down on to them. The problem is getting in close. Had we got close enough to a stag, we would have had a shot. But it was just not to be.

Day two and we reach the top of the hill to find the monarch of the glen himself. I'm lucky, as today it's my turn to take the shot and the stag is a real belter. Stuart is confident that it's a very old beast and should be shot. Stuart is sure that when the rut breaks out properly, this stag will be displaced by one coming in from a neighbouring beat. He generously decides that a stalker in the hand is worth two in the palace and gives me the go-ahead. The ground is steeper than it looks. To get in to a shooting position, I have to crawl onto a sheer boulder and

ghillie Sean Kennerley, who is part of the team, ties a rope around my ankle so I can't fall, and gently lowers me over the boulder.

It's a surprisingly easy way to shoot. Your body clings to the rock because you can't trust the rope so your steadiness is guaranteed by contact with the ground. Then you find the beast through the excellent Zeiss Divari optic and you leave the 'gatherer' side of your brain to fuss about falling. The 'hunter' side of your

Below: The Highland red stag has to be the most iconic of all Scotland's species

Image: iStock

brain zones in on the stag's shoulder as it sits and surveys its hinds. An almost unconscious squeeze of the trigger and the .243 round is squeezed away. At such a steep angle, though the distance is 200 yards, I give it nothing on top. The effective range is 150 yards, which is the rifle's zero. There's the thwack of bullet meeting beast, and the stag slumps forward, dead – another stag for the Royal larder.

Then to the nice bit. Stuart radios the soldiers who at once set about taking the gar-rons up along the ancient path miles below to meet us. No pulling and chewing for me; Sean

Above: Queen Victoria's Highland hunting lodge Glas-allt-Shiel on the banks of Loch Muick at Balmoral

sets to the task with gusto, dragging the beast downhill to a rendezvous with the guardsmen, who will recover the 13 pointer with one of the ponies.

Best of all, we soon have a chance at another beast as the spooked herd pour away. This time its Pete's go and he takes a superb shot at a running stag carrying a limp – but that's another story. Used to shooting running hoofed game on the Continent, Pete wouldn't have taken the shot unless he was capable of it – and he is, the stag is dead.

Then there's the problem of getting Pete's

animal down the 1,000ft hillside and back to the larder. Can you believe it? We're on Balmoral, the most heavily-staffed estate in the Highlands for sure, and we've run out of staff. Pete does it himself, complaining bitterly all the way at my ineffectual encouragement.

Loaded up, the soldiers, stalkers, and two strapped on stags collectively head back to the larder at Balmoral Castle where the Duke will be given a report about the day's stalking. My beast is a magnificent 13-pointer, with well-worn teeth and way past his prime, but Stuart is slightly nervous for such a superb trophy as this to go back to the castle. It will be counted against all the other heads to come in that season on all the Balmoral beats, and probably wouldn't be bettered.

Pete's beast is also an old stag too, so a good choice to shoot. Balmoral is truly a reflection of the British royal family. They do everything bigger and better here. As for me, perhaps the 13-pointer has ruled me out of a knighthood in later life but – Sir Charlie or that stag? – I know which one I would rather have. What an experience, and what a trophy to garner from the Highlands.

On another occasion shortly after the above, I too managed to shoot the best hill stag of my life on the same estate. It wasn't quite as capital a beast as Charlie's stag, but it was my very own Monarch of the glen, a very respectable and ageing 12-point royal.

The day began with traditional Highland weather complete with horizontal rain as ghillie Sean Kennerly and I left the great grey castle of Balmoral behind us and headed out onto the hill in the Land Rover. The previous night I had enjoyed the hospitality of the Scots Guards and ghillie Sean into the wee hours and was feeling a little bit worse for wear.

However, the hangover was soon dispelled by fear as the ground became a good deal steeper and the Land Rover struggled for grip on the gravel incline above Loch Muick. Far below us Queen Victoria's picture-postcard Highland lodge Glas-allt-Shiel towered gracefully on the north west shores of the Loch. It was here that the widowed Queen spent much of her time in mourning after losing her beloved Prince Albert, with faithful servant and famous ghillie John Brown in attendance. I mentioned to Sean that he was actually Brown's modern-day counterpart. The comment was met with much humour and took my mind off our precarious pace up the mountainside. History in the Highlands has often been turbulent and Balmoral is no exception. The very road we were travelling on was used by the young pretender – Charles Edward Stuart, better known as Bonnie Prince Charlie – in 1745 en-route to his disaster at Culloden.

Eventually and with great relief we rolled to a halt beside Alan's hut, which was where the Highland ponies or garrons are stabled during the stag stalking season. We were met by Sergeant Davis and Private Turnbull leading a couple of fine garrons. The two Scots Guardsmen tended the ponies and assisted in ghilling for the castle guests as part of their main posting duty, providing protection for the royal household.

Fortunately the rain had stopped as abruptly as it had started; the fresh washed Highland heather stood out in all its autumn splendour, shadowed by the impressive peaks of Broad Cairn and Loch Nagar. Sean led the way with my TC Icon rifle in a canvas slip slung over his shoulder as tradition demands. I strode on after him with the guardsmen and ponies following on close behind. Our stalking party zig-zagged down the old drovers path, past the picturesque waterfalls on the River South Esk and up into the blaeberry-carpeted woods of Bachnagairn. The gentle ascent became steeper as we left the forest and once more padded onto the peat and heather of the open hillside. Heading up the Glittering Skellies we were met at the summit by our stalker Stuart Donald.

After exchanging pleasantries and a good spy across the landscape, Stuart decided on Glen Doll as our best destination to get to grips with a suitable stag. Descent soon turned to ascent as we wound our way up and along the Altduthrie Burn and onto the open flats of the peat hags. It was here that we saw our first group of stags. We were caught out half-way across the flats when the beasts trotted into view exiting Glen Doll. Our present position was hardly tenable, but for now the deep peat hag hid our stalking party well. Telescopes were deployed and both Stuart and I picked out a huge tall banana-shaped switch head. There couldn't have been a more suitable stag to shoot on the hill that day but the problem was how to get into him. Moments turned into minutes that turned into two hours and still we remained

Left: A puckle of Highland red deer stags. The older stags have already cast their antlers

197

marooned. Eventually it was decided to move the stags. In an attempt to do so the pony men made their way out of the peat hags as we watched on. The ruse worked to a degree as the distant stags did not immediately burst into flight at this disturbance to their browsing, but turned around to head back into Glen Doll.

This pleased Stuart, who was most happy with the result because he thought there was a good chance that we could catch up with them again in the Doll. Half an hour later we crested the summit of Cairn Damff and spied across the corrie to find there wasn't a stag to be seen. Pressing on we carefully traversed the steep hill-side and approached the edge of the precipitous cliffs of Glen Doll. Again, after much glassing, the beasts seemed absent but Stuart felt that they would be hidden somewhere in the dead ground out of sight.

However, Sean soon spotted a lone stag to our right about 150 yards away, working his way through the boulder-strewn, dead ground.

Below: Hesketh Prichard's great-grandson Charlie Jacoby following the path of Nimrod in his ancestor's footsteps

He was an ageing, big-bodied animal but with a poor head so Stuart gave the go-ahead to shoot when a suitable shot was offered. Annoyingly, the beast moved and remained hidden behind a big brute of a boulder. Although the red rut hadn't yet broken out, Stuart attempted a roar and the elusive beast stepped out to the challenge. The stag filled the Zeiss scope, I paused my breath, aimed and winged a bullet on its way, but completely missed. Realising it wasn't such a great place to be around, the beast changed ends and dashed downhill. I instantly changed position and followed the stag in the scope, he paused mid-flight looking back unsure. I took a careful bead up the beast's front leg to the heart and lung region and squeezed off another round. This time the bullet ran true and the stag tumbled spectacularly head-over-heels down the Glen toward the White Water Burn. "Aye your second shot was better than your first one laddie," murmured Stuart, his eye still transfixed on the Swarovski telescope trained on the now still stag. I couldn't offer an excuse for the first miss; I felt I hadn't pulled the shot, but who knows. Maybe it was my precarious position, on the precipitous edge of a 200ft-plus drop that had held my attention more than I had thought. The main thing was the second shot had counted and more than made up for the first.

Stuart dispatched the pony men, who had a long walk around the corrie to drop into Glen Doll, and onto Jocks Road to eventually follow the burn down directly below the fallen stag. Sean made ready to descend to the stag when another beast trotted into view. I deployed the rifle once more onto the Harris bipod and adjusted the magnification on the 2.5-10x50 Zeiss Victory scope. Stuart confirmed that the stag was an old beast carrying a good head that was going back at about 250 yards range. The TC Icon .243 was zeroed 1" high at a hundred yards so I held true onto the beast's heart, held a half-breath and fired. My majestic monarch of the glen absorbed the bullet; clinically dead on his hooves he stood stock still for a moment, before beginning to sway alarmingly and eventually tumbling forwards toward the first stag shot in a similar fashion. "Aye, your shooting is improving and twa stags is a good day," murmured Stuart, still with the Swarovski scope glued to his eye like Nelson approaching the French fleet at Trafalgar.

Sean skipped away down the sheer slopes to bleed and drag the beasts downhill to a suitable place for recovery by the ponies. Stuart and I picked our way down to eventually meet both Sean and the soliders on Jocks Road, where we all admired my two trophies. Both beasts were old animals with well-worn teeth but the second stag had a wonderful dark antlered head of 12 points making him a royal. It had been one of the best stalking days I have ever had and to shoot a royal head on the royal estate in such good company was a fantastic result.

Two more guardsmen joined us – Silva, a Fijian, and Van, a South African – and after strapping the stags onto the ponies we began the long hike back to the castle. A celebra-

Image: Freeimages

Above: A royal beast leaves his forest sanctuary in the mist for the open moor

Right: Ghillie Sean Kennerly and a trio of Scots guards follow the loaded garron back to the larder at Balmoral

tory dram was enjoyed en-route as we passed Stuart Donald's estate cottage Moulzie. More of the same hospitality and further Highland nectar (single malt) was offered and enjoyed back at the larder by manager Mike Muir and head keeper Gary Coutes. All deer are skinned on arrival, as Balmoral venison is, as is to be expected, aimed at the top end of the market. I marvelled as the other stalkers returned from their respective beats and processed the beasts of the day. Casting a glance at the skull mounts adorning the wall it was hard to ignore the sense of history. For the past 150 years kings, princes and leading aristocrats of their time had all sampled the very same sport I had enjoyed that day. I had been introduced to Balmoral nearly a decade before by then head

keeper Ben Fearny. Sadly, he has since passed away, but his two sons Phillip and Arthur are still carrying on the family tradition as stalkers for the Windsors.

Balmoral is a founder member of the East Grampian Deer Management Group and has taken a lead in the contentious management of deer by establishing a deer model. Game and all wildlife are well managed by an efficient team of stalkers, gamekeepers and ghillies under the expert guidance of head keeper Gary Coutes. The estate also produces excellent grouse driving for the Duke of Edinburgh and his guests plus some productive salmon pools on the river Dee. Balmoral is the ideal of the Scottish sporting week and hill stag stalking was practically invented there. In former times many heads of state enjoyed the stag stalking on this estate. Prime Minister Disraeli loved both the place and the sport and often joined the royal stalking parties at the castle. Tony Blair has been a guest but I hardly imagined he donned the tweeds and tested the wind for a stag. But David Cameron – now there's a thought – I wonder if he's had an invitation since he's been in the top job at Westminster. I am sure he would be happy to sample some royal stalking, as he has certainly felt the tug of Nimrod before; he's a keen stalker, fisherman, and I believe enjoys riding to hounds.

Highland hill stags are almost a sub-species of red deer. They are smaller both in body weight and antler than their southern England or mainland Europe counterparts. However, the pursuit of them on the open hill is as challenging a sport as one could wish for in wild lands. This is not an out-and-out trophy hunt by any means: indeed, it is just the opposite, as switch heads and poor confirmation or aged stags are the priority.

That said, one may be lucky, as I was, to take an impressive trophy head from an ageing animal. Either way, switch head or multiple points, any stag taken fair chase on the hill is well-earned and deserves its place above

Image: Peter Carr Collection

Image: Peter Carr Collection

Above: The author (centre) with a royal red stag flanked by Private Turnbull and Sgt Davies on the Bachnagairn beat of Balmoral

Right: The author's mentor Stuart Donald in a happier mood with a loaded garron at the foot of Glen Doll

the fireplace, regardless of trophy quality, it is shooting the right one that counts – for the benefit of the herd. It is a sporting pastime unique to the Highlands, and has changed little since Victorian times, especially when the ponies are used rather than tracked or other all-terrain vehicles. The Highland pony or garron is the native horse breed of Scotland's mountainous regions. It is not known whether these wild horses first spread into Scotland when the last glaciers receded some 10,000 years ago, or whether they were introduced by early prehistoric settlers. What is known is that by the 8th century, horses were in Scotland, and by

800 AD their images were appearing on carved Pictish stones.

In one of Scottish history's most noted incidents, Robert the Bruce, King of Scots, was most likely mounted on a sturdy Scottish Highland pony when he fought and killed Sir Henry de Bohun with his battle axe at Bannockburn in 1314. Highland ponies became the workhorse of the Highland croft and estate. During the heyday of stalking in the late 19th century they served as the most efficient way to transport deer and other moor game from the hill to the larder, with special saddles and panniers being used. Today the Highland pony continues to be used in this role. They are ideally suited to work on the hill because of their strength and agility even over the roughest and steepest ground, or for forestry work where mechanised access is difficult. Many other modern-day estates have reverted back to the ponies, since they are both more environmentally friendly and cost-effective than 4x4 vehicles.

In the First World War the Lovat Scouts used Highlands as army mounts, and they were also used by the military in the Boer War. With the advent of pony trekking in Scotland in 1955, the Highland pony came into its own and the breed became more widely known. As pursuit of wild game in a true wilderness goes hill stalking for red deer cannot be bettered, especially when serviced by a proficient ghillie leading a Highland garron. **PC**

Image: Peter Carr Collection

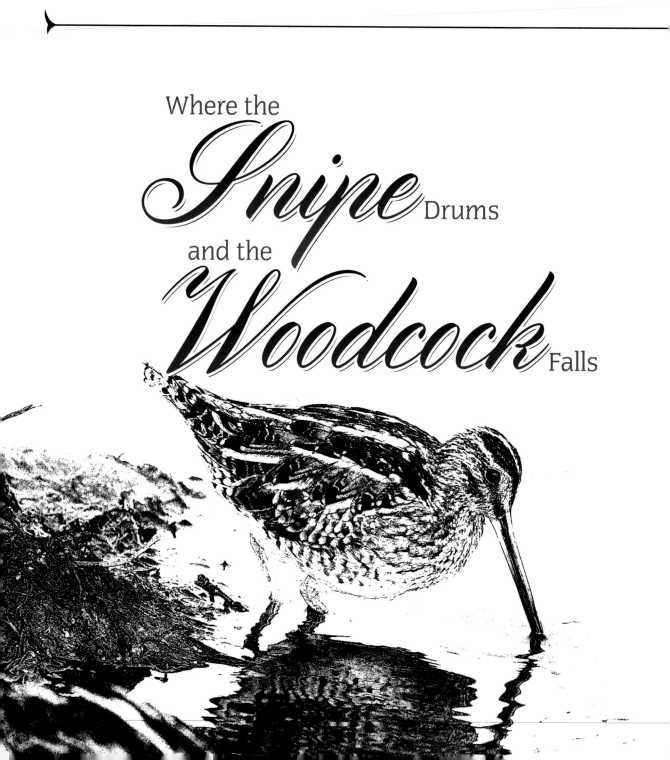

Where the *Snipe* Drums and the *Woodcock* Falls

A bird that gives the highest class of sport when driven, and which one consequently wonders is not more often shot in this fashion, is the snipe. To drive snipe in the centre of a big bog is naturally a fairly hopeless business, but upon certain ground snipe can be driven with great and even consistent success. This method is more followed in foreign countries than in the British Isles, although, curiously enough, it has been introduced abroad by British sportsmen. Provided one can find a river with marshy banks, wherever the marshes are not more than a quarter to half a mile in width, snipe-driving can be reduced to a reasonable certainty. No man can be certain or even guess in what direction snipe, when once flushed, will continue their flight, but their habit of circling causes a fair percentage to go over the guns, often very high. In a wind, there is no more difficult shooting.

Many beaters are not necessary for driving snipe unless they are lying very close indeed, since the best results are to be obtained by moving the snipe, rather than driving. Thus a single beater with two stops set two or three hundred yards away is more likely to persuade the snipe to fly in the desired direction than three beaters walking in line. Snipe, after flying forward for a hundred yards or so, are very apt to circle off at right angles. It is useless to attempt a long drive. Half a mile is quite enough, six hundred yards, or even quarter of a mile, better still, and indeed, it is on birds rising within the last two hundred yards that the most execution is done. These birds often fly low, and some proportion of the shots are frequently at birds that do not rise more than three or four feet above the marsh. Nor are such shots easy, for it is quite a fallacy to think that snipe cease their zigzag flight as soon as some people imagine. A high tussock, the crossing of water, a puff of wind are quite enough to cause snipe that have flown quite a long way to begin their dartings all over again.

One of the greatest difficulties, which is always present at a snipe-drive, is the position from which the shots must be taken. Good cover is an absolute necessity, and in order to obtain this, one is usually forced to hide in the reeds. The reeds are often low, and one often sinks into the mud to the knees or higher. As the shot must be taken in many cases from a sitting position, only about half the circle of fire can be covered by the gun, and the overhead shot is also rendered very difficult. Nothing is more annoying than to have the snipe all passing to the right when one cannot get into a shooting position for that side, owing to the fact that one has sunk well into the mire and cannot move one's feet.

As to cover, after October the reeds have been beaten down by the wind and rain, and a human being becomes a very obvious object in a snipe-bog. Therefore each gun should be provided with a light screen: a piece of green calico, four feet by three, attached at each side to a stick, will be found to be excellent. By thrusting the supporting sticks, which should

be about six feet long, into the marsh, one can obtain a shelter, behind which one can move as much as the nature of the footing will allow. It would, of course, be better still if permanent shelters of some kind be built in the bog, but this is difficult, as they would rapidly subside.

Once the shelter has been successfully erected, a further need arises: as it is impossible to stand up behind so small a screen, one must therefore either sit or kneel. If a man can kneel, all is well, but he usually finishes soaked in December marsh water. At one shoot, the guns were provided with wicker stools upon which they sat, but the ground was phenomenally soft and the stools sometimes disappeared; also the stools were slippery, and a high overhead shot often resulted in the gun measuring his length on his back in mud and water.

I have never heard what the record may be for snipe-driving in Britain, but in Europe 252 birds fell in a day to five guns. I shot this carefully preserved ground in the following year, when unfortunately floods had spoiled our prospects, and our party got eighty odd snipe in half a day's shooting. Four of the eight drives were against a very bright sun, so bright that it was necessary to wear blue glasses, and until you become well accustomed to them, glasses do not aid your marksmanship. The marshes upon which this shooting was done abut upon a river, and one gun – called for the drive the "river gun" – took his stand in a punt under the bank. This gun, whoever he might be, usually made a good percentage of kills to cartridges, whereas the guns in the marsh never did much better than one in three or four – which perhaps was not so bad after all, when one considers that they were often sunk almost to the waist in mud and slime.

The state of the moon is of great importance to the snipe-driver, for if there is no moon the snipe will be busy feeding all day, and will, even after being disturbed, continually return during the course of the drive to their feeding grounds. But after a moonlight night, they are very wild, and if disturbed will fly great distances. The wind is also important, for it is hopeless to try to drive snipe against a strong wind, and a great number will go away at right angles. The best chance is to drive snipe downwind, which, if it be a good gale, blows them over the guns like leaves torn from a tree. The man who can kill one snipe in three under ordinary conditions in a fairly small day must be a shot of the highest class. I say "a small day," advisedly, because if one is killing twenty odd snipe in a drive, it argues that there are plenty of birds, and consequently plenty of the easier kind of chance. But when the birds are few and far between, the gun is tempted to take very high birds; a snipe forty yards up is not out of range, though at forty yards he will, even if the shot be absolutely accurate, usually succeed in flying through the pattern. A snipe killed at extreme range falls with its wings outspread – parachutes down, in fact.

One of the worst difficulties in driving, and one which is unsurmountable, occurs when the birds are in wisps. I have often seen wisps of fifty or sixty, and, on occasion, wisps of two hundred or more. If the snipe are thus packed, one cannot hope to do anything with them, and it is better to leave them for the day.

Snipe can be shot at flighting time, if the gunner knows where to go and does not object to a very large element of uncertainty. I can recall a bed of reeds in a loch into which the snipe continually dropped during the twilight hour. Fishing beside it one evening, I saw a score of snipe arrive. To anyone in the reeds they would have offered very easy shots, as they came in low and quite straight, paused a moment or checked in the air, as if deciding where to alight, and then dropped in like stones. **HP**

Right: The snipe is a
specialist feeder found
in the wild places
across the British Isles

I certainly endorse Prichard's observation on the uncertainty of flighting snipe, although I have been fortunate enough to enjoy some small success in that department of the sport. In the corner of east Yorkshire where I grew up, there used to be a network of small rough pastures. These would semi-flood most winters, and were a huge draw for sinpe. Grazed by cattle for most of the year their dung encouraged the worm-rich areas that the snipe and woodcock adored. Those landed grasses had been there since time immemorial, and any thought of crop rotation, if indeed ever there ever was one, remained just that – a thought. That was until more recent times, and sadly many of these have since been drained, their hedges ripped up, and prime wader habitat fallen under the plough. Thankfully some still remain around the Flambourgh headland, and this is often the first port of call for migrating snipe and woodcock.

However, this former patchwork of rough grasses and seaves (Yorkshire term for rushes or sedge grass), provided the young tyro with ample opportunity to walk-up this diminutive wader with some regularity. And if one positioned oneself between these fields at dusk or dawn, with enough wind to work out their probable flight path between the snipe's rest and feeding areas, really good sport could sometimes be had, but it was certainly a hit and miss affair.

One particular evening I was crouched in a deep hedge bottom, with good grazing ground that fell away down a short hill to Mick's Pltn.

Behind and alongside the trees was a chess board of small, half-flooded, rough grass pastures, which were favoured feeding grounds of the snipe. I was positioned on my shooting boundary with a stiff north-westerly breeze blowing almost across me, from left to right. Behind was a sub-soiled stubble field, and a few hundred yards from that was a rough wet corner, overgrown by rushes, which ringed a pond, slowly being strangled by reed mace. It was this reedy haven that I'd been told, on good authority, had become a regular snipe sanctuary.

Good field craft is essential in snipe shooting, and knowing the habits of your quarry is of the utmost importance. Indeed it takes out what speculation can be taken from what is essentially complete guess work. On this occasion I was extremely confident due to the advanced intel received concerning the reed bed. I was sure it would add more to the hit side of the affair than the miss side. Old Major Cross had noticed snipe in some numbers arriving in the thick reeds behind me at dusk, on most nights during the past week. They had also flown over the hedge I was now ensconced in. What's more, I knew their probable point of departure, as I'd already bagged a few of the tiny waders by walking up their feeding areas previously described, which lay but two fields before me. There was no moon and the wind was ideal. Furthermore, I expected the stiff breeze to direct the wisps somewhere between my ambush place and another higher hedge on my left, which ran perpendicular to the low hedge I was hidden in. What could go wrong, the reader may well ask? Well, when it comes to wild game, 'quite a lot' would be the answer, but in relation to snipe shooting 'almost everything' would be more applicable.

Full of anticipation I took to my station early. Making comfortable, I quickly clipped back the thorns around my natural hide. This was to avoid any hook ups that could ruin my swing. But in doing so I attracted the unwelcome attention of two oystercatchers, whose scolding pipes revealed the gunner to the entire parish. I could do nothing about it and, ever the optimist, hoped the snipe would think little of it. As the evening progressed the orange-billed pied pipers grew weary of their mocking, and retired elsewhere to roost. Then one of those long reflective moments that occasionally happen to most of us, came over me. The combined effects of the whistling wind and the occasional mournful mewing of a gull, soaring somewhere high up in the twilight, lulled me into a daydream. I was half aware of numbed feet in the inadequate wellingtons I then wore, when the first "scaap, scaap" of an airborne snipe focused my attention.

The first bird had lifted and he had flown almost in the right direction, but just out of sensible shooting distance to my left. I pondered on moving, but my now cramped and stiffened legs persuaded me against it. While rubbing some life back into them with numbed hands I soon regretted my decision. A large wisp of fifty or more snipe left the reeds and followed the flightline of their previous pathfinder. Up went the gun, and I tried to pick a tiny target out of the cloud that sped past, like a handful of confetti launched into the wind. But both barrels discharged with a combined two ounce load of No.9s brought down nought. Tears welled in young eyes, and it wasn't solely due to the stinging wind. However all was not yet lost – it seemed some snipe were still at home. Another singleton "scaap, scapped" as it winged its way skywards, taking exactly the same route, as did another a moment after. It didn't need a third bird to convince me to change position. Despair instantly dispelled, and numbness forgotten, I was soon running towards the junction of the higher and lower hedges. Concealment now given up for prime location, I reasoned the near dark would probably be cover enough.

This move proved to be a good plan, and the next snipe fell to a first barrel shot. What followed was a wonderful fifteen minutes of shooting. Alerted to their incoming presence by their fortuitous call (for me at any rate), I'd blot out the little black silhouettes with the AYA's side by side muzzles, and deftly flick the gun through as I pulled the trigger. Most times as not the wader would crumple to fall behind me. Too soon the inky darkness made further shooting unjust, and I happily slipped the gun to go and pick the fallen. A good cast about resulted in six couple being picked. I was ecstatic; twelve snipe to my own gun for an evening flight, a total I have never as yet beaten alone.

One observation regarding snipe flighting I would like to point out is their propensity in Holderness to roost by the various flight ponds

Image: Craig Nash

in the district. Duck flighting has almost been an obsession with me since I first started out with the shotgun, and as such I have taken every opportunity to wait for duck at the ponds, and splashes, artificially fed or not. During that long apprenticeship I have sat at the water's edge in many different counties of all the four countries of Britain, and it has only been in Holderness that snipe have dropped in with any regularity to the ponds. If my memory serves me well, it seemed that it was the norm to expect snipe first as the light began to fade, and most often we were under strict instruction to leave them be and wait for the bigger wildfowl.

I do not recall excessive numbers of snipe coming by, but I cannot remember an occasion when at least one or two didn't spiral downwards and into the reeds with their distinctive call. More often it would be a small wisp, or three or four arriving oddly but all in a tight time frame. Of course I have flighted duck more often in Holderness than elsewhere, and perhaps it's the higher participation percentage that makes the fact linger in the memory. Indeed I recollect the fluttering arrival of a snipe against a setting sun as much as I do the widgeon's whistle, or the teal's piping, when I reminisce of flights long past, so the fact must be so.

Above: Our resident woodcock are bolstered during the shooting season by migrants crossing the North Sea on the full moon

Whatever the reason, their absence was sorely missed in other areas and the mind had to be concentrated if one didn't want to miss the first ducks 'in'. In Holderness one could relax until the little long-billed herald gave warning that the duck would soon be on the wing.

Despite the hours spent flighting this diminutive wader, most of the birds that have fallen to my gun have been walked up. Walking them into the wind is superb fun as they twist and jig away, or alternatively rise like skylarks if the fancy takes them. Sometimes spiralling to great heights until they surrender to the wind and are pushed back over the gun, this makes as difficult a mark as one could wish for. Indeed this often the case on a driven day. More than once, I have heard it tell that when a snipe flushes and begins its twisting deception, one must wait for the third turn before picking a line to swing on. I must confess I have never subscribed to this notion, and my best advice is to shoot as the snipe flushes. It is snap shooting at its best, and it has mostly worked for me.

Other than the occasional drive on a mixed day, I have never as yet had the pleasure of attending a purist driven snipe shoot. Of course one must visit Ireland for this spectacle, and oh what fun it must be. On two occasions I have been invited to join a party shooting at Viscount Brookeborough's shoot at Colebrooke Park in Co Fermanagh, but unfortunately both times I was already committed to shooting elsewhere. Every gun that I have conversed with who has shot at Colbrooke endorses Lord Brookeborough's following comment: "I would say that our quality, if that is what one would call it, is that we have quite special driven snipe and they really are quite reliable". One day I must indulge!

The snipe of course has the longest shooting season of all our game birds and wildfowl. He is as welcome an addition to a formal grouse day, as he is on the last excursion of a mixed rough day on the 31st of January. Before we leave the little snipe as a sporting prospect, I would like to relate a story told to me by Davy Thomas, the present head keeper at Black Corries estate, Glen Coe. Davy has really worked wonders since he took over as head keeper here, and the sporting diversification he has brought to the property is commendable in the extreme. His interest in snipe knows no bounds:

A good few years ago, while working for an estate in the Outer Hebrides, we used to be able to obtain a large amount of cattle blood when it was still legal to do so. This was then spread with bucket and scoop into the popular snipe areas to boost worm and insect life, of which it did with notable results. However, it was an exceptionally grotty job! On one occasion, while out grouse shooting on that same estate, I noticed one of the pointers accidentally run past a snipe, of which lifted and dropped again beside by a pointed rock 100 yards away. No-one else had seen it so, knowing my place, I discreetly told the head keeper. He nodded as he looked at the rock, before pointing at it with his stick. "Jeremy", he said to one of the

Left: Perfectly camouflaged, this woodland wader can often be found in the same roosting seats season after season

guns, "Walk over to that pointed rock, there is a snipe sitting right beside it." Puzzled, Jeremy did as he was told. As he got near to the rock the bird lifted and he shot it cleanly. "My good-ness", he remarked. "How on earth did you know that, the dog never even pointed it?" I have never forgotten his straight-faced reply; "No you're absolutely right young man – I smelt it myself!"

But now lets us leave this diminutive wader and look to his greater cousin, who is something of an anomaly in the bird world. The woodcock is classed as a woodland wader; he

is the only member of the wader kind to gain such classification, and what a following he has. The Frenchman loves him and raves on about the delicacy of his meaty thigh as a gas-tronomical equivalent of Nirvana. Now I agree the woodcock is a tasty bird, and as far as his breast goes he is a meaty one too – when in good order – though the thighs have always tasted a little bitter to me, but then who am I to disagree with a Frenchman? The Germans and Danes have an almost mythical respect for the woodcock, and securing one with a success-ful shot is cause for much celebration, but if

Below: Snipe can often be found alongside small streams, burns and creeks when the ground is frosted

there are two nations who do get right when it comes to hunting traditions it is certainly these two. Americans also, who have their own slightly smaller version of the European woodcock, are arriving in ever-increasing numbers to sample the sporting delights available this side of the Atlantic pond.

British shooters of course hold this bird in high regard too, and completion of that elusive left and right under witness allows one to join the exclusive Woodcock Club, whose members gather annually to swap stories and drink to both the bird's health and sporting attributes.

I cut my teeth on woodcock roaming the Yorkshire coast where I have been based for most of my life. Indeed, almost exactly to the spot where my home is now built, I shot my first woodcock more than thirty years ago. As a youth they were my principal quarry species, closely followed by the golden plover, snipe, and the redshank in fourth place before the 1981 Countryside Act took the latter wader from us. The rough shooting permission I had access to as a youth was, as it says, pretty rough – in both quality of terrain and the resident game therein. Cliff pigeons or crossed ferals were most numerous, followed by woodpigeons, when cropping rotations brought a suitable crop in the drill to attract them. An occasional covey of wild grey partridge teased the tyro with their ability to stay out of shot, as did the snipe and plover. Hares however, were quite abundant, but it was when the November moon came, accompanied by an east wind, that we usually got the woodcock.

Their fall was eagerly anticipated each year, and for a while we would have a glut, and they would become our principal quarry species. Favoured flushing places would be explored year on year, and for whatever reason, a woodcock or a pair were usually to be found in their traditional seats. There is a holly tree in a certain wood not 500 yards from my front door from under which, when a mere bush, I must have flushed and shot at least a dozen woodcock over as many years – when the 'cock' where in.

Shooting lore tells us that the hunter's moon in November is the time to expect the first migrant woodcock to arrive, but this only holds true if the moon is late in the month and accompanied by a north-easterly wind. Basically, when the big freeze hits Scandinavia and northern Europe, look out for a waxing moon and a favourable wind – the arrival of the woodcock will be imminent.

A visit to the lighthouse at Flambourgh Head when the wind was in the east and the moon was approaching its fullness would often reveal a stunned or dead woodcock, which had flown into the light glass – mesmerised by its flashing beam. One could be sure then of a good fall of woodcock if a bird or birds where found beneath the building. Another occasion comes to mind when I think of artificial light and its attraction to woodcock. I was out rabbiting with the .22 rimfire at Sir Lawrence Barratt's Farndale estate accompanied by Raymond, the local landlord. A woodcock actually flew straight down the beam of light we were

using. Amazingly, I managed to actually catch the bird a half second before it collided with the lamp, and it was released unharmed to regain its senses.

Like snipe in my younger days, snap-shooting was the way with woodcock, and pleasant sport it was accompanied by my wayward cocker spaniel Sam. The zigzagging flight path of a walked up woodcock winding its way through the trees is much more of a difficult mark than the equivalent bird on a driven day, when he is pushed from the coverts into the open spaces between the woods. Then the bird often takes a straight path to the next lot of trees or other suitable cover, flapping by like a lazy owl disturbed from his daytime slumbers. When woodcock behave like this, they are a far easier mark to hit. If the gun secures his left and right in this way, it is no less fair play, and still an achievement of sorts, but it can hardly be considered in the same league as a brace secured by a barrel apiece, beating the birds' little jigs between the trees when walked up.

The woodcock is a fascinating quarry which, while technically a wader, has game bird status. Our population swells from 78,000 resident birds to 740,000 with migrants that blaze a trail across the North Sea from mainland Europe and Scandinavia. It is found in high numbers across all four of the home countries, and in former times a number of shoots in Cornwall were managed specifically for this bird's sporting potential. Today this rarely happens in England, though Holkham Hall in Norfolk is noted for its excellent wood-cock shooting, and is of course famous for its wild grey partridges under the custodianship of present head keeper Kevan McCaig.

Wales has its noted woodcock corners, and Ireland is still the primary destination for this species, but other than England's Yorkshire coast, it is in Scotland that I have mostly engaged the woodcock. Here the season is a month longer, starting as it does in September.

Scotland's woodcock shooting statistics are very impressive indeed. One of the Western Isles, Rassay, holds the record bag of 916 woodcock shot in a single season. However, it's the east coast that sees the first 'falls of cock' in any number. The record bag taken by a single gun – some 109 birds – was shot on Fair Isle in late October 1908 and the tally might have been higher had the gun not run out of cartridges! This was made all the more remarkable by the fact that not only was the gun used a .410, but Mr George Stout Esq. was actually a birdwatcher. A month later, again off Fair Isle, a further 127 cock fell to three guns. 1908 was clearly an exceptional year for woodcock.

In Scotland woodcock are pursued in three distinct ways. The first, 'flighting', when one or more guns is stationed along the woodland edge or junctions of forest rides in the evening, involves an ambush of the birds as they leave their safe and secure sanctuaries for nocturnal feeding on the pastures. The second, 'walked up', is when one or more guns walk in line, shooting birds as they flush. If gundogs are used they must be worked tight to ensure

Left: Woodcock crossing open areas between cover when driven often flap like owls, but walked up their jinking twisting flight is legendary

image: iStock

Above: Shooting snipe over setters is the pinnacle of wader sport in the UK

the birds rise within range. The last, 'driven shooting', is the most prestigious and the most expensive way of hunting woodcock. Similar to the more familiar pheasant drives, it is conducted on a smaller scale. Hunting areas are driven by small teams of beaters working with spaniels, the cocker spaniel being originally developed for this type of work, when many more estates across Britain managed their coverts for woodcock. Short, sharp drives

are the order of the day, often with one or two back guns deployed behind the beaters, who work through the traditional areas favoured by woodcock year on year. It never ceases to amaze me that I continue to flush and shoot a woodcock from beneath the same holly bush or rowan tree every year. I usually manage to take at least one bird and sometimes two or three over the course of the season from two places on the same estate.

Three seasons ago it was this very area on Carminnows Estate in South West Scotland that I shot three woodcock with colleague on a difficult day that will live long in the memory. This was hallowed ground, formerly part of the Earldom of Carrick and Bruce. The most famous of these earls was, of course, Robert the Bruce, who notably gave the English a sound kicking at the Battle of Bannock Burn, to become Robert 1st King of Scotland. Everyone can have an off day; things were eventually put right with the union of the crowns and later still, reinforced in a little engagement at Culloden Moor.

Conditions were favourable as we set out on an inclement morning that promised to improve. Scotland is a place of contradiction when it comes to the weather, and I have long since stopped relying on the forecasters. On low ground, I find a 'suck it and see' approach puts more birds (or fish for that matter) in the bag. Far better to just get your head down and give it a try, rather than sitting it out back at the lodge. Daytime is for shooting. Leave the evenings for a dram and a cigar.

Spacing out a few yards apart, we worked forward from the south end of the aptly named Fairy Glen behind my colleague's usually neurotic springer spaniel. The dog for once behaved admirably, quartering through the frosted bracken and stunted grass beneath the birches as if it was competing in a field trial. Reports from the keeper had said the woodcock were in and expectations were high. However, if there is one area in which woodcock are reli-able, it is that they are unreliable. If you're after guaranteed sport, you're probably best advised to head for the west coast or, better still, book your shooting on one of the Western Isles or, if it has to be England, at Holkham in Norfolk.

Sport was slow. The dog worked well, but all we managed to flush before lunch was a wisp of snipe that jinked their way across a small bog to rise vertically out of sight, completely immune to the two double barrel salvos following their flight. A late lunch was in order and a new plan conceived as we broke bread and chewed the fat over how best to maximise our chances. We decided that the evening flight would be our best option, which would entail a long walk back the way we had come and into the distant forestry plantations. Then we could only hope we'd find our quarry there, while most of their number had obviously moved a few miles out towards the coast.

We turned heel half-heartedly and began to retrace our steps when suddenly, true to form, the Scottish sun appeared from nowhere to raise our spirits. Shortly afterwards a clap of wings raised the incentive higher. A woodcock that we had obviously passed by flushed from the exposed roots of a silver birch to begin a weaving flight through the stunted trees. My compadre swung up his gun and folded the bird with a snap shot, proving his marksmanship skills were still in fine form.

A little further on, a pair lifted from the heather clinging to the glen side. I fluffed both shots – much to the amusement of my guest as he had already shot one. This was the third unfulfilled chance of a left and right at woodcock of my shooting career and I could have kicked myself. Flustered, we carried on and I finally broke my duck by taking a bird which flitted back behind me, wiping the loud one's eye in the process – he missed it with both barrels. That little trick certainly silenced the good-natured but derogatory comments from my colleague. Luck stayed with me after that, as the spaniel realised who would deliver the goods and stuck to me like a tick on a deer, producing two more flushes that increased my bag to three birds to the other's one.

Eventually, as the sun was sinking, we took our positions alongside the forestry to wait for the woodcock to come to us. It wasn't until the last of the light that we were rewarded with a woodcock appearance and for a few precious minutes, the sport was fast and furious. We had to be careful not to drop the birds in the spruces, making them difficult to retrieve, but alas, my marksmanship was not up to shooting in the shadows. After a number of shots, I had failed to connect with a single bird. Such is the sport of shooting wild birds in wild places. My comrade took two more birds with the same number of shots to successfully finish a difficult but extremely rewarding woodcock foray in south west Scotland.

There's no doubt that woodcock shooting is challenging, but that's part of its allure. When it goes well, there aren't many quarry species that come close to the pursuit of this most sporting of low-ground game birds. But it shouldn't be forgotten that some of our

iconic game birds and farmland waders are already in the sights of the anti-brigade, whose not-so-hidden agendas are beginning to leak out to the mainstream media. The GCWT, in an attempt to pre-empt any forthcoming calls for shooting restrictions, are heading an in-depth woodcock survey, which is currently a work in progress. It must be applauded for its forethought; the survey will provide concrete facts and figures concerning our resident woodcock and migratory visitors to contradict the whimsical fantasy presented by the anti opposition.

The British record bag of 249 snipe shot in one day was taken on the island of Tiree (Inner Hebrides), on the 29th October 1906 by two guns: Lord Elphinstone and Mr. J.D. Cobbold. Apparently they would have shot many more if the birds hadn't been so unapproachable due to the flooded bogs.

Rassay holds the record bag of 916 woodcock shot in a single season. The record bag taken by a single gun – some 109 birds – was shot on Fair Isle in late October 1908 and it is possible that the tally might have been higher if the gun had had more cartridges with him. What is all the more remarkable is the fact that not only was the gun used a .410, but Mr George Stout was actually a birdwatcher.

A right and a left at woodcock is always an achievement but all credit must be given to Lord Balfour of Burleigh who at Kennett (Clackmannan), had four woodcock flying directly toward him at once and he took the lot to achieve a remarkable double double in the early 1900s. **PC**

Right: The author after a good afternoon walking up woodcock with cockers in the Scottish borders

With *Teal* and *Plover*

The actual shooting of a stalked or walked-up bird, except possibly of a grouse, on the high tops in a strong wind, can never give the same satisfaction as that of the same bird driven. And yet some of the most pleasantly remembered dates in our sporting calendars have been spent walking up our game. Looking back on these occasions, it is never the individual shot that we remember, but the work of some dog, the happy fact that we were on "our day" and made a good average of cartridges to birds, or perhaps and much more likely, it was the weather, the distant snowy hills, or the sight of some clear-running burn that has left its mark upon the memory.

Far be it from the writer to exalt mechanical proficiency with the gun into undue prominence. Few desire to become mere killing machines, and for such, at any rate, these notes are not written. But in recalling many days of pleasant effort, it has surprised the writer to realise how large a proportion belong to the impromptu-drive variety, when with three beaters and two guns or more often with the beaters alone, one has attempted to outwit strange fowl-strange, that is to the "gun", to whom a goose is a goose and a duck a duck even though the later be a red-breasted merganser.

In looking back a scene at once presents itself. It is a wild day, if ever there was one, and even the estuary upon whose shores we stand is covered with waves, the heads of which are blown clean off by the gale. Above us rises a bank of sand dunes, and anyone looking over this would discover a wide terrain of bents with here and there a pool. We are also within a quarter of a mile of the Atlantic Ocean, which just now is thundering on its strands. There are the two of us, myself and a ghillie, Dugald by name, a quiet man, prematurely white-haired in spite of the fact that his fortieth year is still nearly a lustrum ahead of him. We have been out for about an hour, and up to the present have but a single teal to show for it. The teal was one of some forty which rose from the shelter of a jutting bank beside the estuary; they have flown on until lost to sight behind the high bank of the dunes under which we stand.

"They'll be on one of them bit pools likely," says Dugald. "I wadnae fire on the plovers or what-not till the teals is by. It'll tak me twenty-thirty minutes to mak' ma circle and get on the ither side." Without more words he goes and I am left alone. First of all I select a spot where a kind of terrace beneath the dunes gives me a six-foot wall of sand in front. Over this I can look as from a grouse-butt. In the immediate foreground I have a field of fire of about forty yards, beyond which the view is blocked by a large sandhill. On either side of this I can see farther where in a dip of the dunes the west wind is driving the sand and roaring in the hollows.

About twenty-five yards to the left, and all unconscious of human proximity, five golden plover are standing. For a moment I hesitate, for, as may have been guessed, Dugald thinks little of plover and much of teal. I realise, however, that Dugald has gone up-wind in order to walk round by the beach, and the explosion of a 9-inch howitzer would hardly reach him against the wind, which seems to increase in violence with every moment. Goodness, how it blows! Sweet and strong sweeps the breath of the Storm Gods from the green is-

lands of the Atlantic. The plover are facing up-wind. I show myself and as they rise, fire both barrels. Two fall to the first barrel, but none to the second, as they swerve. Then the three survivors turn and come straight over me down the wind. I have only time to shove in a single cartridge, and this I send somewhere well behind their tails in spite of all efforts to hold in front.

I reload and look round. The sound of the shots has stirred up sheldrakes that must have been resting in a bay of the estuary. Their instinct is all for the open sea, so they fly by against the wind and within easy shot. I can see the beautiful markings of the cock very clearly, but the but I have not shot a sheldrake since I was a boy, and they pass unmolested. There is still a quarter of an hour or more to spare before Dugald will be able to begin the drive. Five minutes pass, during which I see nothing but several hoodie crows and a herring-gull. Then two wild ducks, both mallards, as I can see through the glasses, fly in and settle off the estuary. They are a couple of hundred yards away, but may swim this way.

Now another and most unwelcome figure enters upon the scene in the shape of an old seaweed gatherer, who evidently intends to carry on his calling, which, if he stays in the estuary, will completely spoil all my chances. He may, however, be on his way to harvest the great piles of weed that the storm has torn from the rocks, on the seashore itself. In the latter case he will do no harm. Slowly he comes up and I accost him.

"Where are ye for?" I bawl in the wind. He touches his cap, but appears not to hear. He passes on with a tread as slow as Destiny, puts up the mallards, and finally disappears just as a score of curlew come over crying mournfully and well out of shot.

Dugald must have made his circle by now, I am sure, for though he is so far away I see some peewits rise, and then suddenly in a bunch, and travelling at express speed, the flock of teal. This time the golden plover have taught me a lesson, and I fire very far ahead indeed. Three little balls of feathers drop straight into the estuary and two more slant down upon its farther shore. To the best of my ability I picked my birds, the others flew into the shot circle. I send the dog into the water, and his efforts to find the teal, which are drifting fast, have to be aided by the throwing of a stone, an act which loses me a chance at two curlew. Then come two redshanks, wailing, and immediately after them a large flock of rock pigeons, of which I get one. And now I see Dugalds's home-wove cap at the far end of the hollow. A snipe rises and flies straight at me with incredible speed, turns, and gives the easiest of chances as he balances a moment against the tempest.

Then it is over as Dugald walks up. "I heard ye shoot," he says as he surveys the teal. "They came over finely bunched," he adds presently.

This is of course, a successful drive – one of the best, indeed, of the scores I have tried at that place; many is the time that things have gone otherwise, and the birds either have been absent or flown over the dunes two hundred yards wide. On one occasion when shooting in the half-lights, I remember a cormorant, diligently journeying over the promontory, come down to a gun who mistook his bulk for that of a greylag goose!

Another bird rarely driven except in an offhand way, but which certainly is a splendid bird to outwit in this fashion, is the golden plover. In few places is he more abundant than in the lands that lie along the Northumbrian coast. Here, as elsewhere, when the snow is deep, he migrates to the tide-edge, where he falls prey to the shore gunner, who creeps upon him under the shelter of the sea-wall and shoots at him sitting upon the shingle beside the water. At such times, however, the golden plover is so thin as not to be worth powder and shot. He is a very different bird upon the uplands and the Wolds, where his rather sorrowful whistle fits in well with the desolate skylines, and with the stormy winds that make the grass so sweet.

There are certain fields that golden plover seem to love to the exclusion of others, certain spots which they always seek when any are in the neighbourhood, and if local knowledge can point out these places, continuous sport can be obtained, when the plover are in the country, by the shooter taking up his position under some hedge on the central line of flight and causing a companion or keeper to move the plover at their chosen resorts. Thirty or forty golden plover can be killed this way in a day.

Stalking golden plover is excellent fun, but it has the disadvantage that the shot when obtained is usually into the flock and needs no skill whatever to bring off successfully.

Among waders the golden plover occupies a place of its own, and is perhaps as welcome an addition to the driven day's bag as any. This is no doubt mainly due to its culinary qualities, for as a rule a flight of golden plover sweeping over a grouse butt does not provide particularly difficult shooting. Although a couple of birds coming downwind with their darting flight are quite a different matter, and make as difficult a right and left as ever desirable.

So much for the golden plover as an incident in a day dedicated to grouse. But those who only know him thus can have no idea what a splendid bird he is when he exists, as he does on some shootings, in sufficient numbers to be made the primary object of pursuit. There are areas in the Outer Hebrides where a day may be suitably organised with no other object in view than the flights of golden plover, which haunt these windswept isles in great numbers. Here little crofts stand between the moors, the hills and the ocean. In summer great fields of grass, buttercup, clover, and various wild flowers stretch in the hollows of the dunes, and as autumn succeeds summer the wetter portions of these vast meadows become the haunt of thousands of golden plover.

The country is broken up by dykes of earth and stone, and on a windy day a single gunner who knows the lines of flight can fire away many more cartridges than he will get birds, even though he may regularly bring home ten couple still. In the remote Hebrides the plover is still often a very wary bird and rarely indeed does a stand feed up to, or a flight settle in a stalkable position. So the gunner must have with him a companion or attendant, who can move the birds or drive them as may be necessary.

In various parts of Britain, notably perhaps in Aberdeenshire, in Cumberland, and in Northumberland equally large flights and stands of plover may be seen. But in these counties they are usually only shot if a shooting party intent upon some other game happen upon an opportune flight of them. A man in Aberdeenshire shot 28 with two barrels of his 12 bore in 1910. At this time they were spending the better part of the day on the plough having first arrived extraordinarily tame.

But the stalking and shooting of plover en masse as the stand takes to flight, though usually effective, can never give anything like the sport and satisfaction that driving the same birds can confer. By this I do not mean that driving is to be preferred to stalking under sporting conditions, but these conditions are rarely provided by the golden plover.

Very rarely as has been pointed out, will he feed within fifty yards of a sea wall save when first arrived in the remote north of the Hebrides. In Hertfordshire for instance he chooses a large field and the very centre of it. When a shot has been fired at a stand their vigilance renders them safe barring accidents, for the rest of the season.

In order to be successful in driving golden plover a knowledge of the ground is of the first importance. The flocks will not frequent all fields alike, even though the feeding in them may seem exactly similar, and it is necessary for the gun to whom the birds are being driven to host himself in the field to which they are expected to come as these birds do not have a line of flight definite enough to allow much margin for error.

In shooting over decoys the real difficulty is suitable concealment for the gunner, but hidden under a hedge a few branches with dead leaves still clinging to them will usually serve. It does no harm, indeed rather the contrary, to have a few peewits among one's decoys. They serve to attract other peewits as well as golden plover and this is always a gain to the fowler.

Let us imagine it is a morning in late September. The previous day we have driven in along the coast road and have seen hundreds of golden plover in the little fields.

Now two of us, and a ghillie start out to spend the day in pursuit of the great stands of plover. Our shooting is lazy, and as the plover congregate in the fields by the road we take a horse and trap but we have not proceeded in it half a mile before a fine flight of forty or more cross the road, and after one or two circlings settle two fields away in a stalkable spot, where we two guns hasten to approach them. But by the time we have done so, the stand as usual, moved out a little and our four barrels bring down but two birds.

Our next attempt on the feathered ranks is on

an island in a loch. It entails a wade of some two hundred yards through deep mud and water. Thus then we approach so near the plover, but not quite near enough, and this stalk is in vain. Though we make the plover move to our benefit, departing in number over the dunes to a better place to stalk. The third attempt using the low dunes gets one of us within thirty yards and he gets three, while the other lying in the imagined line of flight fails to get off a shot.

And now all this manoeuvring has driven the plover inland and we two guns take our places under a dyke while the ghillie goes round to drive. In the drive are curlew, widgeon, golden plover, redshanks, and a teal. The driven birds come fast and true afore the wind and both guns make good accounts of themselves to make a good bag for all the morning's effort.

We celebrate our good fortune with lunch in the shelter of the dunes facing a foam dotted sea, and both agree that the morning has been as enjoyable as such wild work will ever allow.

I have read many books that when golden plover fly over too high, a shot fired will make them sweep earthwards. This is certainly true, but how often does the gunner gain anything by the horizontal dip? Golden plover shooting downwards in a curve are as difficult to hit as any birds that fly.

And how he captivates one's thoughts, this most soft-eyed of all birds, for the golden plover has a gentler eye than any of his kind, and nothing of the hard, darting glance common to all his cousins. Upon what strange scenes does he look in the short span of his life? He flies high over northern towns into cold mists bred about the

Pole. There during the brief summer he struts in the splendour of his black-breasted breeding plumage beside meres in wastes unvisited by man. When the time comes for his southward move, he again proves himself a great traveller. His advance guards break their journey in Scandinavia and in our Isles, but his main battalions sweep on over the Giralda Tower and Seville to the marshes and vegas of Andalucían rivers. From there he makes his traverse of the narrow seas to Africa; thus the plover that was hatched in the Arctic waste in June may in November fly over the minarets of the sacred cities of the desert.

It is impossible to think of the golden plover without remembering his next of kin, the green plover. The two species are so often to be seen together, an alliance that is all in favour of the golden plover, since the peewit is the better sentinel and infinitely the more wary bird.

There are many who do not regard the green plover as a good bird for the table, and who, therefore, only shoot them upon occasion. Yet of the so-called "golden plover" served in London restaurants and hotels, at least fifty percent are green plover. If the legs are left on the bird when it is served, it is easy to distinguish the two species as the number of toes differ, the golden plover having but three, while his green cousin boasts four. The French have a proverb to the effect that those who have not tasted vanneau (green plover) do not know how good game can be on the palate. Certainly young green plover shot in August and September are as good as almost any bird, and they are without any question wary enough to make stalking them a high art.

The green plover frequently provides a fairly easy shot, though it is wonderful how often he is missed as he flaps over. But if proper advantage can be taken of times and season, of ground and, above all, of weather, the peewit can be made to give shots as difficult as any – indeed on occasion the most difficult of any bird with perhaps a single exception. This does not, of course, refer to the stalked peewit – in that sport the fun is purely getting within range – nor to the ordinary driven bird, but to peewits as they abandon themselves to the wind and are literally blown over the guns.

You must picture an immense spread of dunes covered with little sandy hillocks and raved over by the winds of the Atlantic. Very sweet are the summer flowers on these dunes, and a scent that an islander would journey far to smell once more, redolent as it is to him of boyhood and long summer evenings. This range of dunes is a great haunt of green plover – flocks five hundred strong are to be seen for ever wheeling and settling; single birds beat slowly up against the west wind, and in the

early darkness their mournful cry peoples the gloom.

There are always some particular areas of this great stretch of dunes that the plover favour. Sometimes these are a mile apart, sometimes but a few hundred yards. If the shooter, having discovered these areas, can place himself on a windy day between them and then crawl up fairly close to a flock, while his companion walks down-wind upon them, the birds will often rise to a height of twenty yards or so and then suddenly abandon themselves to the force of the gale and, driven by its strength, pass over the head of the shooter with incredible speed.

One evening, just as it was growing dark, I happened, having returned from a long day's snipe-shooting, to be standing in the lee of a long barn, behind which a high wall running parallel to it divided the waste dunes from the farm-lands and made a barrier some sixty or seventy yards in length. On the south side stands the lodge, and on that particular evening some herd-girls were driving in cattle on the open ground to the north. A stiff wind was blowing, and down the wind, flying low, then rising and topping the barn, came about three or four hundred green plover in little flocks or singly. As the birds topped the barn, they abandoned themselves to the force of the wind, and were whirled into the gathering darkness, giving the most difficult shots at short range that I have ever seen offered.

Great execution can be done upon peewits over decoys, which readily attract them. To anyone with sufficient local knowledge to forecast their lines of flight, their evening visits to the saltings can be made to yield good sport.

I rarely see green plover without calling to mind an episode that occurred at a certain public school. In this episode a green plover played a prominent part. A youth of about fifteen, whom we will call Young Lower Fifth, was wont to pass as much time as possible of his summer and winter holidays with a gun, lying out at night on the seashore and spending every shilling of his pocket-money on cartridges. On each return to school his sporting desires had to be curbed and held firmly in check. But it happened that one wild February brought thousands of plover to the ploughs that lie between the school and the sea.

Twice a week the run, with which football was varied, passed through those fields, and in a moment of temptation Young Lower Fifth made up his mind to try his luck with the plover. This determination entailed the smuggling in of a walking-stick gun, which, disguised as an umbrella – for by the unwritten laws that may not be broken only the Sixth were privileged to carry sticks – he succeeded in bringing back after an "up town" leave. For a moment he considered the bold course of leaving it in the umbrella-stand, but prudence led him to adopt a safer if less gallant course. Finally it reposed in a cunning excavation in the wall of his cubicle in the dormitory.

A half-holiday was, of course, the only suitable occasion on which the plan so happily initiated could be carried out. After a week of waiting, a hard frost set in, football was off, and a run to the sea prescribed for the House. Here, then, was the sportsman's chance! Complete secrecy was an absolute necessity – a whisper of his intention would have run like lighting through the school, and the hardihood and very unlikeliness of the deed would have provoked enough comment to wreck a far less risky scheme. Thus Young Lower Fifth could counsel himself alone. The plover fields were some two miles out on the road to the sea, and the first step was to get the gun to some handy place. At the earliest opportunity Young Lower Fifth, having the gun ready hidden under his clothes, dashed out and cached it in the plantation beyond the football fields that bordered the same road.

The next problem was a question of time, and speed. What with dinner and call-over, it was nearly two o'clock when he started. Usually a lazy youth, it was no surprise that he should bring up the tail end of the run, and the prefect, cursing him for his slowness, hurried on to tick off the first arrivals. Meanwhile Young Lower Fifth, discouraging any companionship, by those methods that serve schoolboys so well, but which we forget in later life, lagged behind, and by 3.30, having recovered his gun, was hurrying at a very different pace on his back track. On his way home from the sea, he had noticed a fine flock of plover in a certain field beside the road, and towards this he set off with the highest hopes. When he reached it, the plover, glorious to relate, were still there, and he stalked them from behind one of the many stone dykes with which the country is seamed. He easily approached within forty yards of them and had a shot which, as his gun was a .410, somewhat naturally did not take effect! He crept on and during the best part on an hour had nine shots, all without result. He then realised that success depended on his achieving an approach within twenty yards, or even fifteen, and to this he set his mind. He had just spotted a flock in a good position, when a single plover suddenly flew over him from the west side of the road. It was quite close, and Lower Fifth threw up his gun and down came the bird. A moment later he had leaped over the wall and retrieved it, rejoicing.

It was a fine specimen, and would look well in the school museum, and there he told himself he would go and contemplate it, and it would be a "good egg". As he scrambled back into the road his heart jumped horribly, for he heard a voice shouting "Hi! hi! hi!" and was aware of a policemen coming over the hill at the double. He knew enough of the law to be conscious that no one was allowed to shoot within forty yards of the high road, and it was certain the policeman had seen the shot fired. Lower Fifth turned and fled. He could move fast enough when he wished to, and for the next quarter of a mile he made good time, but looking back over his shoulder he was disagreeably aware that the distance between him and his pursuer was not increasing. Rather the contrary. He tried to put on a spurt. The twilight was now falling, and through the clear frosty air he could hear the heavy footsteps behind perceptively gaining. At the beginning of the chase he had noticed his enemy was wearing high boots, and he realised that a man who could make good time in high boots would inevitably run him down at the last.

Lower Fifth's next move stands, I think, to the credit of his craft. At this point the road dipped and turned a hundred yards or so, and here Lower Fifth knew he would be below the policeman's horizon. A little farther on the road crossed the railway by a bridge. As soon as the boy knew himself to be out of sight, he flung himself through the hedge and down the embankment, and ran along the line until he was hidden under the bridge.

As he crouched panting in the dark shadow, he was acutely conscious of the possibilities of the situation, not, indeed, as concerned the law of the land – that of the school appeared a much more urgent matter. He had broken at least four School rules, and the face of the Head rose as a vision. At this moment a voice called out:

"Come ye oot fra' under the brig!" Lower Fifth did not budge, and the policeman plunged down to him, notebook in hand. To the demand for his name and address the boy made no answer, but a glance at his cuts and sweater told the man all he needed.

"Ye frae the Collich. I'd better be taking ye back there!" Young Lower Fifth found his voice: "Why?"

"Ye've broken the law."

"Yes and what's the penalty?"

"That's a ma'er for the magistrate."

"What's the most they can fine me?"

"About forty shillings."

"Well, I'll pay you that."

"Ye'd daur offer me a bribe!"

"There's no bribe about it. You represent the law."

"I do!" This grimly.

"But you don't represent the school. Look here —" and then Lower Fifth explained the probable results.

The policeman listened, but his face did not relax. He was a hard man, and his profession had not softened him.

When the youth was finished, there was silence beneath the "brigg." At last the policeman took out a piece of paper and wrote upon it.

"That's where I live," said he. "Bring ten shillings there by next Sa'erday and ye'll hear no more of yon shot. I'll tak' yon gun. Ye can have it when ye brings the ten shillings."

"Thank you," said Lower Fifth with great gratitude.

The hand that paid the money and redeemed the gun was a maternal one. The same hand on the same day took a carefully packed green plover to a bird stuffer by request to act as agent on the strength of the following note:

"Please take it to H—. He'll do it for nothing, because he said he would when I gave him the third little auk I found dead on the beach last month. Tell him to get the eyes right, rather prominent and darker than he usually sticks in." **HP**

The moving story of young Lower Fifth shooting the lapwing is of course a biographical account of young Prichard himself during his time at Fettes. And what a story it is, of the impetuosity of youth, enthusiasm for the hunt, and that who-dares-wins attitude, which would manifest itself in the man – who would become both explorer and decorated soldier. It is also one of quick wit, courage and honesty, very fine and indeed expected attributes of young gentlemen in those days. Once the game was up, young Lower Fifth had the guts to be forthright with the law, and had the speed of thought to confess while offering

a sensible solution to the wrongdoing, without involving the headmaster.

I wholeheartedly agree with Prichard when he says the smaller informal days are oft remembered better for events other than the sport itself. He talks of varying landscapes, good shot-to-kill ratios, dog work and the like. But what really stands out is his preference for birds being driven, but informally rather than the full fig day with shoot staff and a team of guns.

He likes his sport wild, varied and with the minimum of companions or attendants, and I'm with him on that too. Impromptu drives are what stirred the Nimrod in Prichard's heart, and it is a term used often in his writings on sport. Give him a curlew, teal, or plover, coming at him on a good wind, and one can almost sense his pulse racing and his barely contained anticipation on the brink of overflow as he throws up the gun up to fire.

His anxiety is equally expressed when an outsider threatens to spoil his sport too. The first time I read about the unwelcome seaweed gatherer, who threatened to ruin his chances by carrying on his calling, I actually laughed out loud. How often has a similar scene been played out by shooters nowadays? I grant you there won't be too many seaweed gatherers about, but the legions of hikers on hill and foreshore today would probably have caused Prichard to suffer a premature breakdown.

The lapwing, or green plover, was taken off the shooting list in the Protection of Birds Act 1954. And what a loss to the sportsman it was. Often have I been found hidden in some hedgerow, or shivering knee-deep in the questionable seclusion of a field drain, trying to anticipate the flight lines of the golden variety, when nought but its iridescent green cousin screams overhead. Tempting though it was, I always let the crested bird pass, but oh how I wished the game laws were written differently. In my area of Yorkshire the ploughs, pastures and drillings were always an attraction for legions of lapwings during the winter, and even today there seems just as many nesting pairs as yesteryear. However, it is the way of things and this handsome wader is now consigned to the history books as a sporting prospect.

Before I leave my association with the lapwing I must share an abiding memory of this bird, which comes to mind every time I'm reminded of this plover by sight or comment. It was in my very early teens on an extremely windy day that I was first allowed out alone with the old Henry Clarke hammer gun. In those early days I hadn't yet learned to shoot off my left shoulder, the better one for my master eye, and my marksmanship suffered somewhat as a result. Indeed I was a god awful shot, and a late stormy afternoon walking the turnips for partridges and spinneys for woodcock had resulted in one hare for almost a box of 25 Eley Impax discharged. Not a happy average I'm sure you'll agree. Game had been abundant and many a worthy chance squandered. The woodcock 'were in' and I jumped many from the holly groves, but their twisting flight had saved their pin feathers every time. My lack of results were further compounded, after flushing a couple of tight-sitting coveys of partridge, by committing the cardinal sin of 'browning' into them on the hope of achieving a flock shot (to help my appalling shot ratio). This was, of course, to no avail as one must always pick his bird, and the grey birds flew on saluted but unscathed.

The fall of the hare wouldn't win any sporting colours either, and I'm almost ashamed to say that I stalked and shot Sally in her form. In my defence, you must understand my grandfather – the old Sgt. Major – had supplied the cartridges, and he expected results. Ethics were not completely absent however. I well knew that 7-shot was inadequate for ground game so I endeavoured to get as close as practically possible. Back then I was more quick-eyed than crack-shot, and I had spotted puss lying squat with her ears held flat along her back,

Left: A huge flight of golden plover on the estuary. Thankfully this plover is still on the shooting list

head to wind pressed in tight between the plough rows. A laboured but dedicated stalk ensued, crawling ever so carefully along the outer furrow of the new ploughing she had chosen to reside in. Pushing the fowling piece along inch by inch before me, I was eventually within easy shot of puss. After pulling the left hammer back, the click subdued by a cupped hand, I shot her cleanly at the front end (accompanied by a whispered apology for her less than glorious exit) and from the left shoulder out of necessity, due to the angle of my position. I believe from then on I always shot from the left shoulder, and my shooting moved up to mediocre.

However, the above is a very long-winded foundation of my ever abiding memory of the lapwing. After the murder of the hare and near depletion of cartridges, I hung about in the hope some unlucky golden plover would come over my position, secreted as I now was in a long defunct semi-filled well sunk in the bank between two field margins. The hide was perfect for the purpose in hand; however, its placement was of course beyond my control and a little off the main flight line the goldies had been intermittently taking in the day's dying hour. My hope of bagging a few wayward stragglers showed a certain degree of optimism that burns bright in youth and dims with maturity. I had just pulled my things about me in readiness to leave, the rapidly descending darkness and rising gale dispelling any further hope of success, when legion upon legion of lapwings filled the sky.

Right: The green plover or lapwing was lost forever to the shooter in the 1954 Wild Bird Protection Act

Passing low over me in the buffeting wind they numbered in their thousands. If the golden plover's call can be best described as melancholic, his green cousin's efforts are more than eerie, especially in a

collective chorus that rises high above a near gale. This awesome flight lasted some time, and was really something to behold, the birds somehow managing to keep their southerly direction, although their quirky acrobatics due to the wind seemed to be a combined struggle that defied all possibility. I hastened home with the plovers about me until the glow of the street lamps forced them to gain altitude and disappear from both eye and ear, but having left a memory that will last forever.

As a quarry species Prichard was clearly fond of the lapwing. However, it was also one of the birds that were shot indiscriminately by professional fowlers who killed all plovers and kittiwakes for their feathers. Back then there was a huge demand for decorating elaborate feathered hats, as they were all the rage in ladies fashion. My great-grandfather was a professional vermin catcher at that time, and he too devoted much of his efforts to plover and kittiwake shooting outside of his normal warren work.

Prichard admired the sporting attributes of the green plover, and the indiscriminate shooting with large bore shotguns loaded to the max into the resting stands of plover was anathema to him. He lobbied hard and made much noise about it in the right circles, and penned his displeasure in various journals. A Bill was put to the House of Commons on a number of occasions, but was thwarted at every attempt by those with a vested interest in the trade. Finally, his efforts seemed they would be rewarded, after an article he penned for *Pearson's Magazine* entitled "Slaughtered for Fashion" hit the mark with the public. Prichard had also been instrumental, prior to the second reading of the

Bill, in framing and obtaining signatures to a letter in support of it, which was also published in the *Times*, and other papers. This drew support from many people of influence including the Duke of Rutland, the Duchess of Somerset, Canon Edward Lyttelton, Lord Lilford, Sir Herbert Maxwell, Sir Harry Johnston, Bishop Welldon, John Galsworthy Esq, Arthur Conan Doyle, and other notables. Unfortunately, the Bill once again was scuppered by obstruction in the committee stages and war came to Europe. However, after the war the baton was taken up by the *Spectator* and particularly a Mr. H. J. Massingham, who took a third Plumage Bill through to successful legislation, and effectively halved my great-grandfather's income. In the end it mattered little, as he was killed soon after the war by a freak lighting strike that hit the spade he was using to dig down to a rabbit during a ferreting operation, not a mile from where I sit writing at this moment.

Admirable as it was – and the result is certainly to be applauded – the Bill's hangover was the eventual removal of the green plover form the shooting list, echoes of the Plumage Bill being used to do so. Although sportsmen had hunted the bird sparingly, the peers involved in the feather trade turned the crusade against the sportsmen, and eventually had their revenge by taking the legitimate pursuit of this bird away from them forever.

Thankfully the golden plover remained on the shooting list, as it does to this day, surviving the last attempt at removal in the 1981 Wildlife and Countryside Act. This bird has brought me as much pleasure in their pursuit as the species did in Prichard's time. I took my first plover by being in the right place at the right time, which doesn't happen too often with this wary bird. It was with a fresh wind and a hard frost one late December morning in the mid 1980s. I'd taken the gun and spaniel for a walk and was working the hedges for a chance at a woodcock when I heard inbound goldies. I was at the low side of a rise with a high hedge between me and the rapidly approaching plover squad-

ron. The sun was behind me and I'm convinced it was for this reason that they hadn't seen me. My first barrel missed, but I knew I'd fallen short, and swung through harder on the second shot to fold one of the tail end birds. Four more flights in succession followed the first one, and the shooting was fast and furious for a minute or two, and then they were gone. I'd acquitted myself rather well

Below: Prichard thought the American golden plover he saw in arctic Labrador bred in Britain, but the birds are two separate races

Image: Wikimedia Dominic Sherony

with two left and rights and two singletons. It was a happy gunner indeed that day who strode into the boot room with his plover proudly displayed in the net of the game bag. Plover shooting has never been as easy as that since that first taste of success. Indeed I'm smiling and shaking my head as I write these words when I recall the many manoeuvres Holderness gamekeeper Tony Megson and I have tried together to engage this bird. Be it by driving, flighting, waited ambush, or improvised stalk, this little wader has nearly always given us the slip, and the rare taste of success was all the more sweeter for that, let me tell you.

Nowadays most golden plover shot in Britain end up in the game bag as interesting incidentals on mixed rough shooting days, grouse drives, or by wildfowlers on the marsh bemoaning a paucity of duck, and yet they are a wonderful quarry species, with a unique, mild liver flavour. As a table bird, you will require a couple as an appetiser, but the little balls of tasty, fatty dark meat are well worth the effort to prepare.

Their metallic, almost wind charm-like, but certainly melancholic whistle stirs the heart on a winter's day when the wind is fresh on your face and the game bag flaps loosely due to lack of occupants. I don't think there is another whistle like it to raise the excitement, with perhaps the exception of the widgeon's whistle, or a teal's piping. But how often does that promise gamely given by the plover turn into fruitful endeavour? With the widgeon and teal he is usually committed when you hear his whistle close by. The plover, however, is often over the top of you, or more often banking wide when his whistle stirs the blood, but

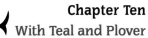
he does lift the spirits nonetheless, and to see wild game and fowl is an achievement in itself is it not? I for one am happy to tramp the foreshore, moors, ploughing and even the high tops on the chance of a fair shot, but if I do return with clean barrels – which is quite often – have I sighted my quarry, or at least seen sign, I have always been contented. How different is that to the latecomer to the sport, often successful entrepreneurs who have made their fortunes on results, who complain aggressively at the lack of action when attempting to pursue wild game. This is the killer of game and fowl, but not a sportsman, and he does us no good.

The coastline of Dumfries and Galloway follows a tortuous route from Gretna to Loch Ryan. The rivers Annan, Dee, Cree, Bladnock and the waters of Urr and Fleet, as well as numerous smaller burns, bring tiny particles of sand and clay to be deposited where the rivers meet the sea. This creates an ever-shifting sequence of mud flats known locally as 'merse'. South east of Dumfries town, the sands of Powfoot look across the narrowest part of the Solway, out toward the Cumbrian coast and the mountains of the Lake District. It was here that Edward Longshanks, King of England, crossed the firth to attack Scotland and lay siege to Caerlaverock Castle in 1300. After their surrender, he had the entire occupants bar one hanged – this lucky survivor was deliberately left breathing to spread the story of the massacre. Here, the mud has been colonised by hardy plants like glasswort, thrift, sea aster and sea spurrey, and is called home by worms and crustaceans. It is a miniature universe, feeding vast numbers of birds. Throughout the year, waders such as golden plover, lapwing,

Left: On the hills and moors in summer, British golden plover winter around our foreshores and adjacent farms

curlew, and redshank can be seen here. At one time, all these waders were on the quarry list; but alas, now only the first among this sporting quartet is still open to the shore shooter.

Until the early 1970s, wildfowl shooting and fishing were carried out here without restriction, but concerned local wildfowlers and conservationists acted together to create what is now the largest Local Nature Reserve in Britain. Wildfowling and fishing are still permitted under strict control, protecting the area's long-term future for fowlers and safeguarding economic benefits to the local community.

The Caerlaverock National Nature Reserve stretches along the coast for 14 kilometres, past the estuaries of Lochar Water and the River Nith, an internationally important wintering site for ten species of waterfowl that arrive here in their thousands. In one small area of merse, about three kilometres long by half a kilometre wide, wildfowl shooting is allowed under controlled conditions, and great numbers of Canada geese are also shot here on the opening day of the season.

My first experience of shore gunning was on the Solway many years ago when I headed to the merse in pursuit of plover. Goldies have always captivated me; they are without doubt a beautifully plumaged wader with a jinking flight that makes them a really sporting shot. Often in still conditions with little wind, when ducks, geese and other wad-

Above: The teal is our smallest duck, but provides a lot of sport and a tasty meal though an adult needs two

ers are out of range, a shot at a flight of plover will see them plummet closer to the ground, offering a second barrel chance. Prichard dismisses this ruse as mere ineffectual fantasy, but I can tell you that it has certainly worked for me on at least two occasions, indeed it happened on my inaugural Scottish fowling outing.

I was heading on to the merse in the small hours, as dawn was just blushing into life on the eastern horizon. I could already hear the melancholic call of vast stands of plover, communicating to each other, far out and unseen on the salt flats. Ghosting carefully into position, I slid into a small semi-dry creek that would provide sparse but adequate cover if I kept low and still.

Soon after, the plover murmured nervously somewhere close to the water's edge and then, with a rising cacophony of whistles, the stands lifted into flight, spurred on by the rising tide. Daylight was now upon us and my anticipation was soon dashed as the clouds of goldies followed the coast westwards and away from my position.

It was a bonny new day, but a flawless turquoise sky was not that good for fowling, and I reasoned any chance of a shot was done. I was very glad to be out, yet a tad disappointed my quarry hadn't played the game. Gathering my kit together I was about to pack up when an errant squadron of golden plover peeled away from the shoreline and headed in my direction, gaining altitude as they came. Pressing myself into the saltings I kept as low as I possibly could to avoid their wary glare, and fumbled two cartridges into the Browning. Then, swinging the gun up, I let off the first barrel with a full length of lead, but without result. How-

ever, the effect of the shot forced the flight to dive down, as plovers tend to do. I made my second barrel count, turning two goldies turtle with one shot, and the flight was gone. Both birds spiralled earthwards like stricken bi-planes, to plump into the moss not a yard apart.

Springing out of my improvised hide with an agility that defied belief, I raced out to retrieve my lucky brace. They say fortune favours the brave, but it sometimes falls on the disheartened too. Even when conditions are not conducive to sport, and motivation is noticeable by its absence, it can pay to remain positive. I had travelled a long way to the Solway and re-lived an excitement not felt since my teens. These two wonderful plover prizes completed a pilgrimage to a very special and unique part of Scotland.

This plover is to be found in most of Britain's wildest places. I have come across goldies on the high tops ptarmigan shooting in late August and early September, on the low moors of Cornwall, Yorkshire, Wales, and even Ireland. But it has been on the Holderness coast and the adjacent drillings and pastures that I've done most with this wary bird. He is vastly underrated as a sporting species, and it would be a great loss to our sport if he went the way of his green cousin and was removed from the shooting list.

The teal is our most diminutive duck, but what sport he provides, and what flavour he brings to the table! Can his gastronomic excellence be bettered by any other British duck? I think not. A widgeon on good grass comes close, as does a flight pond mallard wild fed by falling crab apple, but the teal is still the overall winner in my eyes.

I've been fortunate to have been brought up in good duck country. I live a brisk walk from the East Yorkshire foreshore; ten minutes' drive south and I'm in Holderness, latticed by myriad field drains and flight ponds. Ten minutes north and the flooded pastures and sea cliffs are right on the migration routes of our larger fowl and ducks alike. And through my years of sporting pursuit you can believe it when I say I have taken full advantage of my location.

Much fun was had walking the land drains and jumping the teal at the bends where the current was more sluggish and the high banks made for a stealthy approach. Accurate snap shooting is a prerequisite for this style of shooting, as the teal flush into what wind there is almost vertically. Two guns could make great execution if they set off from opposite ends of a drain section, and worked towards each other on opposing banks. You had to be confident with one another's shooting reserve of course, as this could be dangerous work with an excitable shot that couldn't be relied on to put safety first. He who had the wind got most of the shooting, but on a stiller day the teal, when flushed, would often follow the drain or dyke to the next gun, who was crouched waiting in anticipation, alerted at his companion's shot at the flush, or his low whistle if safety had to demand the gun remain quiet.

Of course walking the drains, and the quiet creeks and puddle rushes of the marsh, is very much a hit and miss affair. Waiting on the foreshore for the morning or evening flight is another chance affair, although carefully placed decoys do help enormously to draw duck if anchored correctly. But feeding a likely splash often returns great dividends, and one would be surprised at how small a splash suffices to draw and hold teal.

Take for instance, the small spring on Graeme Shephard's farm that I begged him to let me feed on the chance I could draw in some duck. His consent was duly given, and the wet "slap hole", a mere nine by six feet wide, one foot deep at one end, but mostly no deeper than six inches across, was fed with barley and potato peelings. The teal loved it. Occasionally we would build up a good flight of mallard too, and I along with young Will Shep would take our share when the feathers, and rapidly disappearing barley, told us we had to be on. But it was and fortunately still is mostly the teal that love that little splash. It is a place one could shoot once a fortnight throughout the season, and no flight pond should ever be shot more than that, if it is not to be ruined. The only exception to this would, of course, be if a freeze came and the puddle became nought but a pane of ice, then all shooting would be postponed.

This very same splash provided one of the most exciting nights I have ever experienced at the teal. It was a strong west wind with no moon. The abundance of feathers showed we had a good stock of teal frequenting our barley-fed puddle, and we felt it was time to reap some reward for our exertions. It wasn't a place one could gain access with a vehicle, so all the feed has to be man-hauled to it on one's back. The wind direction meant we would have to sit on the water's edge at the narrow end of the splash and shoot from a sitting position. A rough headland with a low blackthorn hedge was sixty yards to our front, with a deep drain to our left at a similar distance and open field to the

Image: Shutterstock

right and behind.

Shooting well from a sitting position, especially when one's legs are splayed, is not an easy thing to do. The best advice I can give is use your hip as you would your leading foot. It is a trick I learned on my very first dedicated teal flight on a flooded potato field many moons ago with trawler skipper and keen fowler Frank Powell. It has held me in good stead ever since. This night we knew the teal would come into the freshening wind; therefore I shuffled round to point my hip halfway toward their expected incoming direction. Will's invaluable black Labrador, Bess, provided some welcome warmth as she curled up beside me. The light was failing fast and a cock partridge somewhere out in the drilling called his covey to him. I thought his call so very fitting at the end of another day in the England's green and pleasant land. It is a sound no doubt heard around England's parishes since the landed estates spread across the kingdom at the fall of Cromwell, and subsequent restoration of the

Above: Golden plover are a wary bird to outwit but their pursuit is a very worthy undertaking

Image: Peter Carr Collection

monarchy. It is a sound that shouts out "Old England"!

But the partridge has become quite now, and a barn owl's ghostly silhouette glides past, no doubt looking for a rat drawn to our barley rations. Then, somewhere in the gloom, two snipe approach and pass us by, their "scaap, scaap" flight call receding into the distance. More snipe flit past, and then two of their kind silently spiral down to the water's edge like frosted sycamore leaves in autumn's fall. Bess is now alert, her head turned toward the tiny waders, but our instincts are harnessed. We have agreed to wait for teal, and the little ducks are not long in coming.

Their high pitched "piep, piep" alerts us to their imminent arrival. Bess is sat up, her nose straining skywards – she knows there is work soon to be done – and a "whoosh" is followed by a light splash. The first teal is in – we have been too slow. But our latent movement puts the fowl to wing, and up goes the gun and I fold a fine drake as he makes his vertical bid for freedom, though the second barrel fails to find his hen. As the cartridges are ejected Will is quicker off the mark, and he executes a commendable left and right out of a bunch of four, and issues a warning "stay" toward Bess – her quivering composure threatens a run in. But we have their line now. The fact that the gloom is now lit by a clear, star-studded sky helps us enormously to find our mark. Shooting is fast and furious with the teal coming in pairs or small bunches like driven grouse over the low thorn hedge. The engagement is serenaded the whole while by the eager "pieps, pieps" of the next flight circling in for their

barley. But too soon the squadrons lessen, and we take it as our sign to begin the pick up and be off. To linger would chance spoiling the flight for another evening.

Bess is away with a "high lost" from young Will, but she needs no encouragement and is quartering fast, doing what she does best. The game bag's empty void is soon quickly filled. Twenty two teal we have, and we two gunners and retriever are quickly away, leaving the tail end of the flight coming in unmolested. Hopefully they will build up another visiting posse, which we can be about in a fortnight's time. It has been another exciting flight at the teal in East Yorkshire.

The record shoulder gun bag for teal was shot on 6th October 1913 to five guns: Lord Lewisham, R. Anson, and Messrs. E. Meynell, G. Roadley, and the host F. Meynell shot 398 teal on the Laughton Estate in Lincolnshire.

As for golden plover records, Sir Ralph Payne-Gallway Bt. shot 90 golden plover with a shot from his punt gun. The following quote from the baronet will dispel any doubts the reader may have of the sportsmanship and seamanship involved in successful punt gunning: "To stalk in a punt a number of fowl, whether geese or duck, on broad shelterless waters, will often require the manoeuvring of a general, the patience, silence and cunning of an experienced deer-stalker, and the hardihood and pluck of a lifeboat crew, together with the cool watchful eye of its coxswain."

I can find no reliable records of green or golden plover with the shoulder gun. **PC**

Left: The author achieves a good result on the Humber Foreshore and looks forward to the culinary delights

Heath and Moor Game

What would a really experienced conclave of British sportsmen agree upon as the finest British game bird?

The pheasant would have his votes, but he is an alien. The partridge is too small and homely. We can imagine that such a company would agree on the grouse: a bird really indigenous to these islands, and then somebody would bring forward the black cock; and truly an old male, when he has assumed his full plumage, is the handsomest of all British game birds. If you add that to the extreme difficulty of shooting him, he does indeed take high place.

The season for black cock opens on 20th August and between that date and the 1st September a great many are done to death. At this season they rise regularly from the heather or from some clump of rushes, and are literally not worth powder and shot, but it is a season at which sportsmen are on the moors and it is common enough to hear men say: "Oh yes, we may as well shoot them now, later we won't get a chance." This is very much to be regretted, for black cock deserve a better fate.

The first opportunity of shooting them, when they come to their proper plumage, occurs on the stooks of the great Scottish harvest. How clever the black cock are, only those who have studied them realise. I remember well once when I was staying in the neighbourhood of the River Spean, our lodge was built upon a hill. On the low ground below it was a field of stooks, and looking out one day I saw, what I had been told I

would see, about 20 black cocks sitting and feeding upon the stooked corn. I got my gun and went down after them. It so happened that there was ground which I could take advantage of to bring me up within shot of some of the stooks on which the black cock were perched. That evening I killed a brace. It was an evening or two later that I again saw the stooks were tenanted. I once again took my gun and proceeded to what I thought would be an easy success, but when I arrived the black cock had departed. On several occasions afterwards I attempted to stalk those wily birds only to earn complete failure, and then suddenly I realised that although the lodge was certainly over half a mile away, the old cocks had their lesson, and watched for my coming. I now espied them through the lodge window, and made an approach entirely under cover, and once again I was successful. The next day I attempted to approach them in the open, only this time, instead of going on to finish my stalk, I sat down in shelter and took out my glass. They waited just long enough to have given me time to complete my stalk, and then quietly flew off and alighted upon the moor. Only once have I seen beasts or birds of the chase treat a hunter in this fashion. This was in Sardinia. The Sardinian wild sheep will often allow the hunter to reconnoitre him, and then when the unfortunate man starts upon his stalk and is hidden by the ground, will quietly move off. I know nothing more trying than when one spends three hours in approaching a ram with a fine head, to find that all the time he has been laughing at you, and has entirely taken your measure. There is no doubt whatsoever that these black cock played the same game. The wonderful thing was how well they judged the time it would take me to approach them.

On that particular shooting, where I was the guest of Lord Knutsford, there were an immense quantity of black cock, and the most delightful days could be had in driving the small woods upon the moor. For this sort of sport – and it is indeed sport – one needs the services of but one attendant, but to do it

successfully in this way one must know one's ground. About a four-mile ride from the lodge was a wood of young larch, bounded on one side by a stream and having at its western end a great sea of bracken: to the north of this rose a few Scotch firs, on the other side of the water. Whatever black cock there were were always among these firs, and a single ghillie could move them to a concealed gun as well as, or better than, an army of beaters. The first time I visited the wood I did not realise the lie of the land and so did not drive them, but on the second occasion I had them driven

to me with success. On the next, they went out at a different angle. That is one of the delights of black cock shooting. The quarry is so very clever: you cannot catch him twice by the same ruse. There were in that country a great many watercourses provided with trees, and the finest sport could be had by following these up with a gun on either side. The old black cocks used to sit in the trees and dash out, giving the most splendid shots, but one had to creep along as if one was still hunting, otherwise the birds left before you were within a hundred yards.

Late in the evening sometimes it is possible, by driving a moor, in certain favoured spots, to get a wonderful ten minutes' shooting. There was one very low heathery knoll, over which one evening at least 100 black cock flew. I would have given anything to have been on the blind side of that knoll, but unfortunately between me and it ran a large tributary of the River Spean. I had obviously made a mistake and the keeper was driving the moor to that knoll. I could do nothing, for there was no bridge within a mile.

Of course there are some moors upon which the black cock are very hard indeed to get. The cocks pack early and live, as it seems, always on points of vantage. I know one moor where they saw a pack of well over 150 black cock every shooting day, and fired at it once in two months.

It is memories of this sort of thing that account for the bad treatment the cock receives before he gets his full plumage. There are several points in the British game laws which ought to be altered, but the most crying need of all is that of the capercaillie and the black cock. The capercaillie may be shot from the 1st August, in fact he has only the protection of the Wild Birds Protection Act. The black cock, as I have said, from the 20th. If both these dates were put forward to the 15th September no harm would be done, and we should be spared those rather dreadful scenes, when cocks in immature plumage, nursing mothers, and wretched skinny fledglings, are beaten up from the heather, only to fall into it again, having presented the worst possible shots. It is equally true, although it is a matter outside the scope of this passage, that an extra fortnight in March might be allowed in certain districts of England and Scotland for the shooting of brent geese and other wild fowl, but whether such a law will ever pass, I am afraid it is quite certain that to the really crying need of the capercaillie-black cock scandal, there will be no justice. The Scottish moors are of interest to most people only for August and September, and one can see the opposition that a Bill to take away the smallest of the tenant's rights would arouse. At present, and as things are, capercaillie and black cock shooting in August often becomes the prerogative of the schoolboy, and when you think of the fine birds they would become were they but spared a little longer, it seems truly sad. Better they should never be shot at all than that they should be murdered while half grown fledglings or moulting fathers. **HP**

Chapter Eleven
Heath and Moor Game

I

Prichard would be saddened if he were to see the plight of both the black cock and the capercaillie today. The caper of course did get its own shooting season and therefore the shooting of half-grown fledglings and moulting fathers was stopped for the bigger bird, as his season began on the 1st of October. Alas, it has since been lost to the British sportsman forever, legislation removing it from the shooting list. But the last hope for this bird was its management for shooting. The protection given it by law was conversely its death knell. Bird protectionists are unwilling to control any predators in the caper's habitat, and the last locations where any numbers of these birds exist are mostly in their hands. But enough of caper doom and gloom, what about the black cock, says you?

Heath game, black game, or simply the black grouse has the same shooting season, starting on the 20th of September and finishing on the 10th December, as they did in Prichard's time. Fortunately Prichard's worries of shooting early birds in poor feather were heeded, despite the species' open season dates remaining the same. His and other sportsmen's writings condemning the ungentlemanly practice of shooting half-grown and moulting birds paid off. It soon became very bad form and a more ethical view taken towards all questionable wing shooting practices developed, proving the power of the pen when wielded by credible experts. Also of course, the austere times the nation suffered following the Great War saw the leasing of whole estates on a monthly or seasonal basis rapidly go out of fashion. Instead, shootings

Image: Shutterstock

Left: Watching black cock at the lek is one of the most moving wildlife experiences in Britain

were either leased on a long term basis (typically five or ten years), by the wealthy few, or landowners sold a number of days, keeping the management in house. This ensured almost by default that game stocks were not abused by the outgoing seasonal or monthly tenant. Stock was then managed in a more sustainable and ethical way.

It was more than fifteen years ago when I shot my first black cock in the Galloway hills of Scotland. Then there were many of these birds in the birches that bounded the edge of the heather moors, and among the new plantations.

Sadly, the birds in the area have declined dramatically, mainly due to the closing tree canopy of commercial forestry and excessive predation. Indeed, in this area numbers have halved, and since Prichard's time the British population of black grouse has plummeted a staggering 95 per cent!

Since securing that first black cock, I have followed the progress of the various black grouse recovery projects with some interest. The Game & Wildlife Conservation Trust's (formerly the Game Conservancy) director of upland research Dr David Baines is a dedicated

Right: James Folkard walks to the point on the Black Corries Moor

Opposite: The red grouse the only bird species unique to Britain

Image: Peter Carr Collection

leader in the recovery of this iconic game bird. Thanks to Dr Baines and other leading conservationists, landowners, foresters and not least gamekeepers, future generations may experience the black cock's extraordinary springtime lek (a Norse word meaning 'play') and once more enjoy a shootable surplus in the autumn.

Changes in habitat and land use have been the main cause of long-term decline of Britain's black grouse. In more recent years the maturation and canopy closure of commercial forestry plantations, which actually provided suitable habitat in the early stages following planting, is likely to have driven these declines in many areas. Once a common enough bird throughout Britain's upland birch scrub, pinewoods and moorland areas, it was an eagerly sought incidental in the game bags of both grouse and rough-shooters. A temporary reprieve in decline during the 1950s–70s was noted when large areas of the uplands were commercially planted with conifers. This provided an ideal but short-term habitat for black grouse as, once the trees grow and the canopy closes, the under-storey is shaded out. Currently mature plantations are also counterproductive as they harbour countless predators such as foxes and crows, especially in un-keepered areas. Mature conifer plantations represent the worst habitat for black grouse, for as soon as the canopy closes it provides very minimal, if any, benefit to these magnificent birds. There are many such plantations in south west Scotland today.

Image: Tiffany Chambers

Research has shown that if forestry was feathered 100 metres into the woodland, suitable black grouse habitat would be created, and directly benefit black game. The immanent clear felling of these now mature and harvestable dense conifer woodlands situated on black grouse ground will immediately increase habitat value and reduce the pressure from predators. The re-design of subsequent re-stocked trees after felling spruce plantations should include recommended measures such as widening rides, creating open ground, and thinning tree cover at the edge of compartments. This will then provide the feathered woodland edge favoured by black game. Protecting and establishing broadleaf trees, especially birch, willow and rowan, plus avoidance of planting on boggy ground to improve brood-rearing habitats, are also of high importance.

Black grouse have declined at an alarming rate: in the 1970s there were estimated to be 25,000 lekking males and this had decreased to just 5,000 by 2005. The black grouse survey in 2005 showed a decline of 29 per cent in Scotland, with 3,293 displaying males from the 4,719 estimated in the first national survey in 1995–96. However, Scotland still held a high percentage (66 per cent) of the British population.

The adverse effect of predation is not to be underestimated. This is backed up by a study from Stirling University and the British Trust for Ornithology, which states, "Predation is widely recognised as a major proximate cause of mortality and breeding failure in black grouse, with fox, pine marten, stoat, peregrine, goshawk and corvids all suggested as regular predators." Surely limited licensed control of raptors in local key areas is a sensible request for the benefit of this species? I understand that bird protectionists would not be happy about this, but why should the black cock suffer so?

Only collective efforts and wise management of Scotland's upland margins by estate managers, GWCT, SNH, FC and the RSPB – but led by gamekeepers – will ensure black grouse survival. If the sorry plight of Scotland's capercaillie is anything to go by, I certainly wouldn't entrust the welfare of the black grouse to the RSPB alone.

Most blackcock today are taken by methods of strategy and stalking, rather than by driving. Of course occasional birds are shot from the lower butts on a grouse drive, but these are shot as incidentals. The big bags, taken more than a century ago, were not organised that often. The guns had to be well briefed, and both capable and willing to crawl into their stands, and remain hidden and silent. It would only take one gun to be seen or heard to put the packs of birds out of the drive. In the days of no radios or mobile phones, the disaster of spoiling the drive would be a protracted one, as the keeper may have been unaware of the misdeed until the drive was almost over. Driving blackcock on the scale of grouse or pheasants was too risky an affair to provide with any regularity. Mini drives, as Prichard described, could be successful using a single beater, or walking gun, to try and steer the elusive blackcock over the standing gun. All

I can say is that way of doing things is still as hit and miss as it was in Prichard's time, and their numbers are considerably less.

Shooting this species over pointers only worked in the early season when the birds were young and the adults in moult, and we have already read how this practice soon fell out of favour. A few misinformed keepers, who believed that black grouse were detrimental to his red cousin, carried on shooting the vulnerable birds in this way, but thankfully a more ethical mindset was soon adopted by most.

Therefore most birds were either shot by the spot and stalk method, or by slowly walking up their haunts where the cover is conducive to getting in close to the birds before discovery. Even the famed sportsman Colonel Peter Hawker found this method the most successful:

"Being told that the only possible way to get black-cocks was to creep after them in the morning by daylight, I started off with my friend David Dinwiddie, and after despairing of seeing any, we espied a pack at feed; but the moment we stopped they flew up, although they were on the opposite side of an immense valley from the hill on which we were. After taking a long flight like ducks they perched on a plantation of larch firs, among some stone walls; accordingly, I began to creep when about five hundred yards from them, but having got to the end of my ambush, I found the distance too far; I then, in preference to firing at random, crept over the wall, and succeeded in getting to another, where I had a safe march to a breach within forty yards, with my heart in my mouth,

Left: A perching blackcock is very difficult to approach and a fast flyer, providing top sport

for about one hundred yards, I gained the point, and down I knocked him, a fine old black-cock."

One and a half centuries later that wily game bird is mostly stalked in a similar manner by the sportsman that desires him. There is no other game bird that comes even close to the black cock for caution and self-preservation. He is the equivalent of the curlew of the foreshore for wariness on hill and heath. At Glen Moy he was off-limits, but I have watched his antics there at the lek for hours. I've heard his mating warble bubbling over moors from the Ettrick Valley, west to Dumfriesshire, north to Perthshire, and east to Angus. At Glen Trusta, I have knocked him down on the forest edge, surprising him in the long heather and burnsides as I carefully and quietly made my way round. Erupting at your feet, he is a fair mark accelerating away, and if you can swallow the shock of his rising and keep your cool a snap shot makes him yours. If you miss him, you can bet your wife's virtue he's just been well educated. Try it twice in the same place, in the same season, and I'd wager an empty game bag every time, no matter how careful your approach. Better to try a different dell or burnside, or look for other game, because you won't catch the black cock out twice.

An impromptu drive sometimes works well if you know your ground but, as I've said, it's a chancy affair. Two safe guns working a section of ground towards one another can increase one's chances of a driven bird, and oh how he flies. He is certainly our fastest game bird on the wing, with perhaps the exception of the

capercaillie. A left and right at driven black cock is really something. The late great Sir Joseph Nickerson writes of this achievement in his wonderful book *A Shooting Man's Creed*, and as he was probably the greatest game shot of his generation, there can be no better testament to the bird's sporting attributes.

In the early 1990s I shared a memorable late season foray at both black game and snipe, in the Glen Kens, with a German colleague who desperately wanted to bag a British black cock. The ground was sparse of heather but allegedly a few red grouse hung on to maintain a self-sustaining population. My old springer bitch Moss was a born flirt; she'd work for anyone to a fashion. Therefore I let my Teutonic friend take her with him to his end of the beat in the hope she would deliver some game. It was ten to one against bagging a black cock. The birds were certainly there, but so late in the season they knew all the tricks. In all honesty, he would have been better pursuing black game dog-less at this time and venue. However, I thought the spaniel would produce him a snipe, or woodcock. It turned out to be an enjoyable episode, capped by some hard-won success. I shall let him narrate the event:

My first Scottish foray after the elusive black cock was in the 1990s and late in the season. Shooting at the beginning of December meant that the cock birds would be in full feather and at their best. The shooting was a walked-up affair with just me, a dog, and gun. My host had kindly lent me his spaniel, whom he said would work for anyone, but unfortunately this didn't include Germans, as the dog was oblivious to both whistle and verbal commands.

It was a cold, frosty start to the morning, with a low mist cloaking the forestry. I refrained from shooting the numerous rabbits and odd pheasant that flushed in the rushes by the forest edge. My object was to bag a black cock and I didn't want to spoil any chance of doing so by shooting at other game. The borrowed spaniel soon exhausted itself chasing the countless rabbits and became more biddable as we entered the birch scrub at the moor's edge. The spaniel then proved some worth by flushing a grey hen well within range but I let her go unharmed, having no wish to shoot a female of the species. A woodcock was flushed next and I was sorely tempted to shoot, but again I let it pass by unmolested.

Image: Shutterstock

Left: A black cock displays his powder puff lyre-shaped tail at the lek to resemble a dragoon's epaulettes

Further on and across a steep ravine I then saw three black cocks all perched in a silver birch, no doubt drying their plumage due to the damp misty conditions. Keeping to the forest edge I worked forward and hoped they would sit tight before I could flush them within range of the shotgun. It wasn't to be, as the flash of the spaniel quartering through the heather alarmed them well before it would have been sensible to take a shot and they disappeared into the distance.

A little dejected, I carried on with the spaniel working well and not too far ahead when the dog flushed another black cock almost at my feet. The bird erupted into flight, taking me completely by surprise and accelerated away skywards to safety. I was caught wrong-footed and clumsily missed the bird with both barrels. Now totally dejected, I broke the gun, ejecting the empty shell cases, and watched the black cock angle across the valley. Then the bird dipped a wing and began to beat back towards me. Fumbling with numbed fingers in the cartridge bag I slipped two more shells into the shotgun and glanced up to see the bird approaching overhead. Being much better footed this time, I mounted the gun and swung on to the black cock: following through I shot and hit him squarely, killing him well. It couldn't have been more perfect as the black grouse thumped in to the ground not a metre behind me. I beat the dog to the bird, not wanting her to damage the plumage, and admired the beautiful black cock, turning him over and over in my hands.

I have shot black cock elsewhere in Europe since then, but my first British bird taken that day so many years before in Scotland will remain the most memorable of memories.

An interesting post script to this story is my version of events. I too had been stalking three black cock perched in some wind-bent pines and, using a burn to approach unseen, had come within shooting range of the wary birds. It hadn't been an easy stalk by any means. After using an old tumbled-down dry stone wall that had fallen into disrepair to shield me for most of the stalk, I was then faced with open ground when the wall finally ran out. On my side of the stone dyke ran a shallow gutter running with water over a gravel bottom, which ran into a burn. If I could make it across the open ground undiscovered to the burn, one or more of the black cocks would be mine. Bellying into the gutter I endured the questionable pleasure of the inch deep water running through my shirt collar at various points during the crawl. In the end I surrendered myself to the water, committed as I now was to the endeavour. Eventually I reached the burn, edged myself along it, mindful to avoid crunching the frosted bracken steams and, shivering uncontrollably, I popped two Eley Grand Pix no.5s into the AYA side by side.

Shuffling up a heathery knoll I ever so carefully peered over its brow, and was relieved to see the three black cocks still in residence less than forty yards away. If the widgeon is the dandy of the tide, then the black cock must surely be his heathland counterpart. I watched the trio preen a while, taking in all their glory, iridescent sapphire-hued plumage sheened like polished marble in the misty morning. Unfortunately, admiring my quarry's finery proved costly. I had lingered a little longer than I should have, because my colleague's two barrel salute at his rising blackcock put my three birds to flight. Defeat slapped me in the face as they whirred away over the moor.

Dumbstruck I sat back on my heels and watched them go. Seconds later I was startled back into action by another approaching black cock that topped the pines coming straight for me. I raised the gun. It was the very bird my German friend had missed. But he'd seen me as I'd clocked him and was already dipping a wing to avoid me. I was too late, the blackcock was swerving away out of range when the gun came to the shoulder and I was forced to let him go. A single shot moments after said Germany

1 England 0. Wringing my shirt out, I jogged across the ground between us in an effort to get warm. I needn't have bothered because the "waidmannsheil" schnapps that followed the result quickly warmed one from the inside out as we admired the prized bird.

I haven't shot any black cock in Britain for more than a decade, but I hope to do so again in the near future when stocks allow. The GWCT and dedicated keepers have done a lot to reverse the fortunes of this iconic game bird. At present, most shooting estates quite rightly have a voluntary shooting ban on black game, but let's hope that current conservation strategies bear fruit and the black cock will once again be present in harvestable numbers. It would be a tragedy to see this gamest of birds go the same way as the capercallie and be taken off the British shooting list, never to return.

Below: On the continent black cocks are shot early in the lek but the practice is outlawed in the British Isles

Image: Shutterstock

II

The 'glorious 12th' is absolutely that: it is when the shooting season starts proper. The grouse are 'in', and so are their snowline-living cousins, the ptarmigan, and that delightful but diminutive wader the snipe. Indeed on one glorious 12th, in the nineties on the Glenshee beat of the Invercauld estate, we had the excellent luck to shoot a good bag that included all three species. Soon after grouse come in, the stubbles will provide some partridge sport after the 1st of September before surrendering to the plough. Then things really get going as October comes around, and everything is 'in', but it all starts with the grouse.

I have enjoyed some excellent days on the 12th, or indeed on the 13th if the famous date fell on a Sunday. Looking back through notes made at the time the variance of the weather is immediately apparent: from bright days in

shirt sleeve order, with a light breeze bringing the perfume of the heather blossom, whose purple carpets stretch the four points of the compass and are in turn contrasted by the deep warm green of the bilberry or blaeberry patches (depending on which side of the border one is), to days of driving rain, as bleak as a midwinter storm, when one hides in the butt out of the wind-driven wet. All have their merits in their own ways, and even shooting in inclement considerations can be just as pleasurable as prettier days because the season has 'begun'. Guns have had the dust blown off and seen the touch of brush and oil. Maybe one has had a few forays at the pigeons or 'doo's, but for most the gun will have laid in state since the 1st of February, or the 20th for the fowlers among us.

Driven grouse shooting is popularly regarded as the pinnacle of British game shooting. It is certainly the most expensive, pampered and exclusive of live quarry shooting disciplines available in these isles. There is a certain amount of snobbery involved; I guess that is part of the tradition, but often it makes me smile. On one occasion last season as a drive came to a close, one of the beaters engaged me in conversation and it quickly seemed the snobbery wasn't confined to the actual shooters and their entourage. I was shooting at Farndale with friends, a super little moor that delivers four respectable days' grouse driving most seasons, and an estate where I had once been part of the keepering team. The lovely old gentlemen appeared mortified when I informed him of my former employment on the estate. He couldn't seem to understand the estate's former keeper, and an under keeper at that, could be lording it in the butts and captaining the guns no less. It was a real 'sergeant in the officer's mess' moment. The old boy was very polite, but was clearly struggling with the notion that the grouse butts weren't all filled with big businessmen, captains of industry, or aristocrats.

Ownership of our uplands has changed much over the last half of the past century; the aristocracy no longer hold the monopoly over the heather-carpeted hills of our nation. Uber-successful entrepreneurs – or 'new' money, in old parlance – turned sporting enthusiasts have used the fickle taxation laws to buy up vast, unproductive acreages and allow a much-needed cash injection to the rural economy. Many keepering positions were retained and, indeed, other positions were created by this land change after the Second World War, when most feared a repeat of the redundancies seen after the previous war – a fact that is often overlooked. Paradoxically, it was the inheritance tax laws that saw the break up and sale of many an estate on a scale not seen since the Great War. The aftermath of that war was a watershed for the keepering profession. Many keepers had fallen at the front, and almost as many found their previous positions untenable or no longer available, as landowners addressed their mangled finances hit hard by the war in Europe.

However, those land holding aristocrats that had managed to keep their holdings together

Left: James Folkard's first grouse, but he doesn't look like he appreciates the blooding by Davy Thomas

after two incomprehensible wars led the way in what is fast becoming a real game shooting renaissance of late. From Baronet to Duke, and oilman to manufacturing mogul, our shooting estates are thriving thanks to hardworking keepers and a modernisation in management practices.

Grouse shooting was long known for its cyclical booms and busts, and grouse abundance and subsequent crashes were mostly down to Strongylosis or grouse disease. The cause of the disease is a build-up of the parasitic threadworms, passed easily in high grouse densities, quickly leading to the classic crashes when heavy infestations see the birds succumb. Thankfully, modern anti-worm treatment, initially by catching and direct dosing grouse, followed by extensive use of medicated grit during the closed season, has made grouse population crashes a thing of the past.

Since the millennium, and especially in these last few superb seasons, results have justified the investment in currency, belief, sweat and tears for many a shooting estate.

A dedicated work ethic and due diligence to the law by our nation's hill keepers, assisted by modern advances in parasite control, has at last shown the way to avoid the traditional peaks and troughs of our grouse population's abundance and paucity. This has been a long time coming. Even some of the old stalwarts of the moors – who were initially wary of these new-fangled developments – have come round to thinking that science may just have the answer. Predictable grouse shooting forecasts

may well become the norm. There's no doubt that exciting times are ahead for Britain's hill keepers.

But as exciting as driven grouse shooting is, the really wild way to engage these birds is by walking them up over spaniels, or shooting over pointers. Wild rolling moors, chess boarded by the chequered patches of varying length of heather so necessary to keep an abundance of grouse, have always drawn me. If I was born to one sporting environment, it would be as a hill man, no doubt about it. The wide open landscape, with towering hills, and glacier-carved glens and dales appeal to the wandering Nimrod. Wild sport and a couple of brace taken in the company of a skilled dog handler, to me, equals the best of driven days with the two guns, when the grouse come thick and fast.

Let the reader now accompany me and a couple of colleagues to Glen Coe on a day over pointers. The Black Corrie lodge recedes into the distance, dwarfed in the shadow of Buachaille Etive Mòr that dominates the landscape. We zig zag along the bearly-discernable hill road out towards the Blackwater. After what seems a determinable ride rocking to and fro at a snail's pace we eventually run out of road and the game begins proper.

The dogs are loosed by head keeper Davy Thomas, and we gather our necessaries about us. Filling my lungs with the clear Highland air, I take in the vista around me. Looking south the formidable desolation of Rannoch Moor that appeals to those like me, who like the wild places, stretches away to Loch Ba. The moor is

Left: Paddy brings back his bird after the runner had hidden in the long heather

dotted by myriad trout-inhabited lochans, one of which is the source of the River Etive. I follow that jewel of a spate stream with the eye; its lower reaches have provided me with double figure salmon in previous seasons. Turning my attention to the west the Blackwater reservoir is as low as it has been in living memory. Old flooded shillings and stone dykes, long since a forgotten Atlantis, show their ruins to the sky once more. North is the direction we will be heading so we have the wind on the dogs' side. Here the heather is at its finest, and rising hills repeat one after another away into the distance.

Davy is working five pointers, although one is a young bitch in its first season. Nat is brought out on the moor for her education rather than to help with the sport. Two are English pointers and three German pointers. We are three guns and two go forward with the keeper, periodically one will swap with the third gun in reserve, and the sport alternately shared. The underkeepers bring up the rear, with Mark Shone holding court with his black Labrador ever ready for any retrieving work. Mark is the neighbouring keeper from Glen Etive, my favourite place in all of wildest Britain. Under Mark's expert guidance and tuition, I have enjoyed some of the finest sport I have ever experienced, on river, hill and moor. Furthermore, as far as good company and hospitality goes, there aren't many to beat Mark and his wife Pip.

"Let go Moss", and off races the grey roaned pointer. Possessed by endless energy the German dog quarters the moor in long sweeps as we move forward, me in the rear and Ruth and

James as the leading guns flanking either side of the keeper. It is mid-September, a little late for bird-dogging, and the birds have become wild. A good covey flushes well in front, and Davy shakes his head in disappointment, but loses none of his infectious smile. Ever the optimist, he encourages us on saying "Don't worry, some will hold to the point." But the birds seemingly don't want to play, and frustratingly flush before the dogs have a chance to find them.

The going alternates from easy on the short heather, to tiring in the longer stuff, with the odd precarious burnside cutting its way across the moor to tumble into the Blackwater. Davy releases Ollie, the lemon and white English pointer dog, and he races away. It's interesting to note the different styles of the two dogs' quartering techniques. Abruptly, Moss freezes-statue like and Ollie comes in to back her up. Davy moves forward, directing the two guns as he goes, "steady" he says, almost soothingly to the pointer. With silent hand signals he manoeuvres the guns and, happy with their placement, he snaps his fingers for the flush. Moss inches forward and the covey erupt in a whirr of wings. Ruth gets off a barrel but finds there is plenty of air around a fast moving grouse, James gets both barrels away and folds his first grouse. Davy is rightly pleased and punches the air in victory.

We have a change of dogs. "Let go Lexy", casts off the black German pointer, followed by "Let go Corrie", which sends off the black and white English pointer.

This time I'm one of the forward guns, and

fluff a capital chance at a snipe in full view of the entire entourage. He rose nicely at the flush and flew straight, unusually for a snipe, but I missed him twice. Then, to add insult to injury, he began his twists and turns when both barrels had been spent. It was pleasing to see a good few coveys but the birds were wild and mostly lifted out of range. Occasionally the dogs would give a false point, marking the scent where a covey had lifted way in front, but this is to be expected. We were certainly working for our game, as were the tireless

dogs. Indeed, in the next couple of hours we, the three guns, felt some remorse towards their valiant efforts in difficult conditions, because all three of us missed grouse.

Opportunities were hard to come by and chances missed carried an element of self-inflicted guilt. Davy was the perfect host, making light of our frustration, but inwardly he must have been disappointed. But finally, Lexy made a good solid point, and it was my turn to approach the black pointer stood like a stone. A nod from Davy, with a slight wink – which

Image: Peter Carr Collection

meant please don't cock it up – and I half raised the gun as he said "get 'em up" with a click of the thumb. In went the dark dog like an arrow; up went the five birds slanting away to the side. The gun came into the shoulder, I gave the outside bird a yard of lead, and swinging I fired immediately. The grouse spun to the ground in a lead-induced feather burst. Caught full in the pattern the shot was executed perfectly, and the grouse dead in an instant.

Ruth quickly followed suit, walking into a capital point with Davy, and she took the rising singleton with textbook-like ease with her 20 gauge. Mark slipped his black lab Paddy and the big lab overran the bird, picked up the scent and turned, sticking his head deep into the heather. Emerging with the grouse, he delivered the bird to hand. Ruth's bird ended a wonderful afternoon's shooting grouse over pointers in one of the wildest areas of Scotland.

It was a small afternoon's shooting by anyone's standard if the bag was anything to go by, but it stands out to me for many reasons. The location alone would have had me quartering that moor on the barest chance of a grouse, plover or snipe. The company of the keepers involved was excellent; no one had ever been made to feel more welcome, even though our one and a half brace day could have easily been five or six brace, if our shooting was up to standard. Taking our piece in the bothy beside the Blackwater was like stepping back in time. And both Davy's and Mark's enthusiasm for all things grouse, and dogs, was good to listen to and partake in. And

sharing the day with two great friends, who had both just shot their first grouse, made it that bit extra special.

Real sport is so much more than numbers. I've enjoyed some superb driven days at grouse, some fantastic walked up days, when a forty brace day had been split equally between grouse and ptarmigan with a good sprinkling of snipe too, but that afternoon at the Black Corries ranks as the most enjoyable yet at grouse.

Black game record bags: The British record of 252 black grouse was shot during the 1860 season at Cannock Chase by 8 guns. Lord Berkley Paget holds the personal record as he shot 126 Black game to his own gun shot on that record day in Staffordshire.

The record bag for black grouse in Scotland was obtained on 4 October 1869, when 247 birds were shot by 11 guns at Glenwharrie, Dumfriesshire, of which more than 200 birds were cock birds. The guns were: H.R.H. Prince Christian of Schleswig-Holstein, Count Hompesch, Viscount Masham, Duke of Buccleugh, Lt-Colonel Gordon, lord William Thynne, Lord George Hamilton, Lt-Colonel A. Thynne, The Hon. William Home, Mr Edward Balfour, and Lord Walter Scott.

Record number of driven red grouse is: 2,929 shot on the Littlehead and Abbeystead Moors in Lancashire on 12th August 1915 by eight guns: Lord Sefton, the Hon. J. Ward, the Hon. H. Stonor, Mr. E. Oakley, Major the Hon. J. Dawnay, Capt. The Hon. T. Fitzherbet, Capt. The Hon. H. Bridgeman, and Major the Hon. E. Beaumont. **PC**

Grey Geese

In the Outer Hebrides grey geese are still resident, though, it is said – and, alas, possibly with truth – in ever diminishing numbers! Not very many years ago they nested beside the inland lochs, but now the wise birds – and where in all the feathered kingdom can you find wiser? – more generally seek some uninhabited sea-girt islet with no land beyond it but only the hill and dale of ocean, until the green and mist-hidden shores of Newfoundland are reached, realms where the greylag are replaced by their cousins, the glorious Canada geese of the West.

In olden days the greylags were regularly seen and slain in many a Welsh vale and southern country. They have their place in English history – were not the shafts of the bowmen at Crécy tipped with their feathers? And can't we imagine that the arrow tipped with the wing-pinions of a wild goose clove swifter than that furnished only with the tame? The birds in life flew high in the gale, but never so swiftly as the arrow which rushed from the string of the forest-born man when he loosed his long-distance shaft.

> *"What of the shaft?*
> *The shaft was cut in England,*
> *A long shaft, a strong shaft,*
> *Barbed and trim and true.*
> *So we'll drink all together*
> *To the grey goose feather*
> *And the land where the grey goose flew."*

The Fen country used to be a great sanctuary of the graylag in England, but when civilisation drained the marshes the geese in great measure disappeared, though to this day in favourable weather they may be seen in large gaggles flying against the sky or feeding in some spot so exposed as to be generally quite hopeless of approach.

It is probably safe to say that a very large percentage of the grey geese killed in a year come to the gun, the gun very rarely goes to them. The shelter-pit, the ambushment on the line of flight succeeded ten times for the once when stalking is the method of attack. This is a pity, for the wild goose is certainly harder to approach than the red deer stag. Also, whereas we can kill our stag at two hundred yards, we must go six times closer to the graylag.

My first bout with grey geese was sufficiently inglorious. We had, at the time, taken a shooting upon one of the Outer Hebrides, and one day we repaired to an inland loch in order to determine the species of a pair of divers which had nested there. The divers turned out to be of the red-throated kind. Their nest, so the shepherds told us, had been placed upon an island in the centre of the loch.

There was no boat upon the loch but the weather was warm – it was August – so I stripped off my clothes and, leaving my gun upon them, began a slow progress through the knee-deep water flowing over weed-grown rocks. To swim was impossible among the jagged rocks, so I continued to pick a slow course accompanied by a large and very melodious bee which made several attempts to settle on me. At length, as the water deepened, I was able to swim, and presently arrived in the lee of the island and peered over the heather with which it was covered.

The island was narrow, and I found myself face to face at a range of five yards with a large graylag gander, while on all sides his horrified companions rose with wing-music and scolding clamour. Oh for my gun, divided from me by a hundred and fifty yards of peat-blue water! But of course it was not to be and the greylags – nineteen in all – gathered force and space, swung, rose higher and, finally, headed away towards the dunes while I picked my way back full of the certainty that no bird flew as well worth shooting as the grey goose.

The rest of the afternoon was passed in a careful examination of the shores of the loch, for, as every one knows, the doings of geese can be read in feather and trail more easily than those of other birds. It appeared, however, that their visits to Loch Dunscaur were infrequent, whereas over a line of ridge lay another and much larger loch named Vausory.

This loch at its western end possessed a strand of black sand, that, taken in conjunction with the wild hills of sparse heather by which it was surrounded, gave an impression of curious and brooding menace. From its shore a high and narrow peninsula reached out a lean arm ending in a height of rocks, shaped like a closed fist. Below the first and extending about fifty paces was a space of flat shore covered with green grass. Here at last was the home of the greylags. The grass was eaten short, the black sands were seamed and

riddled with tracks and trails, the backwaters curtained by a mass of feathers. It was now past six o'clock, meal-times in our island paradise did not exist save at our convenience. Certainly, the obvious and only course was to await the return of the nineteen and others, for others there certainly were.

Soon enough heather and sod to give shelter to a crouching form were piled up around a depression in the lee of the Fist, and the gunner and spaniel disappeared from view. A little wind came and a shower from the west, then the sky blew clear. An hour passed and part of another. Far overhead a pair of golden plover flew dunewards, the sun sank and the cold northern twilight began to slay the shadows in the hills. But there was no sign of geese. It was nearly dark. A whistling of wings. Could it be the geese? Impossible. Three wild ducks came over fast and high, right overhead. The gun is thrown up, the leader found, the barrels swing. Bang! The duck crumples up and falls a hundred yards out in the loch. The temptation of that shot was too strong, but the taking of it was an indulgence. The gunner knows that and listens, but when the echoes die away all is as it was before. The spaniel, whose shortsighted eyes were ruined by distemper two years before, is taken to the shore, a stone is thrown in, she swims towards the sound. But, though Molly has no eyes of use beyond fifty yards, her nose is for that reason doubtless quite abnormal. She swims on and on, turns, crosses the wind, the stumpy tail beats twice upon the water and soon she is ashore with a

fine mallard, not yet of course in anything but very sober plumage.

Then once more the wet dog and dry youth go to ground in the heather-scented pit. And now the dark comes rapidly. Another duck passes within easy shot, but good resolutions hold firm and we hear him pitch in the water with a rush not eighty yards away. Then once more the minutes go by, the sky is green rather than blue, and the stars come out like lights behind blurred glasses. What is that? Whish, whish, three mallards coming straight over. They are five-and-twenty yards up, but look of course much higher. By this time the loch – or most of it – is shrouded in chiaroscuro.

Surely the geese will not come to-night, and the wild ducks offer a lovely shot. Better two ducks in the hand than – Bang! Bang! But we do not get two ducks after all. The swing of the gun was either not sharp enough or it was not "carried through." The first barrel was a clean miss, the second a rough-and-ready re-covery, for the last bird slants down hit in the body, but almost before it strikes the water we know and mourn our mistake. Somewhere out on the loch, with a unison of complaint and a creaking of mighty wings, a large gaggle

of geese rise. They must have pitched unseen in the water, and were doubtless swimming up-wind to their accustomed feeding-place…

We rise, retrieve the duck that has lost us our chance of the far nobler birds, and turn sorrowfully homewards – a three-mile tramp. Gloom accompanies us, as it were, hand-in-hand.

But the desire to shoot a graylag is upon us, and the sun is not over the sea-horizon before we are once more on the hills above the Loch of the Black Sands.

We are very young and very keen, but we do not know much concerning the habits of geese. Indeed, we are still a full half-mile away, when a great gaggle of at least a hundred rise from the flat under the Fist. Probably they are not unaccustomed to human apparitions, for they pitch again on the far side of the loch. Out comes the stalking-glass, and a line of approach is mapped out. We make an immense circle, first tying the spaniel in the heather with a handkerchief, and begin a slow and almost ultra-cautious approach.

There is a point which, we believe, will bring the gun within forty yards of the geese, and by steady crawling the spot is almost reached when there arises a sudden and heart-sickening clamour, as, with all the angry conversation so characteristic of startled geese, the great gaggle wings into the air. What can have put them up and off? A moment later that question is answered. A shepherd appears walking on the skyline. On that occasion, at least, we deserved success.

And now follow days and nights too tedious to write of, though glorious in memory. Morning often finds us on the hills. Once we await the incoming of the geese at dawn, in fact we spend hours in the shelter-pit. Only once do we see the geese, and that is one evening when the whole party are picking Alpine strawberries in the garden; they pass "honking, clamouring in their flight," fifty fathoms high in the blue.

The lease of the shooting is drawing rapidly to a close when one afternoon, accompanied by the ladies, we go out to shoot the Loch of the Black Sands for duck. By half-past four o'clock we have finished, and we sit down beside the Black Sands to make tea. We have previously examined the haunt of the graylags, only to find they have deserted it for some time. The kettle boils, and we are sitting, cups in hand, when quite suddenly, and quite low over the hill behind, sweep a dozen geese. We spring for our guns – my comrade reaches his – but on sight of us the greylags have turned, and are swinging rapidly away. Too far! A charge of No.6 rattles loudly against the feathers, and two days later we have departed, baffled, beaten, for the south.

And now we must skip thirteen years, during all of which I never saw a graylag, though I killed many other kinds of geese, both in the old world and the new. Often, indeed, at divers times and by various camp-fires, when the geese had been "plenty" and the luck kind, my thoughts had turned to those British-bred greylags, upon which I had been, so to speak, entered, and I wondered if it would ever be my lot to try them again. I hardly thought so. Thirteen years is a long time. It seemed unlikely, for, from all I heard, more and more gunners, in search of sport, were with each year taking passage in Messrs. David Mac-Brayne's steamers and defying the terrors of the Little Minch. Molly was gone, at the ripe old age of fifteen, to the happy hunting-grounds where leashes are not. Her place had been taken by a succession of her offspring of both sexes, one at least of which gained fame. But in the year 1909 I was presented with a Labrador whose acquisition revived a keenness for the shot-gun which had for years vanished or burnt low before the stronger fascinations of the rifle. If I had been told at the time that I was taking the Hebridean shooting for Sinbad, I should probably have denied the charge *in toto*, but looking back now I must admit that the big black dog was perhaps not without his influence. "To most of us," says Lord Buxton in this connection, "our geese are swans," and I can frankly own that I am happier when my dog behaves well and my shooting is not all that it might be, than when my barrels are straighter than usual and my dog does not reach such standard as is his. Shooting without a dog is truly the egg without salt – an insipid business.

I will not describe the journey to the north and then to the west, or the joy of remembered scenes which even the quick roll of the good ship

Lapwing was powerless to destroy in its entirety. Let it suffice that we arrived on the evening of August the first.

The morning of the second was spent by my companion E. and myself in walking over the portions of the shoot which lay near the house. All was excellent. The marshes, the dunes, and the bays seemed as full of game as ever, but a question as to the geese elicited from the ghillie that "he was not thinking they go any more to Vausory now." Vausory, as I have explained, being the Loch of the Black Sands. This was sad, but

definite.

About four o'clock my friend E., who is both ardent and well skilled, departed to fish one of the lochs, while I, accompanied by my wife and the ever-faithful Sinbad, went for a stroll on the dunes. Of course a gun went too. It was our intention to walk down to Scolpaig Point, and on the way the dunes were "full of in-popping rabbits and up-flying gulls." There were also great flocks of green plover and curlew, the former of which swung high above us, while the latter, the scouts, spies, and watchdogs of the tide-side, fled to sea-surrounded sanctuaries on our appearance.

After walking down the long line of hillocks which abut on one of the farthest-west cart-tracks in the Hebrides, we came out in a great field of potatoes growing in the sand, and, passing through these knee-high, arrived at a final dune, from which the ground falls away into a wide flat plane that here extends to the high bents of the Atlantic sea-edge.

The plain of this early August season was rich with delicate bluebells, and here and there the short sweet turf was dotted with sea pinks and blowing cotton-flowers. Beyond it lay the blue sea, and the silver wonder-strand of the bay. The evening was so beautiful that the truth is we were not troubling ourselves very much about the presence of game, and, for the time, plover and curlew were quite minor interests; but a single glance at the flowered plain caused us both to sink down, while I quickly take out my telescope. What are they, those numbers of dark grey forms standing out there in the centre of the flat? Greylag geese, and over one hundred and fifty of them.

But what is to be done? The geese are in the centre of this large open plain, with not a vestige of shelter within half a mile of them. We have a 12-bore shot-gun and two cartridges loaded with No3 shot, picked out from among a handful of No.7s. The wind is off-shore, we know nothing about the line of flight which the geese, if disturbed, will take. There is nothing for it but guesswork. Nevertheless, I point out to my wife a low outcrop of sand behind which I mean to try and conceal myself, while she attempts to drive the geese to me. We separate, and Sinbad and I, with the line of dunes between us and the geese, hurry on our way. A long run and a cautious crawl take me to my hiding-place, that proves to be a ridge about two feet in height, along the top of which the rabbits have burrowed out a regular warren. There is exceedingly little cover, and knowing, as I do, that I must be, as far as the geese are concerned, very near their skyline, I dare not raise my head. I lie flat on my face in the bents, Sinbad has curled himself up in the trough of a rabbit-hole. While we are waiting several rabbits come out and play, frisking and gamboling within a few yards. And now a few minutes pass, and then I am suddenly aware that the geese are on the wing and coming straight at me. Are there any

of my old friends among them? They say a wild goose lives a score of years, so there well may be! On and on they come, not fifteen yards high and straight for me. Forty seconds more and a brace, at least, will be mine. But, as they near me, one bird and then another notices something which is not as it should be; indeed they can hardly fail to see me from the elevation they have attained, and the few handfuls of bents which I have scattered over myself do not sufficiently hide it. The geese divide into two bodies, one passes to each side; those on the right are nearer, and of then one, a big gander, is nearer than the others. He is but a little less than forty yards off. As he comes level I fire my first barrel at him. But he gathers himself up and, with slower beat of pinion, carries on; nor is he stopped by the second barrel, but he separates from the rest and heads at right angles away over the dunes. He does not clear the summits by more than a yard or two and is then shut out from sight. But no searching, though we search both long and carefully, reveals him. I go home wishing I had never fired, or had swung a little quicker, or any other of the many wishes that crowd into the mind of one who wounds or kills to no good end, and whose victim becomes the prey of hoodie or of black-back.

Now, almost every day we saw the geese, sometimes on the plain, sometimes in the cornfields, or again upon the shores of the estuary, or even out at sea. I do not know how many hours E. and I spent in pursuit of them. We had agreed never to fire unless comparatively sure of success, a promise nobly fulfilled by my companion when he put up a couple of hundred of them, the near-

est at little over fifty yards.

We lay for them in the corn, losing as we waited chance after chance at teal, duck, plover, and pigeon. Once I spent three hours within a hundred yards of them, and then at last came success.

It had been a dreadful day. My diary says, "pouring rain and storm and mist," but towards afternoon the wind chopped round and there shone out one of those blue hours which heaven vouchsafes us only in the Western Isles. The laird, E., one of the ladies and I set out after the geese, news of their whereabouts having been brought in by a drenched horseman early in the afternoon.

We were still over a mile away when we discovered a large gaggle of them, some gathered upon the highest point of a peninsula which thrust out its weed-hung flanks into the ocean. The peninsula itself was capped with short grass and its few acres contained a couple of lochs, one so near the sea that after a gale from the west its surface was covered with great sailing pinnacles of foam, formed of the "spume and spindrift of ocean." E. and the laird at once set off, as there was good cover right up to the geese, while, having placed Mrs. E. as a stop on the dunes, Sinbad and I lay down behind a rolling ridge and waited for developments. The geese rose wild before the stalking-party and presently headed straight for us. They were coming down-wind at a tremendous pace, and being high in the air perceived the ambush, but not in time to save the leading bird, which died in the blue from the effects of two barrels of No.3 shot. The majority of the birds

passed quite low over Mrs. E, and had one of my companions been in her place a right and left was more than probable.

Luck, of course, never comes singly, and on the way home we found a large flock out on the "plain." While the ghillie and the laird drove these, E. and I took up our places in the dunes. Once again the geese came my way, and one was dropped in the estuary where Sinbad and I spent the early hours of night in search, for it had driven ashore among a maze of islands.

And now our luck with the greylags had turned indeed. On the following day A. drove them to me and I fired two long barrels. The shot-at bird, a magnificent gander, a very father of geese, left the flock hard-hit and disappeared "among the solitary downs," nor did search reveal his corpse. Yet when presently, seeing the "postie" on the hill, we hurried back for our mail, it was to find the gander had been picked up by a passing herdsman and by him deposited on the round grass-plot in front of the house.

The next casualty which occurred in the gray-lag ranks was due to a most remarkable shot with a .303 rifle. The flock were resting on the sands when A. pressed trigger and flicked out the brains of an old gander at a little over three hundred paces. He said, with due modesty afterwards, that he doubted if he could do it again! And with that shot let the story of our campaign against the grey legions end. We got many others, but never one but costs its quota of effort and tried the qualities of the stalker. Skoll to the grey goose! Skoll to one of the most sporting birds that fly!

Year by year they say that the numbers of

greylags lessen. Whether this is really so it is hard to determine. My experience runs contrary to this opinion, as on my last visit there were certainly three geese to every one that I saw on my first. This state of affairs was possibly, however, largely due to the fact that a keen goose-shooter had taken the adjacent shootings and with them an island for many years peculiarly beloved of the graylag tribe. Doubtless when he stirred them up there they came to us, and when we pursued them they returned to him. Moreover, we found that when he left at the end of August the geese also left almost immediately, nor in the latter part of September did we see them save on a single occasion when, one day while sailing we were driven by contrary winds out of our course, we fired at a curlew in the vicinity of Goose Island. Straight-way some hundreds of the great birds arose from its salty lawns and that evening were seen in our cornfield, but before the next dawn had returned once more into their sanctuary.

The grey goose's nesting-places have never been shrouded in mystery as have those of certain other birds. As far as Europe is concerned, it breeds in Norway, in Russia, in Denmark, and in Spain, nor is it other than common in the East, though there it is supposed by some to be represented by an allied form, but as far as the British Isles are concerned it has been, like the Celts, pushed ever farther to the north and the west.

In the far north of Scotland, and in the Western Isles there are still wilds where the grey goose constructs her enormous nest, which measures as much as eight to nine feet in circumference. She lays her eggs upon a lining of down plucked from her breast. The pairing takes place in May, and this season, with that occupied by the hatching of the eggs, forms the only period of the year when the grey goose of the Outer Hebrides are not gathered together in flocks. This is no doubt caused by the occurrence of the moulting-season in mid-July, when for some days grey geese totally lose their powers of flight. Fortunately at such times they are protected by the Wild Birds Preservation Act, or it is terrible to think what damage might be inflicted by a single crew of fishermen who chanced to stumble upon some moulting colony, and for this purpose the same spot is visited year after year with the utmost conservatism. The moult is not of long duration,

and the birds have been seen strong on the wing in the end of July.

Few sights are finer than that of a great flock alighting. In the air the glory of their flight lies in its strength and in the wonderful formation of the feathered phalanx, but once a single cautious bird has alighted, watch the rest swinging and swooping in aerial gymnastics which one would fancy all too light and undignified for such grave and revered birds. They swoop and swing like plover, and then, as they begin to feed, mark the short alert step, and, above all, mark that sentinel in whose care lies the safety of the feathered republic. Often I have lain watching geese for hours at a time. Once I saw a sentinel remain unrelieved for fifty-five minutes. They may remain longer, certainly sometimes the period is shorter, for I have known the watcher to be relieved three times within the hour.

There he stood on his point of vantage; presently some other birds came feeding towards him. One of them stood up, and the sentinel resigned his duties and vanished into the private life of the flock. I have never seen the sentinel goose ask for relief by plucking at a comrade with his bill, as some observers record, yet of one thing I am certain, the geese understand each other, and I verily believe converse together.

We have seen, then, that in summer and early autumn, that is from August 15th to the end of September, grey goose or graylag goose shooting is a delightful sport; but as the year closes, and in January and February, the pursuit of this finest of all British fowl reaches its height. A great number of migrant gaggles – both greylags

and white-fronts – from the north arrive, and the keen hunter may see numbers of geese in the day though he may not bag one at all. In Uist, as elsewhere, winter changes the face of the land. Gone are the meadows of clover and of flowers, the reeds upon the lochs become black and the level of water rises. Cover disappears, or at least all cover that has life does, until one is left with nothing but the rocks and the dunes and the irrigation ditches, the last full of water and only to be used by the very keen.

Still, it is at this season when the winds rave over these treeless isles that the goose-shooter comes to the height of his desire, and can spend day after day with his telescope and shot-gun among the dunes, beside the lochs, or laying out upon some island among the sands of the Sound, where his long vigil may at length be rewarded by the geese feeding in or coming in with the tide. Such vigils, however, often entail the spending of four or five hours on the islands, as, when the tide rises, the most frequented of these are cut off by deep water from the mainland.

There are many ways in which geese may be hunted at this season. First of all, there is driving. Graylag geese, and white-fronted geese, in winter, when the lie of the country is at all in their favour, are the most difficult of all British land-loving fowl to outmanoeuvre. The qualifying adjective "land-loving" is necessary, in that the vast tracks of open sand and mud beloved of the brent render their pursuit with a shoulder gun with any reasonable chance of success often quite out of the question. Grey geese, on the other hand, feed largely upon the short grass, such grass as grows upon seaside golf-links, and so it is that some-times the hills, knolls, and hummocks play into the gunner's hand and he obtains his reward. But first and last grey goose shooting means much work, discomfort, and exposure for few shots. The old ganders and geese are as much masters of their feathered squadrons as any German General acting according to plan.

In February 1912, several gaggles of grey geese were to be seen every morning upon the Big Bog. They always took up the same position, one with open and level ground upon every side for half a mile. There, in perfect safety, they were wont to allow the gunner to approach to within 500 yards, when they rise and defeat him.

A certain amount of careful watching at length proved that, firstly, the geese were most plentiful upon the bog at dawn, and, secondly, that shortly after that hour they were in the habit of flying towards Paible over the low dunes, whereas at other times, and notably later in the day, they flew out towards Dunscaur, and the hills and lochs of inland Uist.

About a mile from the marshy sanctuary of the geese their early line of flight took them over some low dunes. Here we placed a line of butts, constructed with care. There were four butts: one was under the wall of a cattle-fold or "fank"; the next was a mere hole upon the top of a dune sixty or seventy feet high, and shaped like a castle pudding; the remaining two were carefully placed about a hundred yards apart upon some more level ground which extended to the shores of an estuary. We were two guns four times, three guns once, and one gun upon no less than eleven

occasions. The line of goose-butts was fortunately not far from the house, but, even so, it took some determination to rise by candle-light and fare forth in the dark to spend an hour or so while John Macdonald went round and stirred up the geese from the Houghary, or farther, side. Also luck was peculiarly unpropitious. On the one oc-casion when we were three, one of us fired a high shot, the geese passed on, but later in the day, a small boy appeared with a large gander which, he said, had fallen from the clouds into Paible Loch. Had we always been three guns, or even two, the tale might have been different and the tally also, but towards the end of the time it was left to me alone to carry on and, morning after morning, anything from one hundred to three hundred graylag geese passed over the butts, but never the same butt, and only once over the occupied butt. One morning, as I strained my eyes from the Castle-Pudding butt, two splendid lots of geese came over the Fank butt quite low. Thinking the others would follow the same line of flight, I rushed down, put off another gaggle by so doing and, when once safely behind the Fank wall, had the chagrin of seeing a lot of five birds pass exactly over the Castle Pudding. In fact, on the whole eleven mornings I only fired once, and then without result, nor was there any morning when between two and three hundred geese failed to come, and usually they came low. In a word, the campaign ended in their favour.

When September is nearing its end, the opportunities of graylag shooting reach their height. At this time of year the geese – if they have been properly treated – have contracted the habit of spending the night on the stubbles and in the patches of uncut corn, which wisdom and cunning will leave for them. They spend the day either by the lochs in the heathery interior of the island, or upon a peninsula which forms the most westerly point of Britain. Thither they fly when disturbed by the carts and cowherds at daylight. As the sun sinks, and long before it grows dark, the geese come down to the cornlands, although they are too wary actually to alight on the stubbles; they take up a position in the open plain within half a mile from whence they watch the farm-hands, until at 6 or 6:30 they depart. Then the geese begin to walk in towards the corn. By lying up before the first gaggle arrive, a shot can be obtained if the area of corn is not too large. But once the shot has been fired, the trick can never be repeated with much chance of success except by moonlight. On the whole, it is better and wiser not to shoot the geese in the corn too often, but rather to study their lines of flight to and from it. More especially is this the case when first the geese come to the corn. They should always be left alone for a week, after that they will bear a good deal of persecution before they will allow themselves to be driven away. Ducks are the

same in this respect.

I have never killed more than two grey geese at a shot, though once, when on the promontory, two of us fired our four barrels at five incoming graylag and dropped four. Only once have I scored a fair right and left at greylags in Britain. This was on occasion of a drive when we put up the geese from the estuary towards the corn. But sitting up one night, at dawn I killed a single goose which flew over, and the moment I had reloaded another which had been disturbed by the shot. I have no idea what other people have averaged with graylag geese, but personally any day when we got a goose at all was a red-letter day, and the best snipe or duck shooting was considered well lost. This point of view, of course, is apt to elevate grey-goose shooting to the plane of big-game hunting, than which it is certainly a more difficult performance. To stalk a hundred grey geese, possessed of two hundred eyes, to within forty yards will call for more skill in stalking than the approach of the wildest four-footed beast to within one hundred and fifty. It has occasionally happened that gunners, disgusted at their failure to approach geese with a shot-gun, have gone up against them with a Mannlicher

or Mauser rifle, and have thus got a bird or two by firing at two hundred or three hundred yards. This course is absolutely fatal to the shoot. Graylag geese are quite aware of the range of a shot-gun, and it does not take them long to appreciate that of a rifle. But, as geese loathe and hate the unexpected, it takes a very few bullets whistling over or among them to cause them to develop a dislike for the country and area in which such things can happen. In a word, they go. Nor must it be forgotten that, at the seasons when graylag shooting is at its best, it is very unlikely that many shooting tenants will be in the north, so that the geese can usually attain a sanctuary. This makes for good, as not many greylags can survive the Small Holdings Act. For years geese return to the same spots, but when on their return they find Progress, in the shape of a croft, upon the ground once dedicated to the sea-wind and themselves, they accept the notice to quit. So they depart and seek new isles; but the supply of new isles is limited and the geese suffer. It is not shooting that is so disastrous, but the fact that in July, when the birds moult, there is a period of days when even the old ganders cannot fly. At such times if they meet man their lot is hard indeed. The fact that to kill geese in July is against the law may or may not weigh with the individual fisherman, usually not at all, so he lands out and beats the young geese on the head with an oar – the parents take to the water where they are pretty safe; but these happenings are for the geese economically unsound, and they are being pushed ever farther to find new sanctuaries where they may conduct their nesting in peace. Apart from all else the human race owe a deep debt to the graylag, for unquestionably he is the parent of all our domesticated geese. Hybrids between the wild goose and the tame are common in the Hebrides.

The early morning is undoubtedly the best time for getting a chance at greylags. It is not difficult to find the places where they pass the night, and a careful study of the ground will give the hunter some idea for a successful approach.

Thus I remember one island where a gaggle of eight greylags were used to spend every night. This island at its western end developed into a promontory perhaps five hundred yards in length by three hundred in breadth. In the very centre of this lawn of short grass the geese were to be seen every morning. During the night there was ample evidence that they patrolled the entire promontory, but daylight always seemed to find them one hundred yards from any possible approach.

Along the north side the dunes rose six or eight feet above the edge of the shore, and it was therefore an easy matter to approach from that side, yet, owing to the fact that the geese were always careful to remain in the middle of the ground, to attempt a shot was useless. Two or three times I got within one hundred to one hundred and fifty yards of these eight geese. When the sun had been up a short time they always rose and left, but in the opposite direction, and never along the same line of flight. I noticed, however, that they always flew east and across a channel of the sea to the mainland, but, as I have said, their line of flight was never the same to within a few hundred yards. The problem now was how to narrow their flight so as to ensure as far as might be their passing over a certain point. I decided to make two scarecrows and set them up in the dark on the edge of the bank, about two hundred yards apart, and then take my place between them. The paper scarecrows were made and tied on sticks, and well before the dawn I arrived to set them up. Now, I should like to be able to say that the ruse was crowned with success, but, as a matter of fact, I had just arrived at the point where I intended to set up my first scarecrow when the geese, moving for some reason earlier than usual, flew clean over me. Hastily dropping the scarecrows I cocked my gun and fired both barrels at the huge indistinct birds. There was a satisfactory plop, but only one, and the geese never while I was there returned to let me try my scarecrows, though I often saw the seven that once were eight through the glass at other points of the shooting. **HP**

In the century that has passed since Prichard first engaged 'grey geese', their fortunes
have been very much reversed. The greylag
especially has chosen to dominate much of our
countryside and that of Europe. Many more now
are resident and choose to stay here in Britain
rather than migrate back to Iceland. Even in my
childhood the breeding range of the greylag was
restricted to north west Scotland – Prichard's old
haunts. But thanks to introductions of wild stock
by wildfowling clubs (initially in the Lake District),
and an increasing tendency for migrants to turn
native, this goose has spread rapidly these last
forty years with a staggering 140,000 British-
breeding birds, swelled by a winter population
approaching 90,000 from Iceland.

The other grey goose that provides many
fowlers with sport is the pink-footed goose.
Its numbers have increased enormously too,
although in my area along the Humber estuary,
a succession of unfortunate poisoning incidents
due to wheat seed dressings in the late 1970s
reduced this bird's local population significantly.
However, its numbers have since risen, especially
on the wash, and many of the surviving old Humber birds were thought to have changed their wintering grounds from the middle Humber to the
wash. In excess of 365,000 birds now winter with
mixed populations migrating in from Spitsbergen,
Iceland and Greenland.

Our last grey goose on the shooting list is
only open to English fowlers. The white-fronted
goose has a wintering population of 15,500
birds, with 13,000 from Greenland (orange bills)
and the remainder from Siberia (pink bills). This

*Left: A sizeable skein of
pink-footed geese join a
large gaggle of greys on
an inland stubble*

handsome goose is fully protected in Scotland and Ireland, and under a voluntary moratorium in Wales. As such he can only be engaged in England.

It is the first two species, however, that will provide the most sport for the shore shooter and inland fowler alike. We will have to travel back almost three decades to the first occasion I engaged the smallest of our quarry goose trio, the pink-foot.

I had traveled up to the Solway, not long after passing my driving test, full of youthful excitement, with a gang of Bridlington fisherman, who made a regular pilgrimage to the firth's goose grounds. We would be staying in a ramshackle old caravan somewhere near Glencaple. The journey north soon passed with much goose talk.

As we were nearing our destination, our cavalcade of three cars passed a field of winter wheat close to the firth, absolutely full of pink-footed geese. The numerous gaggles were constantly joined by more skeins until the combined numbers resembled that "grand army of geese" that BB would often refer too. Taking the initiative, I turned the car around and headed back to Annan with the idea of securing a bottle of malt. I had decided to seek out the farmer and request a crack at the geese, which must have been hammering his crop something terrible. The whisky, I felt, would probably help any negotiations.

After a couple of false starts I found the relative farm house and the young Sassenach bearing gifts was received like an angel from the Lord, and permission duly given. The normal plan of engagement was to cover the creeks and foreshore at flight time, or on the moon if it was favourable. We had three goose decoys between us; these were usually more useful in buoying spirits and raising hope then actually decoying geese. But they would be necessary for tomorrow's foray.

The geese had apparently been feeding every day for the past week on the larger field. A long, weather-beaten and wind-angled thorn hedge straddled a dry ditch, and split the wheat field into two unequal halves. It was here that we would have to secrete ourselves and hope the three decoys drew the pink-footed legions into range of our guns. John Stevenson was using a 10 bore, Tony Morris an 8 bore, me and Andy Lee I believe were using our standard 12 bores. I cannot remember what the other couple of hangers-on were using, or indeed their names.

They grey dawn was already paling fast into a new day when we started hacking into the hedge. For reasons of time we decide to put two guns in each hide, and halve the work. This was soon done, and Tony set up the token decoys as I applied the finishing touches to the hide I would be sharing with him. Now Tony isn't a small lad, indeed he isn't just simply a big bloke; he has shoulders like the green Marvel comic hero, and I soon wished I'd hacked our shared space a little wider.

Anyway, what was done was done, and squeezed in tight we both bent back and snapped off the few hawthorn twigs that impeded our view, or threatened to spoil our swing. Job done, the guns were loaded and placed handily, daylight is upon us, and the flask opened for a quick warming cup of tea.

The tea however is quickly tipped into the ditch as the "wink wink" of approaching pinks sees mugs changed for guns. A huge skein of geese approach fast and begin to whiffle down in a ragged spiral, accompanied by a shrill medley of "wink winks" right in front of the gun line. We wait until the paddles are lifted for landing, and all rise as one picking a bird from the multitude of choices. The fusillade sees half a dozen or more geese fall to the big loads. Due to my cramped position, and the deftness of my colleague rising – which defies his frame – I hadn't managed to get a shot. Tony's 8 bore had, however, delivered him a goose.

Image: iStock

Above: All geese fly deceptively fast but their take off and landing often look difficult and laborious

John's yellow lab Lady was cast off and courageously retrieved every goose to him, before the next skein soared over the horizon from the Solway Firth. The goose noise increased in volume and hearts hammered as the Icelandic squadron turned to spiral down in a crescendo of excited goose conversation. This time I was the quicker one, and had two down before Tony could rise. The report silenced the feathered horde momentarily and the feather-flapped air was replaced by booms as my colleagues on either side opened

fire. A similar return as the first wave saw Lady in action once more. The fallen quickly recovered, we waited anxiously, eyes and ears straining for the next incomers, but then, disaster.

A van pulled up in the distant road and a chap started walking towards our field. Geese were flighting inland on either side of us, and the next skein could now be heard inbound. But the Barbour-clad apparition, who was now rapidly approaching our position, put off the geese in spectacular style. They gained height and parted into two great skeins to pass by high and to either side of our ambush. Not seeing us at first, he stopped at the decoys and scratched his head before looking sheepishly either way and deciding to lift our decoys. It was testament to our camouflage that we remained unnoticed. But he couldn't have been a high achiever because there were enough goose feathers from the fallen to arouse suspicion – indeed it looked like a pillow case had burst about the decoys. A challenging "Oy" from one of our party saw him drop the plastic imitations like they'd become electrified. Looking like a rabbit caught in a lamp he pottered over and sheepishly engaged us in conversation. Apparently the farmer usually let him shoot the land and he'd come to check out the complaints of excessive goose activity to find three lost deeks. Personally, I rather think he looked at the deeks as "windfall" rather than "lost", but who knows. Anyway, he was polite enough and lingered just long enough to ruin the best of the flight before taking his leave.

Watching him recede into the distance we hoped for a straggler or two, but as he'd returned the deeks to their position with, shall we say, a lack of finesse, I didn't have too much hope of a result. But the usurped fowler hadn't even made it across the field when a single goose flying as high as three telegraph poles veered onto a course that would pass right over the hide occupied by yours truly and Tony. It was a job for the 8 bore, and as there wasn't time to stand, my hide partner raised and swung the monster before its 'boom' shattered the scene to silence. As the black powder smoke cloud dissipated I

heard wind rushing through feather, and looking up saw, to my horror, the big bird hurtling earthwards and into our position. "Incoming!" I cried and tried to move. Tony had realised too that we were in a dangerous place and, both trying to heave our way out, we succeeded in becoming stuck together in a flurry of blind panic. There was nothing else for it but to adopt the brace position and hope for deliverance. The goose smacked into the hedge and drilled a hole through the dense thicket of thorns to smack into the earth not two inches behind us. The force split the goose's breast in two, and there was little doubt if one of us had been hit it would have been terminal. And that, dear reader, was the end of one of the best flights I have enjoyed at the great legions of the pink-footed goose.

The biggest grey goose in these isles, and the ancestor of all our domestic geese, is the greylag. I have pursued him by various manoeuvers across much of my home country and across Scotland. Stalking a goose with a shotgun is, as Prichard points out, very near an art form and most often the result is abject failure. He has the eyes of an eagle and a bent towards self-preservation that equals the curlew and black cock. He says that most fall by letting the greylag come to the gun, rather than the gun coming to the greylag, and I concur. But without decoys this too is essentially difficult. Close observation of the bird's habits is the only way to increase one's chances of success. Many times I have tried, by crawling along drains and dykes, to get under their flight, but how many times have they passed

Image: Peter Carr Collection

wide, tantalisingly just out of range. One must never shoot a long-range goose with the 12 bore; these grey sentinels of the sky deserve better treatment.

My most memorable flight at the king of geese was close to the Yorkshire coast on Demming Farm. An old spring there is surrounded by gorse and rough cover, and is often flooded in the winter. Two seasons ago a good number of greylags had chosen to rest there by day, arriving soon after dawn. Their habit was quickly noted, and one fine December morning the trap was set. Graeme Shephard, the farmer, and I covered either side of the long splash, and we both pressed into the willow and gorse cover as an improvised hide. Like clockwork, the high pitched "hooonks" followed by "aahng-ahng-ung", heralded their immediate arrival. Crouching even lower I waited anxiously,

hoping they would come in. Swerving left at a steep angle the skein of twenty or more swung round the big willow and lost height. Changing my footwork to better engage their direction I was spotted, and with a clamour the skein frantically tried to gain height but the Remington auto was already in action. Unfortunately I hadn't given them enough lead and managed only one bird on my third and final shot. Graeme, however, put on a fine display and had two for his two barrels and one more for a quick one cartridge load – it was an eye wipe in grand style.

Eager to do better, I fed the shotgun with the required three cartridge reload just as the next skein arrived on their landing approach. I left the first shot to Graeme this time as I was badly positioned for a shot. I had to turn but another singleton was mine, to Graeme's –

you've guessed it – two. I did manage two from three out of the next skein, but my colleague had put on a fine display and shot five from five. It isn't often one can outwit the grey goose like this without decoys, and despite my erratic skill with the gun on that day, it is still a happy memory, though I am heartily tired of the leg pulling every time goose shooting comes up in Graeme's company. He certainly likes to get mileage out of my marksmanship, or rather lack of it, but it was certainly a memorable morning flight. **PC**

Seals
on the Tide

I

The grey seal (*Halichoerus grypus*) is the largest of British mammals, that is, of course, provided we omit the whales. He is indeed a glorious brute, living upon and around the most inaccessible rocks and skerries, or on the Pembrokeshire and other coasts, in gloomy caves. If there is anywhere a rock upon our western or northwestern coasts, many a sea-mile from the mainland and exposed to the full battering of the Atlantic, it is more than probably visited by grey seals.

Such a spot is Haskeir, a rocky islet so difficult of access that during more than five months, every day and night of which we were ready to start at any hour, we only succeeded in landing upon it twice. Those two landings were worth the trouble and the waiting.

Since that time it seems to have been my fate to see a great deal of the grey seals both in the Outer Hebrides, in the Orkneys, off the coast of Donegal and at another place in Ireland, which I will not particularise, lest some unworthy being, carrying murder in his hands, visit it. I have also met and pursued the *grypus* in the Fro Islands off Trondhjem in Norway, and have seen his big dog-like head excite terribly the Eskimo of Labrador.

But here it is my wish and my intention to deal with the grey seal as he appears in Scottish waters.

First of all, then, few people realise his bulk. He may attain and even exceed ten feet, and his weight turn the scales at six hundred pounds, and even more. He goes by a variety of names – Atlantic seal, sea-horse, sea-bear, horse-head, the great seal, the Haskeir seal – and to him or rather to his female we owe the origin of the mermaid legend.

Scott makes reference to the great seal. In the "Lord of the Isles" we find the lines:

*"Rude Heiskar's seal through surges dark
Will long pursue the minstrel's bark."*

And in a note to one edition of the poems the following:

"The seal displays a taste for music, which could scarcely be expected from his habits and local predilections. They will long follow a boat in which any musical instrument is played, and even a tune simply whistled has attractions for them."

I tried on several occasions the effect of music on seals, and no doubt it is among the many things that arouse their easily awakened curiosity. But being no musician the critical faculties of the seals may have been offended: at any rate I met with no great success.

The subject of the grey seal is one instinct with poetry and legend, and I will write on it as fully as I may in the hope that here and there will be a reader to whom my halting words may bring back or suggest something of their existence on the ultimate Atlantic rocks and isles. After all, it is unlikely that even the few will do more than visit the haunts of the grey seal, whereas I have lived and slept for a week at a time upon the rocks on which they breed, and have watched time and again the sudden emergence of the bear-like head, a rock-cod gripped firmly in the incurved yellow ivory of the huge teeth, and seen the great bulls doing battle for their females, challenging each other with their bellowing and most mournful cry.

The beginning of my acquaintance with the grey seal was made through the rifle, for when Mr. J.G. Millais was writing his book on British mammals, a complete series of grey seals in their different pelages was necessary. The British Museum could not supply the want, being themselves almost entirely unprovided, so, having an adequate excuse, I hunted *Halichoerus grypus* far and wide.

Any of the species, save a mighty bull, has for years now been safe from my rifle. But it is a fact that the fair stalking and killing of a really big bull on the rocks is quite as difficult a form of sport as shooting mountain game, and the recovery of the trophy is always uncertain, for rocks are small, tides rise, and seals are slippery; also, bad boat-

men are undeniably obstacles to success.

The first grey seal that I ever saw was upon the rock, Lagan Maskeir, off North Uist. We had approached in a boat with all the caution that we could drill into the lobster-fishers who owned her, and after a crawl over limpet and seaweed we reached a point of vantage on the low flat rock. In front among a medley of boulders, which are covered at high tide, were exposed some acres of weed and pool; on the farther side of these and across a narrow channel a single seal was lying upon the outermost skerry of Lagan Maskeir.

Accustomed as I was to the aspect of the common seal (*Phoca vitulina*), the bulk of his mighty cousin, now seen for the first time, fairly amazed me. As a matter of fact, he was not a very big bull, certainly not above seven or eight feet in length, but he must have weighed more than twice as much as the largest common seal, which rarely exceeds six feet in length or weighs over 200lbs. This seal before me may have weighed 400. But it was only for an instant that I had opportunity of observing him, for, disturbed by the Gaelic voices of the lobster-fishers, who were backing their boat from the rock, he plunged into the water, and when he appeared again his head made a mere blot upon the sapphire surface of the sea. Here he was joined by another seal, but both were so wild as to render an approach within 300 yards impossible.

The rocks, or rather the two separate groups of rocks, known as Haskeir lie exposed to the full force of the Atlantic, some seven and a half miles north-west from Griminish, the north-western extremity of North Uist or the Long Island of the Outer Hebrides. Between the two groups is a channel of the sea about a mile in width, and the five bare grassless rocks which compose Haskeir Eagach, or Little Haskeir, are all divided by deep water. The grass-topped cliffs of Haskeir Na-meul, or Great Haskeir, rise to a hundred feet above the sea, and upon this rock or island scarcely half a mile in circumference is a spring of fresh water. "The derivation of Haskeir," writes Mr. Erskine Beveridge, in his admirable work on the historical monuments of North Uist, a book which must always remain the standard work on the subject, "is obviously Norse representing haf-sker or deep-sea skerry."

The one end of Haskeir, the Reverend Donald Mc-Donald of North Uist informs me, is according to local tradition known as Ottair's Castle, and the other end as the walls of Crimmon's House. He adds that, although it is impossible to establish the historical identity, or even existence, of either Ottair or Crimmon, yet local opinion favours a Norse origin for the name of Ottair and allows him to be the mythical Odin, husband of Freyja.

There is no shelter between the western Uist coast and Newfoundland, and the winds blow there as they rarely blow elsewhere, so that for many days after our arrival on the mainland, Odin's Isle – I like that mythical derivation – remained unvisited, until at length one morning just before dawn a red-capped lobster-fisher threw pebbles at my window to awaken me and, when I rose and looked out, shouted to me the one word "Haskeir." An hour later we were aboard the huge stone-ballasted boat and taking turns at the sea-oars to row her over the oily swells. She progressed through the water as a saw makes its way through knotted wood, and over our heads the northern sun beat down through the thin atmosphere and awoke decaying odours from among the stones at our feet.

Slowly, almost imperceptibly, Haskeir became enlarged. As we approached it, and while still five or six miles off – for we had started from Scolpaig, a thirteen-mile row – the rock was wrapped in a mirage which made it seem to hang two hundred feet above the ocean. At length, however, the slow monotonous rowing was abandoned, for a slant of wind blew up out of the east and helped us considerably upon our way. Before it died down, we were within a mile of the main rock, and now with word and gesture we impressed the necessity of a silent approach upon the red-capped lobster-fisher and his mates. They agreed, in voices that rang across the water, and we made for that point of Haskeir Eagach from which, if the approach be noiseless enough, a shot may be obtained at the seals basking upon a flat rock which lies at its foot. But when we arrived, the rise and fall of the swell, although by no means great, caused the inevitable outbreak of Gaelic gabble, and a thumping and smashing of the boat-hook against the rock. In another moment we leaped ashore, but not before the seals were all in the water.

Of the tragedy that occurred next there is no need to write. Suffice it to say that my companion went very near to getting a magnificent bull, which he shot, and which, had it not been for the amazing incompetence of the boatmen, he would certainly have secured. Later in the day, having spent a long period in watching the seals, which held to the surf on the Atlantic side of the island, my companion shot a six-foot male upon the main island. As I hoped to visit the rock again I took the precaution, before leaving, of washing away the blood from the place where this seal died. After which we set forth upon our long and wearisome return to Uist.

There can be very little doubt but that on this occasion my companion would have retrieved one of the splendid animals which he shot had the boatmen been of the most ordinary calibre. But they were terrified of the rock; and, even in our irritation and anger, it was amusing to see how much more cheerful men they became when their

boat's nose was once more pointed towards the Uist dunes.

My next visit to Haskeir was paid about a fortnight later, and for it I had the good fortune to secure the services of a really admirable set of boatmen. This time we started from Houghary, and after running out of the rather dangerous channel between the reefs at the mouth of Houghary Bay, headed off for Haskeir in fine style. It was a very calm day and we had to row every mile of the twelve; not once was there wind enough to fill our patched brown sails. Still as the weather was (and indeed as it had been during the two previous days), the swell had not subsided and was quite heavy as we neared Haskeir. In face of the same conditions, the red-capped lobster-fisher and his mates would have denied the possibility of landing. Not so the Houghary men. There was one among them, Donald McClellan, quite the best seal-hunter I have had to do with in the Hebrides.

With him at the prow, the boat was manoeuvred to the point on Little Haskeir where we had landed on the occasion of our previous visit. Here, without pause, he sprang on to the rock, where a moment later I was beside him. The crawl up was under cover and quite easy, and on the top of it I raised my head by imperceptible degrees until I could see the flat rock upon which I hoped to find the fathers of all the Haskeir colony asleep. There was the rock, full in sunshine, but not a seal upon it.

"They haf been frightened, they haf gone!" said Donald. "Perhaps they shall be found on Haskeir Na-meul. When they are killed there, they come here; when they are killed here, perhaps

they go there."

So we entered the boat and rowed across the mile that main separates Little from Big Haskeir. On the main rock we effected a beautiful landing, and Donald and I crept along its surface until, among the puffin holes, we found a pinnacle of rock from which to spy. The boat had gone into hiding. Silence reigned, save for the occasional outcry of two great black-backed gulls which circled and laughed fifty yards above us.

In seal-hunting the tern, the black-backed gull and the oyster-catcher prove terrible thorns in the side of the stalker. The curlew often give the alarm; but so restless are they, and sometimes at such a distance do they fly before the approach of danger, that their warning passes unheeded. The

black-back and the tern swoop and scream above the stalker, their shrill anger an advertisement to all and sundry that all is not as it should be. As to the oyster-catcher, he is of all birds the most persistent, and will follow the intruder upon his domains, hovering within ten feet of his head and screaming his alarm and disgust with hardly a moment's cessation, literally for hours.

But black-backed gulls, if you give them time, will often transfer their attention elsewhere. Besides, they frequently swerve and laugh over their prey or their food, and thus discount their power of communicating uneasiness to other creatures. In the present instance, Donald and I lay still, and in about a quarter of an hour's time the gulls swung away. The wait was not unpleasant, for the sun

struck warm and I had plenty of opportunity to spy the beaches and bays on the shoreward face of Haskeir for seals. This is always a long business, as the rocks are dark, uneven and gloomy and sometimes a seal will go upon them, or even upon some ledge of the cliff of Haskeir itself at high tide, and remain there until the tide rises again and lifts him off it once more. In the black shadows of the cliffs which surround these ledges a seal is very nearly indistinguishable, at least this is so if he is of the black-coated variety, or even of the marbled. But on this particular day the telescope disclosed

nothing, and when the gulls had ceased their clamour we crossed the central chasm of Haskeir and were almost immediately aware of a fine bull seal which had risen quite unconscious of our presence near the rock. After looking about him lazily for some moments, he dived again, and I ran at once to the spot where I thought he would appear, while Donald signalled the boat to be ready to pick up the seal should I succeed in killing him.

In the present instance the bull grey seal or *grypus*, as I have come to call him, rose within fifty yards of the rock and began to swim very slowly along in the most favourable possible position for a shot. The boat was out of sight of the seal, but I could see the men ready to pull to the spot the instant I gave the signal. Donald must have lain down, for he was nowhere to be seen. After the seal had been upon the top of the water for some seconds, I fired. The brain of a seal lies very far back, almost though not quite as far back as that of a walrus. On this occasion the shot, which was a very easy one, was successful, and I do not think that the seal could ever have felt the swift and merciful passing from life to death. Donald bounded to his feet and waved his ragged cap in wild gesticulation, a strange figure against the gaunt and gloomy background.

The boatmen, in answer to his signals, plunged their oars into the water and came like a champion four-oar towards the spot. Meantime the seal rocked gently in the swell, which here was very slight, and the crimson patch about him grew ever wider. I had run down to the nearest point, a ledge some ten or fifteen feet above the sea. Had I not been certain that the boat would retrieve him, I would have taken no chance, but have jumped in, swum to the seal and held him up till their arrival. But Donald assured me that the seal would float, and I was pretty certain of the fact myself; also I had no change of clothes, and it was a case of jumping in "all standing," since the time necessary to unlace a pair of shooting-boots would enable the boat to come up. And so the golden opportunity passed away. The seal had sunk a little, but I verily believe would have floated for five or six minutes more when the boat drew alongside. The captain of it, a man well used to seals, shot out his

hand; but at the same moment a well-meaning member of the crew seized the boathook and, instead of bringing the boat to the seal, attempted to bring the seal to the boat. I shouted in horror, as I saw the wood of the boat-hook thrown across the body of the seal. Donald, too, raved on the rock. But it was all too late. The voice of the captain came up from the boat. "I had him, I had him by the hand!" And then the boat backed away and there began a period of useless staring down into water a hundred fathoms deep. At this moment the voice of Donald:

"There is another seal! Shoot! Shoot! Shoot at once!"

But as the seal which I had killed had disappeared, a resolution had formed itself – never again would I shoot at one of these glorious creatures as he swam in the deep water. I had seen five killed and four lost. Unless I could shoot them on the rocks I would never again fire a bullet at a seal of Haskeir, So the seal which had showed itself, and which looked like a three- or four-year-old, was permitted to depart. Then once again the boat went out of sight and I lay upon the eastern cliff of Haskeir and watched the seals sporting in the surf below. Although they were at no great distance, a shot at them, as they raised their huge heads in the crashing swell, would have been a criminal folly. They were not much disturbed though rather uneasy, as, though the shot had been fired towards the other end of the island, it is not many hundred yards in length.

I had a splendid opportunity of watching the grey seals fishing and feeding, and one which at any other time I should have enjoyed more; but on this early afternoon, the loss of the bull, which lay dead upon the sea-floor of the Atlantic, had produced that sense of utter depression which the loss of a fine trophy coupled with the useless destruction of a fine life inevitably inspires. And this I could not shake off either then or during the homeward voyage. One thing I determined. I would yet kill the grey seals I desired, but I would either shoot them on the rocks or in shallow water, if a haunt of the *grypi*, where the water was shallow, existed round the British coasts.

During the rest of that season in North Uist there was never a day calm enough to land on Haskeir again, and from a couple of visits to Lagan Maskeir a clean rifle was brought back; for although seals were seen, they were out in the deep water.

After this a number of years passed during which I was fortunate enough to discover in Ireland a haunt of grey seals such as I had dreamed of, but naturally enough the desire to kill a specimen on the scene of my disappointment remained strong. It was this, in part, which took me back to the Heb-

rides twelve years later. I went there in August in the sure hope that one day, during that month or September, the weather would permit me to land again upon Haskeir Eagach. But the good boatmen were gone and even the lobster-fishers had departed, and although I made arrangements with their successors, the weather was never, in their eyes, favourable enough to allow of the venture. Certainly it was an extraordinarily stormy year – so stormy that about the time of the annual fights, when the seals mate, the parties of males driven from the island rock came farther inshore than usual. Thus it was that, for the first time within the memory of man, numbers of grey seals came fishing round the bays of the Uist mainland, a state of things of which we took advantage.

One day early in September, on a calm morning, following three or four days of equinoctial gales, a friend[1] and I went to a mainland bay in which I had seen several small *grypi*, but none large enough to shoot, a week or two earlier. A point of high duneland, ending in a promontory of rock, formed one horn of this bay, and gave shelter

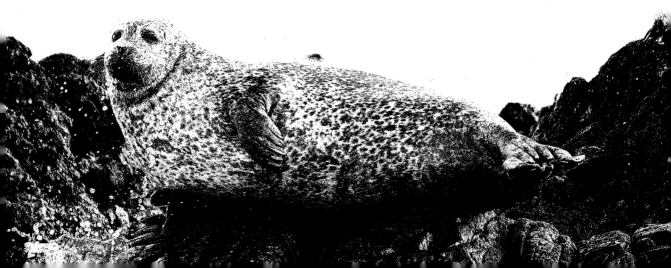

against the winds from the west and north. It was from this vantage-ground that I had seen the small seals. We made our way to this promontory on the morning in question, and lay down while still afar off, on a sandhill, from which we used our telescopes.

"I see three seals!"

"I see four!"

"I see five!"

"One looks like a *grypus*!"

"And a bull!"

"He is a bull!"

After that it did not take us long to get across the intervening turfland and stubbles and out upon the high bald dune, above the bay.

Here once again the telescopes were brought into play and, after five minutes of careful spying, the exact situation became clear. There were five seals, all of the grey species, at a distance of from one hundred to two hundred yards from the beach. Of these, three were small animals, while two looked like mature specimens. The large white spots upon the neck and breast of one of these larger animals shone in the sunlight, while the other was of the black or marbled type, it was difficult to tell which, for when their skins are soaked with sea-water both colours look very much alike. There was no time to be lost, and A. and I tossed for first shot, the coin falling in my favour. We then stalked round to the sandhill lying nearest to the rock on the beach from which we had decided to fire. Here we paused for some moments, as the seals were not making long dives and seemed to be quite undisturbed. There was now a distance of some eighty yards entirely devoid of cover which

we must cross, but in order to do this without being seen it was obviously necessary to wait until *all* the seals were under water at the same time. This, of course, was precisely what did not occur; and at last, as the seals seemed to be edging away from the land, we seized an opportunity when the only seal on the surface had the back of his head towards us to run down to the edge of the water. Arrived at the rock, I put over the safety bolt of my rifle; and as I did so one of the small seals rose within twenty yards of me. As we were well hidden and the wind was favourable, he did not perceive us, and after him the seal with the white-spotted neck arose about a hundred yards out. I was thinking that I had better shoot at once when the large black-headed one came up also. To shoot at either, when both were up, would have ruined my companion's chance of a shot, and while I waited for one of them to dive, I saw a figure show for an instant above the skyline about half a mile away. Now on that morning we were expecting G. to arrive from Oban and had left our man David at the house with instructions to bring him down to join us at Seal Point.

Although we were very well hidden, to G's eternal credit be it said that he espied us, and realising that he was on the skyline, and might be visible to the seals, lay down at once. Soon the spotted seal dived; and after waiting an instant I fired at the big black fellow, and put the bullet through his brain. At the point where I killed him the water was not above fifteen feet in depth and the wind was right on to the shore, so that I felt an agreeable certainty that we would succeed in picking him up. This feeling grew stronger and stronger as I realised that he

[1] *Capt. A.C. Gathorne-Hardy, who died gloriously leading his men at Loos in 1915*

was floating beautifully and drifting inshore. But after the one glance at him, I turned my attention to await the reappearance of white-spots. A. was nicely in position before two of the smallest seals rose almost simultaneously, and one (getting the wind of the blood from the carcase) dived with a resounding smack. Then farther out the large head of white-spots appeared, bobbing up and down on the swell. The seal was in a standing or tread-water position when my companion's unerring bullet entered its head. It sank at once, but in an even better position (as far as depth of water was concerned) for ultimate recovery than mine.

As we had no intention of shooting any of the other seals, we rose from the rock in time to see David, who had begun to strip with cries of delight the moment my seal was killed, come racing across the sands and rush into the sea. Meantime the black seal was drifting steadily in, although the water had nearly closed above it. The gallant David reached and seized it by the flipper and dragged it to the nearest rock. It was a bull and measured 7 feet 5 inches from the nose to the end of the flippers in a straight line, and just under 8 feet when the tape was taken over the curves. Having hauled this seal up the sand to a spot above high-water mark, we next turned our attention to A.'s. Although it had sunk almost immediately, the wind being right on-shore and the tide rising, we had every reason to believe that it would not take very long in drifting ashore, unless it should chance to become wedged under a rock. Even in this event its recovery at low tide, with the aid of a boat, was almost a certainty. So – very pleased with our good luck – we went off to get a cart in which to take the seals to the house.

On our return with a commandeered farmyard vehicle we found A.'s seal lying on the edge of the water. It proved to be a splendidly marked female 6 feet 11 inches or 7 feet 5 inches in length, according as the measurement was taken. I was unable to get the weight; but she was undoubtedly heavier than my bull, and it took the united efforts of four of us to hoist her into the cart. Her skin was one of the most beautiful ones that I have seen.

The temptation to swim for the seal which may have been killed or seemingly killed, at a time when no boat is handy, is sometimes very strong; but it is certainly an unwise and risky thing to do. I remember a case which occurred at the same spot that I have been writing of in the same year. On that occasion my wife had shot a nice young grey-seal bull. The distance was fully 150 yards, and the approach and shot did her the greatest credit. The bullet (from a .275 Mauser) seemed to enter the brain; and as the shot had been well and coolly timed to the moment when the seal's lungs would be full of air, the animal floated splendidly. The water was not deep; but though the wind was favourable, the tide was falling, and A., with an instant and most chivalrous realisation that this was probably the first grey seal ever shot by a lady, only paused to tear off his coat before he plunged into the water. Being a powerful swimmer – clothes, boots, and all – he soon reached the seal; whereupon, as it seemed to be slowly sinking, the three of us on shore who had not gone in, but had contented ourselves with saying that A. was a fine fellow, began to aid him with shouted directions and advice.

"A bit to the left!" we all yelled in chorus, when the voice of the swimmer boomed out over the water:

"Yes, that is all very well, but the creature isn't dead!"

A. drew off, and the seal suddenly began to splash and wriggle; finally it disappeared. Not many hours later it was driven up quite dead upon the sands of the bay. The bullet had passed through both eyes. I think there can be very little doubt that a wounded seal would be an exceedingly nasty antagonist, and that to take any risks of this kind would be almost certain to end badly. A man could not survive a single one of the wounds such as I have seen inflicted by the gigantic ruling bulls on the bodies of the smaller Haskeir males.

As all seals killed in the water are shot in the head, there must be a considerable number of cases in which they are momentarily stunned, and it is from this fact that the danger arises. I remember with great distinctness the case of one enormous bull which was shot in deep water by a companion. As there was no hope of the boat reaching him in time, and my companion could not swim, I had begun to take off my clothes when the seal suddenly recovered and made off. It rose two or three times as it rapidly put half a mile between itself and the rock, nor after that did we see him again.

It is not a difficult matter, once one is sure that a seal is dead, to bring it ashore; for although it may be a very heavy animal it is easily supported

in the water. This is nevertheless always a dirty business, as the seal bleeds very freely and there is no swimming position in which it is easy to keep clear of the blood and oil. It is not a bad plan, if one makes up one's mind to swim for a seal, to take out a handful of stones and throw them at the carcase before approaching it too closely. Dogs can occasionally be trained to retrieve seals, or so it is said, and although my Labrador, Sinbad, will swim out to a seal and do his best to pull it ashore, yet, unless he is fortunate enough to happen to catch it by the flipper, he is very apt to drive the carcase under water in his attempts to get a hold of it. No doubt he could be taught to take a seal habitually by the flipper, but one does not shoot enough seals for this sort of fancy work. Still he did once fairly save a seal which would otherwise have been lost. This was a five-foot-long specimen of the common species.

The absolute lack of knowledge, or rather of accuracy, which is to be met with among fisher-men and others who have spent their lives in seal-haunted waters is amazing. No wonder the statements on points of natural history obtained from such sources are regarded by many with scepticism. A Uist man, who certainly knew a good deal about seals, again and again stated positively that there were three kinds of seals in those waters: the Haskeir seal, *Halichoerus grypus*; the bay seal, by which he meant *Phoca vitulina*; and the offspring of the inter-breeding of the two. The fact that the grey seal brings forth its young in Novem-ber, whereas the common seal does so in May, and that the common-seal babies can swim at birth and those of the grey variety not for three weeks, made no manner of difference to this auburn-bearded student of the herds of Proteus.

From time to time I have seen it stated that seals can be killed with the shoulder shot. Once, in the days of my youth, I tried this shot at a com-mon seal which was lying some five feet above the water, upon a rock. I am perfectly certain that the bullet sped true, but the seal reached the water and was never recovered. Again and again, in shooting stags, sheep, or any other game of the land, one sees an animal after its heart has been shattered by a soft-nosed bullet, gallop forward fifty yards from the spot where it was struck, and then collapse quite dead. This convulsive rush in the case of the seal upon a rock would certainly enable it to reach the water, and once in the water a dead seal is hard to recover.

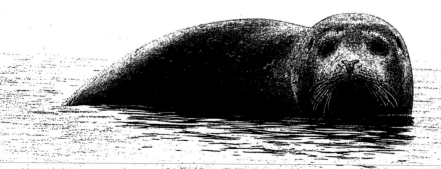

A seal should be shot through the brain, and, provided the right spot be hit, a solid bullet will do all that is necessary and will not spoil the specimen in the horrible way which is inevitable when an expanding bullet is used. As to the most suitable rifle for this sport, it is a very open question. Personally, I fancy a .256 Mannlicher; but anything in skilful hands from a .300 rook rifle to a .350 Mauser would not be out of place, although the last is unnecessarily heavy. In seal-shooting it should be an invariable rule never to fire until you are fairly certain, not so much of killing your beast as, should you do so, of recovering him afterwards. It is, I think, quite a legitimate thing, and does no harm to the race, to shoot an old male when occasion offers, but those who pursue grey seals may expect hard work and little success. Fortunately many of the haunts of the *grypus*, such as Haskeir, the Scilly Islands, and certain favoured resorts in Wales, are in the hands of private owners, who protect them as *far as they can* with enlightenment and ability.

II

It is a perfect day in August – a day upon which the worst of sailors might even enjoy the crossing of the terrible Little Minch, that dread threshold to the delights of the Outer Hebrides. In these islands of Britain, we are – some of us, at any rate – forced to pay for our pleasures: the North Sea guards the reindeer and the salmon, the elk and the trout of Norway; the Irish Sea the snipe and woodcock of Kerry and Mayo; but neither can promise a more appalling experience than the Little Minch on a really stormy day. Well can I remember standing on the deck of the *Flowerdale* – strangely inap-

propriate name! – as we heaved and tossed off Ardnamurchan, when a voice, one of two that were carrying on a conversation behind me, said:

"When he got sae far, he wouldn gae on and face it. He left the steamer at Canna, and was housed for sax days in a croft. Oh, man, there's that in the Minch that would drive a Navy sailor frae his food!"

But to return. The scene on which we look is not the Minch, but the Atlantic, over which in their season rave the winds that rock the world. To-day it is peaceful. The blue sea breaks in white creamings on the white sands, there is a glitter on the waters, Heiskeir and the Monach Isles are half lost in the heat-haze, and the lighthouse thereon seems to have no base, but to be a fairy palace suspended in the air.

Take a glass and let us see what moves upon the face of the waters, while we lie in comfort on the scented dunes to focus the telescope.

Let us begin with Hanglun, that promontory which forms the southern horn of the bay. There are some curlews on the farther side; the glass shows the hunched outlines of four. Probably there are more out of sight. A huge black-backed gull is sitting on the beacon which has been raised above high-water mark, and there are both oyster-catchers and redshanks in the miniature bays running by the edge of the tide. Off the end of the point, an eider duck with a family of eight is sending the calm water in ripples from her breast.

Next we flash the glass for a moment on Langashkeir – a low skerry, haunted by grey seals. It is a mile and a half away, and almost shut in by the haze. Skerelebaun comes next, some half-mile out.

There are many cormorants ranged upon it, and – stop! – what is that thing like a gigantic yellow slug, which sprawls on the seaweed shelf? A seal (*Phoca vitulina*) – not a grey seal, but a common seal, and that is not the only one, since careful observation enables us to make out four more. They have all been there for some considerable time, for their skins are dry. Now there is another approaching the rock. With two quick jerks he throws himself out of the sea and takes his place beside the rest. He is just like a black slug, and not until he dries – which will take from forty to sixty minutes – shall we be able to tell his true colour.

It is very interesting to lie here and watch the seals. How many days have we passed in such employment! Yet the best opportunity we ever had was on the first day we came here – now twelve years ago. We had made the horrid journey, starting from London on Thursday night, Oban at noon on Friday, the *Flowerdale* at 6 a.m. on Saturday, our island port at ten that night, and the seventeen-miles drive with the plover and the curlew crying from the fields beside the road, or through the silence of the moorlands – a silence only broken by the whistling of the wind in the telegraph wires. And so on to our arrival at 4 a.m.; then sleep till lunch, and after that a walk to this spot.

Do you see that little rock there? Yes, that one not a hundred and fifty yards away. The tide was out, and only touched it on the side facing the sea. Well, upon that rock, on that Sunday of long ago, lay thirteen seals – most of them huge old males – and we lounged among the bent-grass and watched them all the afternoon. Those were the days when I longed above all things to shoot

a seal – a desire now passed away. But curiously enough, never did I see seals again occupy that rock until 1912.

To return. The seals on Skerelebaun will be interesting, presently, for the tide is rising. They have all clambered or flippered, or whatever may be the correct term to describe the land-progress of a seal, to the highest point of that outlying part of the rock, and lie there in the attitude of riflemen about to shoot from the recumbent position. Presently, the water reaches them; one by one they float off until the big old bull alone is left. He arches himself into a bow, only his head above water; then it becomes too deep for him, and he joins the other doglike heads swimming round the rock.

In this bay the seals have regular routes, which they usually follow when fishing. Thus a seal appearing to the north, off Paible Head, will almost always fish right inshore and pass between the rock on which we saw them that first Sunday, and another upon its landward side. The channel between these two rocks is a very favourite fishing-place, for the fishing seal will often come up two or three times in passing through it – sometimes with a fish, that it devours before it dives again.

Common seals are very widely distributed round our coasts. My own experience of them has extended (I refer only to *Phoca vitulina*) to the Northumbrian coast, North Uist, Skye and Harris in the Hebrides, the Orkneys and Shetland Isles, and many spots upon the west coast of Ireland. The same animal is also plentiful in the Newfoundland bays, and is known as the harbour seal; also in the fiords of Labrador, where it is abnormally wild owing to the ceaseless persecution it undergoes from both the Eskimo and the white settlers, to whom the skin is of great value. It penetrates up the rivers far into the Labrador peninsula; and when exploring the Fraser River in that country, a few years ago, we saw (and chased without success) a common seal which had travelled over many rapids into the higher waters of the river. The failure to kill this seal was attended by regrettable consequences, as an Eskimo we had in our service became so homesick for the coast at sight of it that he deserted during the night, and returned to his home beside the salt water. In Norway, *Phoca vitulina* is well known, though there also it is very wild and hard to approach – as it may well be, since it is pursued with great diligence by professional hunters. Yet its value – except in Labrador, where the skin is used for the making of boots and the flesh to nourish the Eskimo – is small, ten to eighteen shillings being about the highest figure.

As a sporting beast, a worthy quarry for the big-game shooter, the common seal, under certain circumstances, stands quite high. It should never be shot in the water, except when it is killed as vermin at the mouth of salmon-rivers or in the neighbourhood of nets. In the water, where it has not been much persecuted, the

common seal is apt to allow its bump of curiosity to overcome its instinctive fear of man. It will rise and stare at a boat again and again, sometimes venturing quite close. Similarly, when bathing in Balranald Bay, I have often had seals all round me, and they occasionally accompany a walker on the tide-edge right along the strand at a distance of one or two hundred yards out in the ocean. The seal is supposed to be a very musical animal and to draw near and appreciate the playing of musical instruments or of singing, but this is probably but another phase of its curiosity.

There are other reasons why it is a pity to

shoot common seals in the water. The most important of these is the number of seals which sink at once when killed, and are lost. The sinking of the carcass is by no means certain, as the animal is undoubtedly more buoyant than the grey seal (*Halichoerus grypus*); and whether it sinks immediately or not depends largely upon the position in which the animal is swimming when it receives its death-wound. If it happens to be swimming *along* the surface, as a man swims, it will generally float – especially if it be shot soon after rising from a dive when its lungs are still full of unused air. If, on the other hand, it is in what may be called the "treadwater" position, it will – particularly if it has been up long enough to have expended the air in its lungs – sink at once. But if – except when the animal is shot in the interests of salmon-protection – a rule is made never to shoot a common seal in the water, very little harm will be done to the species by sportsmen; for once on a rock, the seal becomes an exceedingly difficult creature to approach.

To attempt to approach within shot of a basking seal down-wind is hopeless; for a seal has a nose which is rather keener than that of red deer. It also has excellent ears – indeed, considering the creature is amphibious and that the sounds which herald human approach are duplicated in nature by the sound of the sea moving shingle or lapping against the rocks, it is wonderful how slight a noise will ruin a stalk. The eyesight of *Phoca vitulina* is not particularly developed in British waters – the reason for this being that here it has not many enemies, but in Norway or Labrador a very different state of things exists.

On the other hand, the reason why a basking seal is so ready to take alarm, conveyed by sound or smell, is that on land no seal feels safe; he is always nervous. This is not to be wondered at, seeing how handicapped he is on *terra firma*. In the water he knows his own powers and feels comparatively secure. Thus very rarely indeed do seals lie up on rocks which can be reached from the land through shallows; some low skerry, half a mile from shore, is usually the selected spot, and for no apparent rhyme or reason seals will use one skerry to the exclusion of others which seem just as, or even more, suitable. Thus in the three bays, of which Skerelebaun is the central point, and where on most days one can see twenty to thirty seals, there are in all only seven skerries on which they are in the habit of basking. At least ten times this number of skerries exist in the bays, but the seal is a conservative creature. "My fathers did this, gentlemen, and so shall I," is his motto.

There is one skerry much beloved of seals, from which a shot may be obtained, or perhaps it should be said might be obtained. On this one August day, seven seals, including some fine old males, had been descried. No shot had, so far, been fired that year nearer than the far side of Hanglun Point; so we put to sea in the lobster-boat with high hopes. The wind was right, the tide low, and very propitious for a successful landing. I will not take my readers over the whole approach nor describe how artfully some curlew, that were in the way of the stalk, had to be moved; nor how only the most definite words prevailed in preventing the lobster-fishers from closing in upon the covering rock with masts up – a vigorous

advertisement of our progress. All these things, however, were done, and it only remained to pour a continuous stream of water upon the rowlocks to prevent squeaking. Then a jump on to seaweed, a slip of one's light tennis-shoes, a recovery, and while the boatmen break out into hoarse and bearded whispers – harmless only because the wind is strong in their faces – we creep into position. This is what we see. Divided from us only by two hundred yards of water, the seals are lying – some near the tide, others higher on the rock. Upon its very highest pinnacle are two bulls, which surpass all the others in size. Both are dry

and have been long out of the water. There is, of course, a strong temptation to shoot, lest something untoward occur. We look back. The lady in the boat has somehow or other reduced the boatmen to silence. All is right in that quarter, so I – who am to shoot – use the glass. I have never at this time shot a seal, but I have graduated in a good enough school to be aware that the best in view is the *only* permissible mark, so I examine the seals with great care. One, the lower, is a fine big seal of the black and white variety of colour; the one on the summit of the rock is a heavier brute, and has that yellowish tinge in his colouring which many of the old males on this coast seem to attain. His head is resting on the rock, his under-jaw and neck sprawled out. He is every inch of a hundred and eighty yards away – probably he is a little over two hundred. I cock the Mauser .275, put my cap under my hand to lessen the upward jump of the rifle – for a rifle which touches rock throws high. Then I get the sight on the seal.

I have been told and know that the brain of a seal lies far back, almost in the neck, and for this I aim. But before I can shoot, the big yellow bull lifts his head and keeps moving it. I have a mark of about six inches to aim for, and now that the seal's head is up, the possible chance of ricochet off the rock, in case I shoot low, has gone. The heat haze dances, and I feel it is a hundred chances to one against my lonely bullet ever finding its billet. The rifle shakes, too, not from any buck fever, but from the effort to concentrate. And then I am aware that the seal's neck and the white bead on the rifle are in line. Another second and the die is cast, the bullet has gone upon its way. On my retina are visualised half a dozen badly frightened seals hurling themselves towards the water, as many pops like drawn corks as they plunge in and

are swallowed up. But on the top of the rock the place of the old yellow bull is empty. His is one of the swimming heads that just show ere they depart. I have missed, and I shake my head abjectly at the boat. The sun is clouded with disappointment. I allow myself no excuse. I have missed a fair point-blank chance at a range at which in practice I would probably have scored a hit.

That was over twenty years ago. Looking back at it now, I am aware that few marks in the whole realm of big-game shooting are so difficult as the head or neck shot at a seal at anything over a hundred yards. To kill a stag is child's play to it; even a moufflon offers a mark three times the size. Consider, after all, that you are shooting at a mark about the size of a curlew, an object against a background of almost the same colour as itself. It is this extra difficulty that demands the necessity for a high quality of marksmanship. To shoot a seal anywhere but in the brain is useless and cruel; a chance shot might smash its backbone and render it incapable of movement, but the heart-shot would not have the same result. Certainly not always. A stag with his heart shot to pieces will often run a hundred or more yards full

speed before he falls never to rise again. Similarly, a seal shot through the heart can, and will nearly always in its final effort, reach the water. Only once did I see the carcass of a seal shot through the body recovered. It was lying some fifteen yards from the sea on the top of a rock, and the bullet struck it fairly enough through the heart; for all that it reached the water, and was only picked up at low tide by a lucky chance. So it is clear that it is absolutely necessary to shoot a seal in the brain if one wishes to secure the skin.

A common seal, which attains a length of six feet from the top of its teeth to the end of its hind flippers is a very large specimen, and should weigh somewhere about two hundred pounds; whereas a grey seal may measure eleven feet, and weigh six hundred or six hundred and fifty pounds, some say even more. As an article of diet, it is not eaten in this country, although a decoction made of its oil is numbered among the local remedies in use on the far western Celtic fringe. It is taken both internally as well as used externally for rheumatism. In Labrador, on the other hand, *Phoca vitulina* is a much-prized delicacy, especially the flippers. Like our grouse and pheasants, these are cooked after being "hung." In 1910, a flipper was "hung" so effectually by an old Innuit lady that neither she nor the guests she invited to partake of it survived the meal. I myself have attempted seal; but, though in good training and hungry with a twenty-mile walk and a hunter's appetite, I was unable to swallow it. It tasted rather, I imagine, as a badly cured oilcloth might taste.

All seal-hunters should be able to skin their own seals, as they may be called upon to do so by lack of other help; though all over the west of Ireland and Scotland and in the Hebrides men can be found who will do it after a fashion for a fee. Never shall I forget the insight into the character of my Irish fellow-countrymen that a certain episode connected with seal-skinning gave me. It occurred several years ago, on the last occasion on which I shot common seals.

Some skins were wanted for illustration purposes, and I had promised to get them if I could. During the day my luck had been extraordinary, and everything had "come off." The result was that about four o'clock on a frosty February afternoon, we made harbour just as the sun was sinking behind the bald green hills, with four seals in the boat. The boatmen, being asked if there were a seal-skinner in the village, offered to do the job themselves.

"What do you expect to be paid?"

"Ten shillings, sorr. There does be a deal of work on them great big brutes."

"All right."

I then went up to the hotel and had some tea. Half an hour later, I came down to see if the boatmen were skinning properly. To my surprise, I found them both gone and an unknown hump-backed man at work.

"Where are the boatmen?"

"They're after going home, yer honour. They got me hired to finish skinning out the bastes."

"What are they going to pay you?"

"Five shillings, yer honour."

After assuring myself that the new hand was capable, I went back to the hotel, but returned to the beach in the twilight.

The five-shilling man had disappeared. He had sublet the skinning to two gawky youths, and had engaged to pay them a shilling each.

About seven o'clock, I came out for the last time, and found two old women skinning. They were working by the light of an old oil-lamp in an empty shed. They had taken over the reversion of the seal-skinning, and were to be paid threepence each!

Next morning, I examined the skins. They were quite well done in spite of the large and varied staff that had expended their efforts upon them. It was all very Irish indeed; and when I told the boatmen that in future I should employ the two old women direct, they produced the most fantastic excuses: told me that had they had any idea that the humpback would lease the job, they would have remained themselves until it was finished, even if by so doing they suffered financially in a high degree. When it came to payment, I gave them half-a-crown each and the extra half-crown to the old women.

They accepted the decision with good humour, even indeed with humour, and promptly offered me the use of their boat on the morrow at half-price, The truth was they were very much afraid that I would employ the rival boat, and they one and all loved sport. I had, however, made up my mind not to shoot any more common seals, and at the announcement of this resolution the boatmen became very dejected. They did not believe me in the least; and when I left, presently, on a side-car, one of them said, "Well and all, God bless your honour when you do be shooting the seals in the south."

But since that day, now many years ago, the common seals have been unmolested as far as I am concerned, and will probably be in the future, Yet, in a way, I regret that my seal-shooting days are over, for the pursuit of seals takes the hunter into the most delightful surroundings and the sport is of a high class.

In St. John's *Wild Sports of the Highlands* I find the following:

"A farmer, near the coasts here, seeing several [seals] basking on the sandbanks, and not being possessed of a gun, hit upon what seemed to him the excellent plan of setting a strong bull-dog at them, hoping that the dog would hold one of them till he could get up and kill it with his spade. The dog reached the seals before they could get to the water, and attacked one of the largest, The seal, however, with a single bite, completely smashed the head of the dog, and, flinging him to one side, scuffled away into the water, leaving the farmer not much inclined to attempt seal-hunting again."

One remark in this account of St. John's is of interest, and that is that he describes the seals as "basking on a sandbank." On the west coast, I have never seen a seal take the sand; and, probably, counting one time with another, I have seen some thousands of seals. On the east coast, however, I believe, seals do lie upon the sandbanks and may often be seen doing so.

Although the common seal exists in far greater numbers than the grey seal, we must always remember that, inhabiting as it does estuaries and quiet waters, it is much more open to successful attack. The most part of the seals killed during the year fall victims to the rifle or the shot-gun, and it is to be feared that the latter weapon has blinded many a wretched animal. To shoot at a seal with a shot-gun loaded with small shot is an action the cruelty of which is only equalled by its abominable stupidity. Unless the seal is very close – for this kind of shot can only be taken from a boat at a seal rising suddenly within a short distance – it is a thousand to one that the creature will not be killed, yet a hundred to one it will be hit by the scattering charge.

I well remember one hardy Scottish hunter, a man as adamantine as the rock on which the foundation of his house stood, who, literally for years, would rise for snipe-shooting long before the dawn, walk ten miles to his ground, and sit by the roadside, or upon a milestone, till the light became strong enough to shoot by – surely a very knight of candle-light rising! This man killed great bags of snipe, woodcock, geese, ducks, and widgeon; and meeting him ten years after our first acquaintance, I asked him about the progress of his life's passion.

"I shoot no geese nor snipe now," said he. "In fact, I have given up the shot-gun altogether. The rifle's the weapon. Why, man, the post-mortem's so much the more interesting!"

Such men do not shoot at seals with shot-guns. This gentleman was a true sportsman in that a bird that went away wounded and which he did not recover would cloud his satisfaction all the evening.

Finally, here is a story of the war which would not be well regarded by the Prussians, who have, we are led to understand, undertaken this war in part with the hope of delivering the world from the ideals of the British sportsman, in order to replace them by that *Kultur* which is the birth right and monopoly of the "children of Odin." A young British officer, wounded in the thighs, announced the fact in a letter thus: "Dear —, — Both legs down. Coming home with the Pickers up." **HP**

Above: Seals, once worthy quarry, are rarely shot nowadays but their numbers have increased dramatically

Since Prichard's time both species of seal found in UK waters have increased in number dramatically. During his era they were not as common as now, and were often killed indiscriminately. The grey seal was slaughtered arbitrarily by west coast islanders during their breeding time in September to November. It is at this season of the year, when the white pups are helpless, mothers nursing, and the big bulls often lying with their families, that the annual "clubbing of the seals" took place. This bloody tradition was anathema to Prichard. He was very vocal about the abhorrent practice and supported a bill to outlaw it and introduce different shooting seasons to protect both species – as they pup at different times of the year. Prichard and influential friends of his lobbied hard and a bill eventually passed. However, there was a lot of frustration before they were successful and Prichard's writings at the time were very telling of the political scene, concerning the burying of certain proposed bills, and the forcing through of others – in his words

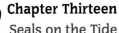

some of the most expansive National Parks in the world. A fact conveniently overlooked by today's protectionists.

But let's get back to the seals. As I have recorded above both British species eventually received separate close seasons to give them peace during their different breeding cycles. Temporary protection came and went on a number of occasions in different localities for decades – until the Conservation of Seals Act 1970 came into being nationally for England, Wales and Scotland. This provided a nationwide annual close season for grey seals, that is to say seals of the species known as *Halichoerus grypus*, extending from 1st September to 31st December inclusive, and an annual close season for common seals, seals of the species known as *Phoca vitulina*, extending from 1st June to 31st August inclusive. From an ethical viewpoint this was admirable and I'm certain if Prichard was alive at the time he would have considered it a great victory. It was a sensible act based on well-informed foundations. It provided protection for a species when vulnerable and allowed its legitimate pursuit at other times of the year, and therefore allowed some form of population control. Unfortunately recent legislation slipped through a couple of years ago that negated the 1970 Act, and effectively banned seal shooting altogether – without a mention in the sporting press. Now an individual license must be applied for for a problem seal in Scottish waters, and only marauding seals are allowed to be shot specifically at salmon nets in English waters. This is a tragic turn of events when both species of seals have become a real menace to vulnerable

"during those days of 'speeding up' legislation by gag and guillotine", a turn of phrase which I rather like. Then, unlike today, most wildlife warriors were well-informed sportsmen who cared for both their quarry's future and its habitat. The likes of Prichard, Roosevelt, Selous, Finch Hatton, and Corbett are some of the most successful yet unsung conservationists the world has ever seen. These sportsmen, against great odds, were very influential in securing species protection, outlawing wildlife exploitation, and helped to form

fish stocks and threaten livelihoods. The biggest threat to our migratory game fish today is the expansion of our two seal species, and the prevalent threat to the seals themselves is disease caused by overpopulation.

However, it is what it is. Fortunately, I am still able to do my little bit by providing protection to vulnerable salmon netting stations on the east coast of Yorkshire. Before there is a protest against my support of coastal salmon netting by those readers who favour casting a fly and wetting a line to tempt the king of fish – I actively fly fish for salmon too! In defence, my heritage is very much entwined with commercial fishing. Indeed my father was one of the east coast's most successful trawler skippers and the family boat sustained the livelihoods and mortgages of five crewmen for much of my younger lifetime.

A large proportion of my early working years were spent commercial fishing, and I (as did my twin brother) worked a T&J net part time for migratory trout and salmon. He still does when time allows but I gave mine up a year ago. I absolutely agree with the buying up of estuary nets and drift nets to let more fish pass for sporting purposes and, of course, from a stock preservation point of view. I fly fish for salmon myself and I really do understand the plight of this magnificent migratory game fish. It is the increase of farmed fish and the associated parasite and pollution problems that go with that vocation, plus the increase in predators – avian and mammalian – which is the real threat to wild salmon and sea trout stocks. It is definitely not the few traditional coastal netters who work their nets away from river mouths, and harvest small numbers of fish each season. These men really are the last of their breed; new licenses are no longer issued. When fishermen relinquish their current rights as I have done, or indeed die, their netting license is then discontinued forevermore. Fishing nets are expensive and time consuming to rig, it is a dangerous occupation, and an onshore wind in a small boat can mean disaster for nets, boat and fisherman alike. Marauding seals robbing hard-won fish and damaging expensive equipment are a real menace in the short season, and irregular weather windows, in which these men are able to ply their trade.

It is during the protection of these nets and their precious catch that I have shot most of my seals, both the common and grey variety. This, though, is one of the few points in which I differ to Prichard. During his time he reports grey seals, unlike common seals, do little damage to salmon netting concerns. It is my experience that both varieties of seal do great damage with equal measure. Of course the numbers of both species are massive now in comparison to a century before. Also perhaps the grey seal's habits have changed more towards marauding nets than in Prichard's time. The common seal is certainly the bigger bandit (in terms of his marauding) and is not averse to entering a salmon river, and patrolling up stream to take advantage of fish congregating in the pools during their journey to spawn. I have never known a grey seal attempt this brazen enterprise.

When I first left college I was unable to secure a keeping position on a suitable estate so, for a

Image: iStock

while at least, I took to the sea instead. Working a small cable with Ned from South Landing on the Flamborough Headland, we fished for sea trout and lobster. It was an interesting life full of adventure, hard work yes, but mostly rewarding. Ned was a hard task master with a short temper, but it was a successful venture. One time on an uncomfortable day hauling pots into a stiff wind, accompanied by some significant spray, I was complaining vociferously about my wet hair blowing into my eyes. I sported a Bryan Ferry-type fringe at

the time, which was, as can be imagined, sodden with salt water. Every time I turned into the wind it was blown back to irritate and sting my eyes, which soon became quite sore. Ned, having heard enough of my bleatings, grabbed the troublesome fringe in one hand, pulled my head onto the pot hauler, and with the other hand severed said fringe with a gutting knife in one fluid movement. I was quiet after that.

Our salmon net was anchored further to eastward of the cable landing at Old Fall. It was

Above: The common seal is much smaller than the grey seal but found in more locations

an interesting but lucrative place to fish. The net was nicely inside of the tide edge, and just out of the backwash from Steel End, a great scar or skerry that ran out towards North Buoy. Here we had nine hours of ebb (most fish are caught on the ebb tide) rather than the usual six hours because of a fickle outset in the tide caused by the great Smethwick sand bank. Unfortunately, when the weather came in it was a very bad place to be, and a few hairy moments were encountered. Another disadvantage was it was the first net any marauding seal would come to that worked south from their headland haven. When we were not at the net or the pots, we were on the cliffs spying for seals. The byelaws were much more

relaxed back then, and if one was about early, all the likely coves could be searched from Stacks right round into Selwicks bay, hopefully stopping any seal before it got to the net. Nowadays we are only permitted to shoot seals actually at the net when actively engaged in stealing fish or damaging fishing gear. It wasn't very often I was allowed a shot in those early days – to miss a seal could have dire financial consequences by making the marauder more wary, and even harder to hit during his pilferings. This was difficult shooting from a high angle but Ned was an effective shot and most seals that came into his sights paid the ultimate toll. Interestingly, nearly every seal shot on the ebb would wash up at low tide a little further

Image: iStock

to eastward at Truck Way and recovered.

When, a few years later, I was granted my own netting license the recovery of shot seals was very much harder. The last thing one wanted was a dead seal washing up on a popular tourist beach with a severe head wound. Every effort was made to secure a shot seal before it sank and this usually involved a wetting. However, as Prichard correctly recorded, the seal's aspect at a successful shot is crucial in how long it will float. Most often when a seal shows himself at a net, he is usually upright in the water, especially if surfacing with a fish. If he is horizontal in the water the seal is usually swimming along the net and therefore a much more difficult shot. Nowhere on the east coast from Grimston to Speeton was the recovery of a sunken seal as easy as it was at Old Fall. It was always an anxious time following a successful shot if the seal wasn't immediately recovered. Many man hours ensued on the ebbing tide glassing the receding shoreline for the beached marauder, but more often than not the search ended in a successful seal recovery with an ATV.

There were a few places that the common seals hauled themselves out on the headland, but almost none for the grey variety. Common seals are, as Prichard recorded, much easier to approach than their bigger cousins, and any flat rock, skerry or scar would suffice for a pull up. On this part of the coast they seemed less inclined to haul up onto the sand, and I never saw a healthy grey seal on the sand at all. However, not so far south, the grey seal rookery at Donna Nook, on the other side of the Humber Estuary, is on sand banks, and home to one of the largest European grey seal nursery areas. There are one or two almost inaccessible places where grey seals do pull up onto the rocks around the Flamborough headland. These are hidden under the towering chalk cliffs of Speeton and Bempton. Why these few places are favoured and other suitable-looking slabs forsaken by the fussy grey variety remains a mystery to me. I also suspect that some seals actually pup under these cliffs in the deep caves chiselled out by the ceaseless wave action.

It was on just such a scar top that I enjoyed a memorable stalk into a huge grey seal bull. The net had been anchored as far as to eastward as we dared under the immense chalky heights of Speeton. It was on a spring tide with much bigger ebb than normal, and full advantage was taken of nature's irregular anomaly. The fishing had been good with a few sea trout running, and a marauding grey seal bull had soon tuned in to the struggling enmeshed fish. He was a canny leviathan though, and had no doubt been driven off by the Scarborough and Filey fisherman operating further north. Checking the net on the ebbing tide I caught sight of him working the net as my brother waded out in the chest waders and oilskin to collect the catch. It was impossible to shoot the bull while my sibling was about his work. We both had to endure the sight (my brother at close hand), of the seal bull robbing fish after fish, biting out the soft part and discarding it immediately for another one. It was an aquatic version of the fox in the hen coop – thieving and killing for the sheer sake of it. There was little I could do at the time, but I vowed to engage him

Left: The true colour of a seal's skin is only apparent when it dries out on land

Right: Seal rookeries are always In inaccessible places

Image: iStock

on the morrows tide.

There is something absolutely delightful about being on the northern shores of Britain at daybreak. It doesn't matter if the weather is fine or foul, the experience is always uplifting, and the varied inhabitants of the foreshore always provide an interesting spectacle. On this particular morning my attentions were focused on the sea surrounding the net. I had carefully gotten into position during the dark hours and was glad of a fair wind. An hour later I watched the amber orb of a fresh new sun spread its golden glow across the North Sea, eventually bringing the vista of Filey Bay to life, and illuminating the great white crags of Speeton cliffs behind me. The tide was flowing up and high water would be a while yet, but I was in position and ready for the marauding bull to enter the scene of coastal tranquillity. Puffins and razorbills whizzed by, returning birds bills packed with sandeels, passing outward-bound partners returning to sea on a relentless errand to feed demanding chicks. Gannets had found a shoal of mackerel or herring close inshore, and dive bombed into them from a great height with folded wings, while the feeding bonanza lasted. The kittiwakes' relentless mewing provided the audio, occasionally drowned out momentarily by the raucous cacophony of a close-by gull, herring or black back – we had them in abundance. Strangely, the gulls here are so used to hikers and the like about the cliffs that they pay little attention to a half-hidden rifleman. The same species in Scotland would betray one in an instant.

The anchor buoys and net floats were straining to ride on the surface at high water. Indeed the offend that formed the crucial net pocket or trap, was threatening to go under. This was a concern because any fish trapped and unmeshed would escape over the headline; I made a mental note to allow more slack on the anchor ropes at low water. As slack water came through at the top of the tide, the buoys and floats thankfully bobbed in a more satisfying fashion. Not long after, my attention was drawn to a black football-shaped object that surfaced momentarily and then disappeared.

My quarry had arrived, but he was wary. At different lengths of the net, his black head would break the surface for air and he would look to the shore before pointing his great Roman nose to the sky and slipping vertically below the turquoise surface once again. This was one cautious adversary, and there was little doubt he'd had a bullet past him before, and he knew from which direction danger threatened. There seemed to be little to interest him at the net because he quickly covered its length. I next saw him surface quite a way away and heading to eastward. This behaviour told me there wasn't many, if indeed any, fish running at all, but the ebb was to come, and with it usually came the fish – then he would be back.

I was enjoying the morning. It isn't too often one gets a perfect sea, with a light south easterly breeze – a perfect salmon wind that pushed the fish inshore in search of the sand eels. The North Sea looked like the Mediterranean. I lazily scanned along the shore with the draw scope searching the shallows and skerries for anything of interest, and then I saw him. The big brute had pulled himself up onto a sloping scar about

Above: Only in shallow water can shots be taken like this, otherwise the seal will be lost to the depths

half a mile to eastward. I was convinced it was him; most seals look alike but this was a big bull, Roman-nosed and dark as jet (although all seals look dark when wet). He'd drawn himself out near some of our other anchor buoys, which were a second alternative to set the net. Interestingly, two years previously I had also seen a grey seal bull basking on this very same scar. A stalk was on – I had the wind on him, and he was close enough to our fishing gear to be a legitimate target. I felt sure he was just biding his time to let the net fill with fish before returning to rob them.

Leaving all non-essentials behind, I strip down to shirt sleeves, and pull my cap peak down to shadow my face, which might give me away at the crucial moment. Resting the rifle in the v of my arms I crawled towards the beach from my vantage point. Forward motion provided by elbows, knees and heels, I eventually made it unobserved. One may wonder why I took such

cautious action with the seal nearly half a mile away. Seals have excellent eyesight and I wasn't leaving anything to chance. My position in the mossy turf had been excellent for covering the net below me. But if I'd stood up and clambered down to the shingle, my profile would have been immediately obvious to the seal.

Now I was safely out of sight I took full advantage of the dead ground and raced across the shingle and sand to where the great limpet-clad skerries stretched into the sea. Their limestone fingers were sharp and slippery, hung as they were with curtains of bladderwrack. The hard moonscape rock held shallow pools of seawater that soon soaked through the shirt. Quickly becoming saturated, I regretted discarding my jacket and my elbows suffered terribly on the rough surface. The rifle was handled with extreme care: I didn't want sand or saltwater to enter barrel or action and ruin the firearm. This consideration slowed me somewhat, and I had a growing concern that the bull would soon return to the net. A cautious peak over the scar top confirmed he was still loitering on the rock. He continuously looked nervously about him, and although his head looked akin to that of an obese basilisk joined to a gluttonous lump of a redundant body, he moved with a sinuous grace.

A short sand spit separated the next set of scars, which would have to be negotiated in the crawling fashion. I was soon ploughing a furrow with my chin through the smooth sand, punctuated by countless worm casts made by the lugworm. Slowly but surely, the distance was shortened by trial and ordeal. Occasionally, good ground could be made quickly skipping between and behind the big rounded chalk boulders, but I had to be careful not to dislodge any stones or rocks, the crack of which would have alerted the bull in an instant. Only once did I question my commitment to the cause, and this was on entering a deeper trough between the skerries that meant a thorough soaking. Wet as I was, I abandoned myself to the elements and, waist-deep in the briny, inched myself across the gap on my derrière. Holding my musket at face height to avoid getting it splashed, it was a fine balance between the rifle remaining dry and keeping it below the seal's line of sight.

Shivering now despite the summer sun, I felt I should be within ethical range of a shot at the bull. Making comfortable, I angled my shoulder towards his probable position and inched the muzzle over the limestone scar. Fitting to the rifle I angled it down to bear on the seal. He was

closer than I had expected and for a moment the great bull filled my scope, but then it was empty, followed by a loud slap as he splashed into the sea to safety. He bobbed for just a second to stare at my impudent intrusion, and was gone. A glint of the sun off my rifle barrel, or a flash of a white hand, had given me away: I wasn't sure which and it mattered not. But for a long minute I sat there sodden and dejected in disbelief to have come so close to success, and be beaten by the superior senses of the seal in the last seconds. He had kept his skin fair and square, and I never saw him at the net again. I figured he'd gone on to bother some other netsman not so hell-bent on his murder, and chalked the experience up as an exciting result by default.

The last seal I shot very nearly went badly wrong. My brother had anchored his net well to the south of Bridlington on the Holderness coast. The in-end of the net was secured to the massive angular concrete tank traps placed there during World War Two to stall any possible invasion by German forces along this stretch of coast. The low dunes and boulder clay cliffs here offer good level vantage points for the rifleman. However, as flat as they were, there was little in the way of cover to take advantage of regarding a shooting position. Again, the excellent fishing soon attracted the attentions of yet another grey seal bull that delighted in the ruination of my brother's hard-won catch.

High water and first of ebb is the best time to shoot net marauding seals. This is mainly because the water is as close to the cliff as it's going to get, and in turn encourages the seal to swim nearer to the rifleman. Due to the lack of cover I was donned head to toe in a military issue ghillie suit. My brother, also suitably camouflaged, acted as spotter with the binoculars and draw scope.

The seal had been in attendance on our arrival but he soon returned when we disappeared from sight. He was a big marbled bull; dappled in shaded blues and greys he had a handsome skin. Everything looked good for a shot, we just had to wait for him to come into the in-end and stay up long enough for a shot. The only worry was two members of the general public, who were walking the dog on a windswept beech. We had to let them pass of course, and let them get far enough away for them not to be bothered by the report. Even a moderated bang is a bang, and can be quite disconcerting for those who do not understand firearms. Anyway, the couple braving the elements passed a few feet below us, completely unaware of our presence. They had perhaps gone three or four hundred yards to our left where the coast angled in, when the seal rose in a perfect position close to shore. He came right out of the water for perhaps half his length and, with all the boxes mentally ticked, I took the opportunity for a shot.

The bullet found his brain and flung the bull backwards where he floated in a growing slick of dark blood for just a few seconds, his flipper flapping spasmodically before sinking beneath the surface. Unfortunately the report, despite their distance from us (acoustics are often unfathomable) attracted the attention of the dog walkers who turned around and headed quickly in our direction. This was a situation I had tried hard to avoid. As they closed in with uncanny accuracy I decided to reveal myself rather than risk one or both having heart failure when they saw a bush at close quarters move and turn into a human being. My brother left me to it and I fenced off the barrage of questions with a polite explanation of what we were actually about, and reassured them that everything was in order and perfectly legal. Still not satisfied, they stormed off in a huff and I watched them through the binoculars as they walked to my vehicle, circled it, and made a note of my registration. I knew then that a visit from the constabulary was imminent.

Sure enough, just after we packed away, we met a police van heading towards us on the cliff road. In fairness the two officers were very polite and professional, and after checking the vehicle details, both my firearms certificate and my brother's salmon netting license, they let us go on our way. I occasionally see one or both of the dog walkers in town and they always scowl at me with little-disguised loathing. It is such a shame that these people do not understand the ways of the countryside and foreshore. The two constables were delightful in comparison, and were genuinely interested in what we were doing, and the damage that seals could do. They were a real credit to their uniform. Once they had established that our operations were within the law they wanted to learn as much as possible about what was being practised on their patch. It was good old-fashioned community police work.

Before I leave this chapter I would like to relate a near-death occurrence that befell me when I was attempting to photograph some local

Right: Grey seals favour the same scars and skerries to haul out on

328

seals for this book. The chalk fault of Flambourgh Headland that runs westwards into Filey Bay encompasses Flamborough, Bempton and Speeton cliffs. Along its length are a number of hidden but precarious descents down the cliff to the shore. These have been passed down by generations of fisherman and the old 'egg climmers'. Many have interesting names such as Newcombe, Roll Up, and Gull Neuks.

One of these above Mossy Shelf is known locally as 'Artley's Shut' and it was here I came close to falling to my death. It was named after a local fisherman who salvaged a HMS submarine G3 wreck that foundered in 1921 close by. He used this access to haul up valuable gun metal and brass via a davit he fixed to the cliff here, and the holding bracket is still in situ. To this is fastened a rope that enables one to descend around a precarious cliff ledge and into a natural chimney that in parts is carpeted by coastal turf. A careful descent from here leads to a narrow chasm that has to be leapt across and, once this is successfully negotiated, the final part is a clamber down a steep mossy bank.

Below here is one of the few places that seals haul themselves out, but the last time I had made my way down to the scars below was some thirty years before. Coastal erosion had played its part here in a big way and the chasm that once could be leapt across had become a canyon. Realising the route down was no more; I turned to head back up and lost my footing on the guano-greased shelf. Panicking, I grabbed wildly for the rope swinging idly in the breeze, and fortunately found it. Gripping on to the very end of the rope

Image: iStock

with both hands, my body angled out at forty five degrees over the precipice, with my feet perilously balanced on the slippery edge, it was the very definition of the term 'cliff-hanger'. Using the caution normally reserved for disarming improvised explosive devices, I gingerly worked my way up the rope and heeled into a firmer footing. It was a very near run thing indeed. I thanked the almighty out loud when my safety was assured, and sank to the ground with a definite dose of the jelly legs.

Sheer abject terror immediate post survival or on the cusp of death is quite different from fear. I have heard and feared the crack of incoming bullets passing close singing certain death – fired by desperate Africans plundering their country's wildlife to fund whatever their current cause was. I have felt the cold abject sweat of fear and deathly concentration when dealing with an enraged elephant bent on pounding all concerned into the bushveld on cropping operations. However, these experiences are expected, albeit no less dangerous, but the body has a certain degree of adrenalin induced control and acceptance geared towards real danger. Unexpected near-death happenings are what induces abject terror. I have felt it only twice before, once after crashing an antiquated motorcycle similar to the one that Aircraftsmen Shaw (better known as Lawrence of Arabia) met his maker on in similar circumstances. The other occasion was the result of a negligent discharge actually inside my Land Rover at the hand of a very old, and extremely unpleasant, German ex-artillery major who had survived Stalingrad and seemed to be trying his very best to

kill me on a roebuck hunt in Scotland. His safety behaviour was absolutely shocking. His hunt was the only one I have ever had to call a premature end to on unacceptable safety grounds. But, thankfully, I am still here to tell the tale.

Seal hunting can be a very emotive issue. In former times the seal was considered a worthy quarry on our coastline. Few support the despicable practice of clubbing helpless grey seal pups to death and that is the image the antis have successfully seared into the minds of most of our country's populace, sportsmen included. But stalking and ethically shooting seals is a far cry from the other barbarous practice no longer carried out in this country. The seal is a significant threat to our migratory game fish and other commercial fisheries. Both grey seals and common seals are thriving around our coasts and due to recent legislation (mentioned earlier in this chapter) that has slipped through negating the 1970 Conservation of Seals Act – which contained shooting seasons for both species – pursuit of seals for sporting purposes alone is now banned. Exception is made for marauding seals to protect nets and localised fish stocks, but current legislation is a real minefield. For those who have experienced their pursuit it is a very satisfying sport indeed. Seals are unique in that they are a truly wild marine game species that could be pursued on Britain's wildest windswept foreshores. Their numbers have expanded to disproportionate levels since Prichard's time, and this soon must surely be addressed by government and management passed back to the landowner and sportsman. **PC**

Left: Seal hunting is a wet, cold sport followed by many in Scandnavia but mostly unavailable in Britain thanks to ridiculous legislation

Ground Game

Image: iStock

Chapter Fourteen
Ground Game

I

The Mountain Hare (*Lepus timidus*), is also known as the Blue Hare, Tundra Hare, Variable Hare, White Hare, and Alpine Hare. Most of these names refer to its pelage or habitat and all of them, in their respective ways, are very apt. In the spring and summer months the coat of the mountain hare undergoes two moults, a browny grey through to a deep slate grey, but during autumn in preparation for winter hares moult into white pelage. Interestingly, the Irish Hare subspecies (*Lepus timidus hibernicus*), which is very closely related, stays a brownish-grey colour all year and only rarely do individuals develop a white coat. Some scientists believe that the Irish Hare should be regarded as a separate species. Brown hares (*Lepus europaeus*) moult only twice a year and, surprisingly to many sportsmen, they are a long residing but alien species to these isles – introduced from across the North Sea sometime during the Iron Age.

Britain's only native Lagomorph is the mountain hare, present in Scotland and Ireland since the Ice Age. It has also been introduced to Shetland, England, Wales and the Isle of Man. Most introductions of this species, and they have been in many different parts of Britain as far south as Staffordshire in England, west to Snowdonia in Wales, and east to Northumberland, have been by sportsmen for shooting purposes. Translocations of Highland stock have also occurred to many Scottish islands. Most of the English attempts ended in failure with the exception of the peak district population, that prospered and spilled over into the high moors of Cheshire, Derbyshire and Yorkshire that

Left: The mountain hare is a truly wild British species left here from the last Ice Age

joined together below the massive television mast on Holme Moss. Introductions to the Scottish lowlands also met with limited success, though some border hills hold reasonable numbers. But the stronghold of this species has always been in the eastern Highlands. Western moors have a much higher annual rainfall and this doesn't suit the hare. Mountain hares can stand extremely low temperatures and snow thanks to the protective properties of their long coat. However, persistent rain and sodden fur negate the air trapping effect that provides insulation against the cold, and the hare suffers accordingly. That is why the dryer eastern hills and moors are favoured by this species, and it is here that I have engaged the white hare the most.

The Angus glens were once a haven for the mountain hare. Annual hare hunts achieved quite large bags here and the population controlled well by managed regular shooting. Traditional keepering favoured both the hare and the grouse and the two species prospered side by side. I used to take many guests, British and foreign, to Angus on these organised hare drives for many consecutive years during the nineties. Unfortunately, since then, more intensive grouse management has seen the hare relegated to the ranks of vermin and they are often shot on sight in many areas with rifles to reduce their grazing effort. Also, in an imagined conflict with grouse, mountain hares are being blamed as unwelcome tick reservoirs. It is a shame to see this turn of events after witnessing the white hare in its glorious heyday. Monoculture of grouse at the exclusion of other species could be our undoing one day, but I hope those with influence will understand and address the issue before it becomes a reality. Species that have lived side by side in the past must be allowed to continue to do so.

I have relished driven and walked up hare days on many a Scottish estate, including Invercauld, Glenshee, Abercairny, Rottal, Drumlanrig Castle, Glen Ogle and Glen Moy. But it was at Glen Moy with my old mentor Stuart Donald where I enjoyed most success. Reasonable fitness is required for this kind of work, as it is for any sport on the Highland hills. Land Rovers and tracked vehicles can only take you so far out, and most of the way will then be on 'shank's pony.' But I do so enjoy working for one's game, the physical demands make it all the more fun, and any success is well won.

It was the first weekend in February in the early 1990s and we were about to start the first of our annual hare hunts on the Earl of Airlie's vast estates. This involved a weekend's hare driving on two separate beats. On this day we would drive the Dog Hillock on Glen Moy, and the following day's excursion was to be on the White Hill next door on Sandy's beat.

Striking out up the Shank Hill our team of guns snaked ever higher following our guide, head keeper Stuart Donald. It was a long pull uphill in this wild environment. A flock of snow buntings flitted forward before us and alighted again and again, almost taunting us to keep up. The wildlife here obviously scratched out a harsh living in this unforgiving, windswept landscape. Good grouse stocks were evident by their numerous marks yet quiet, no "gadow, gadows" today, until the odd pair or trio erupted at one's feet and whirred away, issu-

Image: Peter Carr Collection

ing their agitated "gada, gada, gadarrr'" alarm call. Apart from the startled grouse and the melancholy whine of the wind, the only other sound was the occasional "kronk kronk" of a stratospheric raven passing overhead. It was almost like the desolate landscape had held its breath. This truly was a very wild part of Britain.

Eventually the heather and peat hags gave way to rock strata and scree and we finally reached the brow of the hill. Here Stuart Donald left the first gun, after reminding him once more of the safety instructions: no swinging through the line, only shoot behind when the horn sounds, and do not move from your shooting position until collected. Every fifty yards or so another gun was placed and given instructions. Today we were shooting eleven guns and the sixth gun was perfectly placed at the summit marked by a cairn, followed by me at number seven. I had drawn a good position at the top of a narrow gully that cut through the peat hags before me. White hares usually bolt uphill when disturbed, making them relatively easy to drive. They readily use the topography to their advantage, usually using recognised routes. Gullies, burn sides, and deer trods are all natural passes uphill, and hares will race or canter along them to gain the top of the brae.

I waved to both guns either side of me to be sure that we were all aware of each other's positions. Safety concerns attended to, I un-slipped my 12 bore, checked the barrels were clear, and slid home two Eley Hymax cartridges in shot size three, and awaited for events to unfold. A piercing note from the keeper's thunderer whistle indicated that all the guests were in situ and it was now safe to shoot. The thumbs-up was then passed from gun to gun. I glanced along the line contentedly to see the full team had been perfectly placed and was effectively covering the brow line.

Looking below me into the east glen I observed Stuart Donald descending rapidly downhill, with the agility and constitution of an ibex. He was endeavouring to join his line of beaters in a commanding position on their far right flank. I knew that the beaters would be strung out in a perfect line along the East Moy Burn awaiting the order to start. The keeper, from his vantage

Above: The author after a prosperous hare drive in the Angus Glens during the 1990s

At first the mountain hares looked like spots of cotton wool zig-zagging erratically across the slopes, but they soon headed higher and the first shots were heard. A steady cannonade of shooting indicated that the drive was going well and my anticipation was heightened. Almost immediately a hill hare raced up the gully before me, I mounted and swung but missed a yard behind, confirmed by an explosion of peat. Taking a swift second snap shot, I was fortunately awarded some success as the hare cartwheeled forward dead, just as another trio of its kind tore up the same gully. I quickly executed both a record re-load and two of the three hares with an instinctive left and a right. Then my marksmanship left a lot to be desired, miss followed miss as the shooting became fast and furious. There seemed to be no time to lose, hares were everywhere, I swung and shot, ejected spent cases, reloaded and shot, some hares fell and others fled by unscathed to relative safety.

The crack of the beaters' flags could be heard now and above the shooting the keeper's voice bellowed "hold the line." This created a lull in the proceedings and I realised I had become flustered and this had affected my shooting. The sound of the horn indicated no more shooting forward so I turned about to take any hares passing me by and consciously calmed myself. Stuart Donald's voice once more rose above the whistle of the Highland wind, "bring on the line." My shooting improved and I cleanly took a further three hares before the close crack of the beaters' flags reached me, signalling it was time to unload and the first drive was done.

Guns made safe and returned to their slips,

point, slightly ahead and above his beaters, could control both speed and direction of the drive by barking his orders down the radio, not unlike an impatient Rommel at Tobruk. Woe betide anyone who got out of line or opened up a gap where the hares would most certainly make their escape. If there was ever a man at home in his environment and vocation, it was he.

Blowing some warmth back into my numbed fingers it wasn't long before the first signs that the drive had begun caught my attention. The whole face of the hill that was moments before a seemingly lifeless landscape had now become a hive of activity. A countless procession of red hinds numbering in the hundreds crossed the march into Hunthill estate, almost like the wildebeest on the Mara migration. Pairs of grouse flitted and alighted back and forth, following the contours of the face, and then came the hares.

we had a quick gather-up of the fallen game and shared lunch with the beaters out of the wind in a dry peat hag.

The final drive of the day would be a return drive, bringing back the other side of the hill. Stuart Donald once more placed each guest precisely, as his team of beaters split into two groups and disappeared downhill on either flank of the gun line. My luck held, as did my resolve, and although not as many hares came my way I shot much better, taking my tally for the day to twenty two all out. An admirable final bag of 133 white hares was a good day's shooting in anyone's book. The following day's hare driving was equally as successful as everyone seemed to be on good shooting form, taking another hundred plus hares on an almost two to one shot ratio.

Mountain hare populations appear to be both local and cyclical. When the hare populations are high the surplus has to be shot hard to avoid disease and starvation. This is conservation at the coalface and visiting sportsmen are actually assisting managed estates to help the hares and other wildlife. Driven Highland hare hunts are good value shooting of wild quarry in an untamed wilderness at a time of year when most game shooting has closed. The experience is certainly unique and I would recommend every sportsman who favours wild quarry in the wild places to try it if you can find it. Hare numbers have, as I've made mention earlier, become too pressured in some parts because they have fallen foul of the 'new' way with grouse. Some traditionally managed estates still shoot them when numbers are up, and it is on these holdings that one may find some marvellous sport.

A walked up day at white hares is equally as much fun but one really needs a strong attendant for each gun to carry the bag as you go. These attendants are often hard to come by as 'once

Left: Another good day's snow hare driving on Rottal with Yorkshire fisherman friends and colleagues of the author

Opposite: A great day among the snow hares at Glen Moy with the author's colleagues, friends and clients

bitten twice shy' certainly applies to walked up hare shooting, and if you do manage to engage a willing 'Sherpa' please tip him well – he will have earned it! The inclusion of a hare or two, white or brown on a mixed walked up rough day, is always a welcome sight in my eyes, and if shot well forward I often take a hare home at the day's end when offered game by the keeper. A hare of either variety really does make a superb meal, and easy enough to prepare by students of Mrs Beeton.

I am always amazed at the lesser distinction we British shooters give to the hare, compared to its revered pursuit by our continental cousins. Of course, our fellow sportsmen in our own lands who choose to follow the hounds, rather than take up the gun, delight at the wonderful work involved in hunting beagle and harrier packs, and they hold the humble hare in as high – if not greater – regard. But the majority of British sportsmen see hare driving as a seasonal perk for the farm staff, beaters and keepers after the game bird season closes.

Many of my fellow hunting guests over the decades have been foreigners who feel privileged to hunt both species of hare in numbers they could never attain in their home countries. During my time as an outfitter and sporting agent, I let any number of days to Italian, Maltese and Greek hunters. But it was the German, Austrian and Scandinavian guests that really respected the hare, and indeed all legitimate game. I have always admired these sportsmen for their respectful traditions towards fallen game, and often thought it is something we have missed out on here in Britain. Blowing the hunting horns in salute to the har-

vested game, and to send it to the next world with goodwill and respect is a practice I have always found very moving.

Prichard mentions with a degree of ridicule in his chapter on curlew, Frenchmen in the Channel Islands blowing their hunting horns over unknown game, but he suspected fieldfares as the fallen quarry. I rather think his scorn was directed at their desire to hunt the thrushes though, as opposed to the use of horns to celebrate their passing. This brings to mind an incident in Bedfordshire that befell a long-standing friend of mine that was, and still is, the head keeper at an estate in the area. I had brought a small team of French sportsmen to stalk deer and decoy woodpigeons with him. All went well until we started at the pigeons. Two were left to their own devices in a well-built hide in a good place, while we split up with a guest apiece. On returning to the first pair after a good morning at the woodies, we were horrified to see that one gun had taken advantage of the blackbirds passing by. As can be imagined, the keeper was not very pleased at his indiscretion. The Frenchmen were always keen to eat what they shot, which was commendable. On this day my friend plucked and trussed the songbirds and delivered them to the offending gun with a telling statement "I hope you enjoy these, as they will be the last birds you'll shoot or eat on this estate," this being his take on the Entente Cordiale. The Prichard papers contain an amusing anecdote to the detriment of an unfortunate Frenchman. In a letter to Lady Elizabeth, he wrote:

"I went fishing with a float today and caught one fish – three-quarters of a pound! – in a pool. It

Image: Peter C... collection

was a bad looking fish so I gave it to a French-man." Apparently Prichard's assumption of the fish was quite correct, because the Frenchman was heard shouting "medico, medico", from his bunk the following morning.

By far the best driven brown hare days I have enjoyed have been in the Lincolnshire Wolds on the famous Rothwell Estate known for its record bag of 2,119 wild partridges shot on the 3rd October 1952 by the late Sir Joseph Nickerson and five guests. 151 hares were also shot on what would be known forever after as 'The Great Day'. For the past twenty years the estate's game shooting interests have been managed by the Nickerson family's redoubtable head keeper John Pyle. I feel privileged to have been a member of a mixed gun team composed of German aristocrats, foresters and a token Austrian captain of industry on their annual hare shoot at Rothwell these past few years. Indeed the weekend is best described as an epic event rather than a hare hunt because the après shoot shenanigans have become Lincolnshire folklore thanks to the efforts of their group leader – forest director Jost Arnold. Jostie

Above: A good day's brown hare driving enjoyed by the author and his friends at Rothwell, Lincolnshire

and I have enjoyed many an African adventure together, but it is when I visit Germany and he visits Britain things get really interesting. The pursuit of sport must be ethically rewarding and above all a pleasure to take part in. Jost Arnold is the personification of fun, and his drinking skills are legendary on four continents. But, like me, he likes his game wild, and the wilder the better.

Jost is a superb rifle shot, but struggled with the shotgun for some time, until an investment in tuition put him right. Indeed I remember on one Rothwell hare shoot seeing Jost really saddened by his inefficiency with the shotgun. This was a very rare event indeed – that is, Jost saddened, rather than him missing! There were three of us in the gun trailer at the time, Me, Jost, and His Serene Highness Prince Gustav Wittgenstein-Berleburg, when in a weak moment Jost decided to share his failings and disappointment with the 12 bore. Prince Gustav was a sportsman of note, and always ready to share in a joke. Indeed, between the two of us, we had already convinced one of the other guests he would be a walking gun all day – after he'd conveniently skipped his turn one drive on the previous day's hunt. Seeing Jost suffering a humour bypass due to his absence of shooting prowess was an opportunity just too good to miss. Therefore we took full advantage of his despair, offering every kind of imagined advice – mostly at Jost's expense – but as always he took it well. Thankfully, since then, Jost's newfound skill with two barrels has opened up a whole different range of sporting opportunities to the former rifleman. I too have been carried along with him on the tide of excitement that came

Right: The brown hare is an Iron Age introduction to Britain from the near Continent

with it and enjoyed many a sporting invitation with the big German.

Driving brown hares is much harder in operation compared to their Highland counterparts the white hare. That said, I'm sure the beaters would disagree! The white hare will generally run up hill and over the crest. Brown hares will go every which way, especially if the guns are placed down wind. Therefore far more staff are needed to successfully get the hares to go where they are wanted. Prime places for the guns are on

Image: Wikimedia 3268zauber

gateways or green bridges over dykes and drains. These escape routes are well known to the local hares and full advantage should be taken when placing the guns.

On this day we had been given our safety talk and had the numbering system explained by our tweed-clad head keeper, looking resplendent in his deerstalker, and naturally exuding an air of authority over the shoot staff and his loyal lieutenants – the assistant keepers donned in the same tweed. Speech over, Phillip – Baron von Wambolt – clicks

his heels together and nods his head in respect to the keepers and his fellow guns, and then offers each a tot of Laphroaig single malt to dispel the cold February chill before we march out to our respective stands. It is gratefully received by all.

I'm soon in the centre of the line but it matters not, as the action can just be as hot on the flank as in the middle. Looking north I can see the Humber estuary below me, and as the crow flies I'm almost in line with the shoot that my old friend Tony Megson keepers on the north bank with its wonderful widgeon shooting on the foreshore. The mudflats and banks stretch along the great river, under the monstrous suspension bridge, and on past that mecca of wildfowl haunts 'Read's Island'. It was on this island that the former owner of the shoot where we were now engaged shot an amazing bag of ducks as a lone shooter aided only by a loader. Sir Joseph was shooting with a pair of 28 bore shotguns, making the result even more remarkable.

The pops of gun reports either side of me tore through my thoughts of bygone days back to the job at hand. The hares had lifted and were heading to the line. Some skipped and cantered along, concerned but not yet worried. Others, probably surviving veterans from previous seasons, are already in all-out panic and heading out towards the west side, to be nicely turned back by a skilful flanker who knows what he's at. Cracking his flag frantically and sprinting forward to bring on the flank he keeps the game in. I keep low, pressing my back into the hedge and pull my cap down to avoid the hares seeing, and subsequently avoiding, the glare of my pale face.

Image: Wikimedia R. Altenkamp

Right: Brown hares can reproduce to pest proportions in the east but are scarcer in western counties

Hares in numbers are coming to the guns, the regular pop, pop, of shooting along the line reminded me of what a front rank of Wellington's best at Waterloo should look like. Then it's my turn as one hare beats my neighbour and angles towards me at full speed ahead. Picking him up with the muzzles, but with the gun still lowered, I begin to swing with him. Mounting, I fire as the gun touches the shoulder and the hare rolls forward, instantly dead, the full pattern taking him at the front, as it should.

I'm pleased with myself, and I treat a few more of his kind accordingly, all killed clean. The group as a whole is shooting well, there is no pitiful screaming of hares shot too far back, and all concerned are letting the hares come in close before delivering their shots. It is as it should be; these chaps are experienced shots that respect their quarry, and conduct themselves in an ethical manner.

The way with hares is to let them come in, keep still and low if at all possible, and keep the face covered: masks are too much in company, but a neck gaiter or muffler will hide your features. Failing that, pull your cap peak forward as I do, to throw shadow over your face. Always think front end when shooting hares and an extra flick of the wrist sometimes makes all the difference to ensure an effective, quick kill. Hares are often moving faster than the brain registers. I watched in admiration as my neighbour Johannes Rohl – head forester on the great Wittgenstein-Berleburg estates in Westphalia, Germany – calmly shot successive lefts and rights at hares heading for a gap in the hedgerow close by him. Then the whistle goes as the beaters close in, we turn and take a few hares behind, and the drive is done.

The camaraderie after a successful drive with like-minded friends is always infectious. Everyone has been in the shooting and a good head of hares taken off the first drive. Unfortunately the second drive mostly fails as we are forced by the boundary to drive them into the wind. The hares, as expected, scent the waiting guns and break back or break out each side where the flanking guns manage some shooting. But it matters not to the gun team; all and one are sportsmen and gratefully accept another wee dram from Philip's flask. Next drive I'm placed alongside Austrian entrepreneur Gerhard Annawatt. We have a lot of sport shooting each other's hares as they try to get past us. This is something one can only do with a like-minded friend and definitely not in strange company. We have all shot well once again and the head keeper is pleased at our collective performance. It is worth mentioning, had Gerhard and I stood in the open as we'd been placed, we would have had very little

shooting. I'd taken advantage of a fallen tree and used it as a screen, Gerhard too, in a similar vein of thought, had squeezed into the corner where two hedges met and nothing got past us. That is how to maximise one's chances at hares.

It was great to see a lot of partridges left after the season's end, and a number of paired greys were a grand sight not often seen in these days of modern intensive farming. Young Count Erbach was smiling when we walked back to the road, making it obvious he'd enjoyed some good shooting. It's very satisfying indeed to see a young sportsman with access to some of Europe's grandest game really enjoy some home grown wild British sport. Gerhard and I were of the same opinion as we walked back to the trailer and listened to Georg's animated account of the drive.

The afternoon beat was the best yet, though I suspect it was something of an ordeal for the beaters crossing a big acreage of winter plough. Their boots soon gained a mass of weighty mud and I remember thinking their Scottish hill hare driving counterparts might just wince at that questionable privilege. The hares clapped down in the furrows as the wind gusted, and I'm sure many were passed by, but abundant numbers provided excellent sport to complete a very fine day at the hares, and the weekend closed with a very respectable bag indeed.

Before we leave hare driving, I must stress that every endeavour should always be made to recover any wounded hares. Of course this should go without saying, but on a few shoots I've noticed fellow guns give injured hares little thought. I don't think it was them being cavalier – perish the

thought – I rather think it was through a lack of observation. If a hare flinches at the shot or shows any telling behaviour that he may be hit, follow him with the eye. If the hare has taken a pellet in the lungs it will soon roll over dead, and if he doesn't and enters cover you will be able to direct the picker up accordingly. On well managed estates there are always a sufficient number of pickers up in attendance to sweep behind the gun line. But the sportsman can help massively by letting the staff know of any wounded hares and the direction they took, and if no one is available mark the spot.

The Lincolnshire Wolds must be considered the tamest part of the country included in this book about sport in 'Wildest Britain'. Indeed some may even question the area's inclusion. However, I wanted to provide a comparison to mountain hare driving, rather than just dismiss the lowland practice out of hand. No one could question the wildness of the open moors and high tops where the white hare is found, but his brown cousin also deserves his place as a truly wild quarry. Furthermore, the adjacent Humber bank is as wild a place as one can imagine in inclement conditions.

Brown hares are of course found away from arable agricultural areas, often making their abode on that marginal ground between farmland and moor. Here the brown hare may be sought by the rough shooter, and most welcome he is too, often the hare being the only addition to the game bag on a lean day. Both brown and white hares as a sporting species deserve more respect by sportsmen than is generally given. I have enjoyed many rewarding hours in their pursuit, alone and in company. If the guns are experienced at hare shooting, or newbies well briefed and conscientious, then back end shooting and the pitiful off-putting experience of a wounded squealing hare with smashed hind legs will be avoided. I will leave the humble hare with a thought provoking ode from that fickle Ayrshire bard – Rabbie Burns:

Image: Wikimedia Friedrich Böhringer

ON SEEING A WOUNDED HARE LIMP BY ME,
WHICH A FELLOW HAD JUST SHOT AT

Inhuman man! curse on thy barb'rous art,
And blasted be thy murder-aiming eye;
May never pity soothe thee with a sigh,
Nor ever pleasure glad thy cruel heart.

And then with thought to the wounded hare he
continues:

Go live, poor wanderer of the wood and field!
The bitter little that of life remains:
No more the thickening brakes and verdant plains
To thee shall home, or food, or pastime yield.

Seek, mangled wretch, some place of wonted rest,
No more of rest, but now thy dying bed!
The sheltering rushes whistling o'er thy head,
The cold earth with thy bloody bosom prest.

Oft as by winding Nith, I, musing, wait
The sober eve, or hail the cheerful dawn;
I'll miss thee sporting o'er the dewy lawn,
And curse the ruffian's aim, and mourn thy hap-
less fate.

Mind your face, remain still and let him come right
in, think forward, and you will avoid the above.

Left: Walked up hares
if not harried sit tight
on approach and give
straightforward going
away shots

Opposite: Driven hares
mostly offer crossing or
approaching shots but
are often quite fast

345

II

The common or European rabbit (*Oryctolagus cuniculus*) is a comparative newcomer to Britain. There is no mention of 'warrens' in the Doomsday Book, that great survey of English and Welsh Landholders and their holdings, completed in 1086 on orders of William 1st, also known as William the Conqueror or William the Bastard. The latter designation is due to William's illegitimacy, born out of wedlock to his father's (Robert Duke of Normandy) mistress Herleva. He was not named by – though one could be forgiven for thinking it – the conquered Anglo-Saxon earls, whose lands had become forfeit to William for supporting their fallen King Harold at the ill-fated Hastings engagement, or the subsequent evictions during the Doomsday book collation for tax evasion – trumped up, outdated, or otherwise. William had used the earls' and barons' evasion of tax, that he claimed was previously owed to Edward the Confessor, as an excuse to seize their lands. The book was a complete reckoning of a man's holdings and their value, but as no warrens were listed at all in the Doomsday Book we can be certain the rabbit was absent in 1086. However, other slightly later Norman records show warrens were established soon after William's death, and were a useful income for many landowners. Therefore we can be quite sure the rabbit was brought over to Britain from the continent by Norman nobility sometime after the great manuscript's completion, which incidentally was just a year before William 1st met his maker.

In subsequent centuries, escapees from arti-

Right: The rabbit has occupied nearly all of our isles since Norman times

ficial warrens multiplied unchecked to populate county after county, until the rabbit inhabited most of the country. It is hard to imagine today the massive pre-myxomatosis numbers of conies that could be found, not only in the farmed heartlands, but also in the wildest corners of Britain. Prichard barley mentions them in SIWB, with just an occasional remark regarding bagging a few among the dunes, but the common rabbit back then was the source of much sport to many a gentleman and farmhand alike.

The big rabbit battues that were regularly organised in the Victorian and Edwardian eras of sporting excellence were real eye-openers. Systematic stinking out of warrens was necessary to achieve a 'big bag'. This took place a couple of days before the shoot date, and was achieved by stuffing down balls of paraffin- or creosote-soaked newspaper into the windward holes (to help the smell permeate the warren), taking care to leave one or two main entrances clear to let the rabbits depart. Other deeper warrens were ferreted and the rabbits allowed to bolt, the holes then stopped to prevent the rabbits' return. A simple method of split sticks with a piece of white paper fluttering in the wind at the hole mouths would be sufficient to stop off a bury for a day or two. When rabbits were being driven out of cover, the guns generally stood with their backs to the beaters for reasons of safety, and shot the bolting rabbits as they sped past them. Bags of 1,000 or more conies were commonplace.

Prince Victor Duleep Singh, son of that great sportsman Marajah Duleep Singh – last Raja of the Sikh empire (exiled) – dubbed the Black Prince of Perthshire, and rated the fourth best shot in England, certainly inherited his father's love for sport. He shot mostly in the manner described, in excess of 75,000 rabbits in in a single season to his own gun at the Elveden Estate, which he inherited from his father in Suffolk. Prince Victor was also one of the shooting party that shot the record bag of 6,943 rabbits at Blenheim Palace, Oxfordshire, on 7th October 1898. The five man gun team included the host, His Grace the Duke of Marlborough, Prince Victor and his brother Prince Frederick Duleep Singh, Sir Robert Gresley, and Mr. Stephen Wombwell. The night preceding the shoot was fine with a dull sky, and a dry wind; ideal for shutting out the rabbits from the warrens. This was a slightly different practice from stinking the conies out. In the right conditions (as described) rabbits will feed far out from the warrens and diligent keepers would block off the holes by stuffing them with hay. This ruse wouldn't last for long, but if successfully achieved the night prior to a shoot, excellent results comparable to the alternate method could certainly be achieved.

Some keepers in my early shooting career attempted to stink rabbits out by rolling pine cones soaked in Renardine down the windward holes, in a similar manner as practised in the past. I have never been part of the shooting party after this method was employed, but it was said to be successful. That said, I doubt even treble figures were recorded with any regularity. Rabbit numbers have never reached the density of pre-myxomatosis days. Populations build up and crash almost with cyclical regularity, as the terrible disease returns over and over again. It is hard to believe that, in the first half of the last century, there was as many full-time warreners and rabbit trappers as there were game keepers. The disease certainly had a knock-on benefit to agriculture, indeed this was why it was spread throughout the land. However, that benefit may not be as much as one may think, since many small farmers also made a reasonable side-line living out of the rabbits themselves. Despite the questionable benefits, the original and deliberate spread of this disease by Frenchman Armand Delille was despicable. Germ warfare employed against man or beast is a heinous crime in the mind of any moral man,

sportsman or not.

I think it would be fair to say that the majority of sportsmen that came into shooting during their youth started out on rabbits. I was certainly no exception. After a brief period of prohibition for shooting starlings off a neighbour's TV aerial one Boxing Day, I initially stalked and shot rabbits on the stubbles during, and immediately after, harvest time, with my pride and joy a BSA Airsporter S. After a short break when the stubbles went under the plough, the campaign would be pursued once more on the sprouted drilling. Interestingly, I inadvertently trained my cocker spaniel Sam to point at the time. This was no small thing to do with a spaniel, and I

Left: Bolted rabbits can and mostly do provide fast sport – snap shooting is often the order of the day

Image: freeimages

have no doubt had I set out to do this deliberately I would have failed. However, my repetitive pattern of working the wind, spying and stalking the same quarry put her into 'rabbit mode' and I soon marvelled at her ability to point. There was none of the paw-up or tail out (difficult when docked) habits of a true pointer, but when she froze in a certain way I knew we were on rabbit. This was a habit on which I capitalised on numerous occasions, even more so when I progressed from the airgun to the shotgun.

Most of the rabbits Prichard shot were as incidentals according to his game books and writings on sport. Occasionally, they would feature highly by figure alone on the more formal driven days, but they were certainly pursued with interest at impromptu times when walking them up. These are the type of days that I have enjoyed in the wild places.

Once a year at the beginning of October, a great day's rabbiting could also be had at

Above: Walked up and driven rabbit shooting provides a variety of shots and is mostly exciting, but summer nights with the rimfire take some beating too

Glen Moy in the company of that very stoic of keepers Stuart Donald. There was a rough old pine plantation on the edge of the moor called the Cuilt (pronounced Cult) Wood on the lower slopes of Craigthran. Four guns could walk in a slow line between the tall pines, and shoot the rabbit infested wood steadily, from the lower end to the top. The smell of the pine trees, and the peat impregnated turf disturbed by our footfall was strong in the nose as the guns moved quietly forward. Below the canopy the sound of our tread seemed muffled, rather than quiet. A lone wren occasionally put up an alarmed "tic, tic, tic, ticking," more annoyed at our presence than anything else, but that would be it until a rabbit bolted out of the brash, and was instantly followed by a shotgun report, or an expletive if the gun was caught wrong footed. A lot of very enjoyable sport could be had this way. But it only worked once in a season as the rabbits quickly grew wise, and found the sanctuary of their buries far safer than running the gauntlet of guns above ground. Thirty or forty rabbits could be shot in this way, and I have often thought since that this would have been a great place to try the pine cone and Renardine method of stinking them out. Renardine however, it must be noted, has since become illegal. On another note, this wood had a massive population of adders, and we would only work the dog here after the first frost to avoid snake bite, and the adverse canine complications involved.

Once we'd finished walking up the Cuilt Wood, we would drain, hock and couple the rabbits before heading up Glen Moy proper and stopping for our 'piece' (packed lunch) at the bothy below the Shank Hillock. After we had taken our victuals, and a steady ten minute pull up the pony path, we would line out to the right side of the hill toward the East Burn of Glen Moy. Now out on the open hill proper, what a difference it was to the almost foreboding, closed canopy of the lower plantation. Great vistas held sway in whatever dircction one looked, majestic heathery carpets chequered across the slopes of glacier carved hills and crags. The muffled sound of our progress below that oppressive canopy was now replaced by the grouse's chortle and distant curlew's chime. The moist, musty smell of disturbed peat and pine was replaced with the freshness of heather, and blaeberry now felt underfoot.

It was from here Misty, Stuart's exceptional black and white springer spaniel, would come into play. Walking forward among the heathery knolls, Misty would then work tirelessly, quartering back and forth. Never more than twenty yards in front, she worked with a dedicated purpose flushing the rabbits. Snap shooting was the name of this game, and what fun it was, flushing and shooting. I'm certain that the spaniel enjoyed it just as much as we did, and even more certain that many of those rabbits lived above ground in the heather, as there were very few evident holes.

After we had worked the right had side of the path to the level, we would turn and re-line towards the west burn and take a line back down the Shank to where we had started from. Stuart was always in the middle of the line, and all guns had to carry their own game bag, though on the way up a pile of rabbits could be left half way along the pony path, to be distributed among all taking part on the return leg back down. These were happy days, and if ever there was a spaniel that was a rabbit specialist, it was Misty. A lot of sport could be had here in a spectacular wild place, and all in great company. Indeed, although I have been fortunate enough to have enjoyed some fantastic rabbiting forays, from the Holderness coast shooting the conies among the dunes and stunted hedges, bolted by young Will Shep's ferrets, to semi-driven affairs on some of England's great estates, it is at Glen Moy with that marvellous spaniel Misty that I have the fondest of memories, which are as clear now as if they were enjoyed only yesterday.

Risk of ricochets is always prevalent when shooting ground game for obvious reasons, therefore due regard must always be given to rocks and stony ground. Dogs and ferrets likewise must constantly be given total consideration when working them for rabbits. Further-more, I subscribe wholeheartedly to Colonel Hawker's advice when he writes about shooting a rabbit "always consider the foremost half of him as your target, or he will probably be shot in a slovenly manner; and if there is an earth near, most likely scramble into it, and make his escape." Hear, hear to that.

The reader will remember, in the plover chapter of this book, Prichard recounting a story of a fifth form schoolboy who shoots a lapwing illegally, and after a long chase is finally apprehended by a policeman under the 'brig' or bridge, where he courageously cuts a deal. When I first read that particular passage, and whenever talk turns to shooting rabbits in one's youth, a similar story comes to mind involving another fifth former but some eighty years later. This time the tale is set in Yorkshire, but the youngster's shooting permission had similar elastic boundaries to Prichard's, perhaps stretched even a little more so on occasion.

An east coast rail line ran alongside the eastern extremities of home farm. It was con-tained by a fence that marked the boundary. However, a deft vault over said fence, followed by a practised slide down the embankment, left all thought of any remorse behind, and brought one down to the railway itself. And what a fruit-ful place it was to walk along and bag a bunny or two after the 07:50 to Scarborough had passed. Unfortunately, the regular reports of the newly acquired AYA 12 bore around breakfast time each morning upset Mrs Busy Body, who lived in a bungalow on the opposite embank-

Right: The author thanks young Will Shephard, an accomplished ferreter working the Yorkshire coastline

ment. She was a little more than anti-minded and didn't appreciate the echoing 12 bore broadside accompaniment to her daily Earl Grey and tea cakes at 8.00am.

A call was put in to the local constabulary and the trap was set. If Yorkshire Fifth was guilty of anything else but poaching on this occasion, it was complacency. The policemen of the eight-ies were a lot less fit than in Prichard's time, plus they had been waiting for the "poacher" to come from the road, and hadn't expected him to approach from the fields behind them. And so it was, the 07:50 rattled past and whistled its approach to the level crossing. Seconds later, Yorkshire Lower Fifth slid down the embank-ment, popped in a couple of green Eley Hymax No.4s into the AYA (he used to err on the heavy side of caution when it came to loads), and began stalking along the line for a plump rabbit with a devil-may-care attitude. That would soon change when he rolled over his next coney and his whole future hunting career hung in the bal-ance for an anxious half hour.

There was a report, and the rabbit fell dead, followed by a huge commotion coming from the siding a few hundred yards ahead as two policemen fell over each other in their haste to turn about. The shot had surprised them from behind, but they were now gathering their slack and vocally venting their displeasure. Situation instantly assessed, Yorkshire Fifth decided on leaving the shot rabbit where it lay, and took to flight. Bursting directly up the embankment through a briar patch that would have stalled a tiger tank, he made good his escape. Distance was soon put between him and his now flagging pursuers, but his way home was barred by a patrol car. He had to get to school for his fate would surely be sealed if he didn't turn up, but what to do with the precious shotgun?

It was a hard decision, but the gun was disassembled and dropped into a convenient horse trough. A crawl under the hawthorn put him onto the highway, and a twenty minute dash brought him to the playing field fence that was soon scaled, and access gained to the science block tutor room, just in time to gain his mark before lessons began. Fortunately for him that was the end of the matter; there was no visit to the school by the constabulary, he kept his certificate, lost a rabbit, ruined a gun (recov-

ered later), and learned a very valuable lesson. It could have easily gone the other way, and a whole way of life denied him if a prosecution had been brought and lost him his certificate as a result.

The story was only shared with one other. Guilt at the loss of the gun had caused him to fret intolerably. It had been gifted to him by an old Sgt major. Seeing the youth had lost the instrument that had brought him happiness and freedom to enjoy his wild sport in the great British countryside, the same Sgt major, at the confessional, pressed £100 into his hand to put towards a replacement gun. It was accompanied by a simple but stern line of advice: "don't be so complacent in future". **PC**

Image: Blaze Publishing

Afterword

Hesketh Prichard lived only forty-five years. Thirty of these separate two scenes which, for me, illuminate the character of his life. One is a scene on the shore of a bay in Jersey. A boy of thirteen, carrying for the first time a hired 10 bore gun, is walking along the sands on the chance of a shot. A raven comes within range and he fires, and the raven falls into the sea. He realises it is being carried away by the tide, and strips to swim for it. As he does he sees a curlew, thinks he can just reach it with the 10 bore, stands up naked to shoot, brings the curlew down into the water and is himself knocked down by the gun. He gets up and rushes to the water, but the curlew is a long way out, and when he has retrieved both birds he is dragged out of the shallows by his companion, a fisherman who cannot swim.

The second scene is a room in a house in Hertfordshire. A very tall man whose clothes hang loosely about him is talking rapidly and eagerly of rifles and sights, of *papier mâché* masks, telescopes, the men who sniped from the trenches opposite him. Above his high cheek-bones his grey eyes look into the distance. He sees something you do not: you have seen a look a little like it in the eyes of other men back from the war, but this is the eye of a man who is in a world of his own – a world of a dream? He is back, suddenly, to some tiny practical detail of a bolt-action. And suddenly, too, he changes the subject. Wild geese, the West of Ireland, Achill Island, the Atlantic – will I come with him to the islands in the west after wild geese, when he is better? He must get better soon, The doctors must find out – they have already found out – what is the matter with him; and next year, he means to go to the West of Ireland. He is looking again into the distance; and I who listen have guessed the truth[1].

Right: The last known photo of Major Hesketh Prichard DSO MC, shortly before his death

[1]*Written in 1924 by his friend Eric Parker in the introductory to the book* Hesketh Prichard A Memoir

Recommended *Reading*

Instructions to Young Sportsmen in all that Relates to Guns and Shooting by Colonel Peter Hawker (born November 1786 – died 1853) first published in 1814 (author's reference). This book was an all-encompassing book on sport, particularly wildfowling, which Prichard paid much attention to as a boy.

A Tideline Books 1985 limited edition is available at www.tidelinebooks.co.uk

The Moor and the Loch by John Colquhoun (born March 1805 – died May 1885) first published in 1840 (author's reference). Colquhoun acquired vast experience in matters of Scottish sport and natural history, which was really quite exceptional, as he had hunted over most of mainland Scotland during his sporting lifetime. This book, along with the following work by St John, set the benchmark for future sporting writers. Prichard was one of the few that surpassed them.

Free download available from https://archive.org/details/moorandloch00colqgoog

Short Sketches of the Wild Sports and Natural History of the Highlands by Charles William George St John (born 1809 – died 1856) first published 1893 (author's reference). This sportsman's work was recognised as that of an accurate observer and a writer of talent. His style is clear and direct, sober details based on factual experience are wrapped in a genuine appreciation of scenery. His writings incentivised many a Victorian and Edwardian lover of wild sport to visit the hills and moors of the north.

Facsimile Edition available published by Ashford Press Publishing, Southampton, in 1986 . ISBN 10: 0907069673 / ISBN 13: 9780907069676

The Wildfowler in Scotland, by J.G. Millais (born March 1865 – died March 1931) published by Longmans, in 1901 (author's reference). Prichard had a great respect for Millais as naturalist, artist and sportsman, and he appears in SIWB. It was J.G. Millais who introduced Prichard to Balranald estate in North Uist, where much of

Prichard's wildfowling and seal hunting was done.

2nd edition by Tideline Books: facsimile Reprint 1974 - 167pp. Advertisement leaf and new foreword by the publisher www.tidelinebooks.co.uk

Autumns in Argyleshire with Rod and Gun by Hon. Alfred Erskine Gathorne-Hardy (born February 1845 – died November 1918) published by Longmans in 1900 (author's reference). This book I personally believe set the style for SIWB. It is a collection of 30 years' worth of sporting reminiscences, at Poltalloch estate in Argyll. Many of the honourable gentleman's musings had been previously published in the *Field* and *Cornhill* magazines.

Paperback and e-book available. ISBN 10: 1162784350 / 1-162-78435-0. ISBN 13: 9781162784359 Publisher: Kessinger Publishing

Record Bags and Shooting Records by Sir Hugh S. Gladstone (born April 1877 – died April 1949). London – H. F. & G. Witherby, 1922 (author's reference). This book is an excellent reference to the big bags of yesteryear with the speed and weight of birds etc. The evolution of the sporting gun and marksmanship are also covered.

Paperback version and kindle edition available. Published by Read Books, United Kingdom, 2007 ISBN 10: 1406789593 / ISBN 13: 9781406789591

Hesketh Prichard A Memoir by Eric Parker. This is an in-depth biographical study of Prichard's achievements as Hunter: Explorer: Naturalist : Cricketer : Author : Soldier. A must-read for anyone with an interest in this remarkable sportsman.

Published by Fisher Unwin Ltd LONDON 1924. Scarce but sometimes available

The Black Grouse by Patrick Laurie. An excellent study on this declining and iconic gambird, lively natural history writing by Patrick.

2012 Merlin Unwin books ISBN 978-1-906122-43-0

The British Deer Stalking Bible by Peter Carr. This book takes an in-depth look at not just the six deer species available to the rifle hunter in Britain, but also the wild boar, feral goat, Soay sheep and the fox. Valuable advice from a hunting perspective is given on each species, and includes many interesting anecdotes from the author. Specialist chapters on equipment, deer dogs and best practice are also covered. An essential read for both the novice and seasoned stalker.

ISBN 978-0-9549597-8-4, available from www.virtualnewsagent.com

Sporting Rifles: A Guide to Modern Firearms by Peter Carr. A comprehensive guide to 37 sporting rifles for every application from foxing to big game hunting. Covering a range of models and popular calibres, it's an easily-accessible reference for both the beginner and experienced rifle shot alike.

ISBN 978-1-910247-03-7, available www.virtualnewsagent.com.

Acknowledgements

I would like to thank two of Hesketh Prichard's descendants whom, without their total support and help, this book would not have been possible.

Venitia Lascelles, Hesketh's granddaughter, kindly allowed me access to the 'HP' library, and to stay on many occasions at her late father Michael's home in the Lake District. Netia, I thank you enormously for your support and help tidying up the Prichard papers.

Secondly, a massive thanks to Hesketh's great-grandson Charlie Jacoby for your suggestion and sanction to rummage through and use the Prichard papers to produce a modern version of *Sport In Wildest Britain*, and for your company on many a sporting occasion. I shall never forget you attempting to press a suit crumpled beyond recognition with a four inch travel iron, prior to our attendance at the House of Lords for a function, and for actually managing to blag your way in at the Black Rod's entrance after losing your invitation. It was a fine display of a classic CJ 'comedy' tour that is a treasured memory.

Nicola Turner, my deputy editor on *Modern Gamekeeping* magazine and editor of this tome – as always I cannot thank you enough Nico for your diligent, professional work ethic at all times. And to another Blaze Publishing colleague, Steve Dawson – who worked wonders on designing the transparencies to antiquate Prichard's section of the chapters – for your relentless work at all hours to bring this project to completion. I appreciate your efforts immensely.

To Lt. Gen. Sir Barney White-Spunner KCB CBE, and the current executive chariman of the Countryside Alliance, I thank you for your kind and inspirational words in the foreword.

Also to a different, but equally commanding (and demanding), 'general', publisher Wesley Stanton for his patience, and financial backing to publish this project. Thanks Wes. I found your comment, "It better not be vanity publishing, and on your head be it!" immensely inspirational, uplifting and reassuring as always.

To my wife Debra for her continued support, and tolerance above and beyond the expected call of duty of most wives – thank you x. **PC**

Left: Co-author Pete Carr and his mountain hound Jeager contemplating the climb up Ben Starav